CAPTAIN JOSEPH BOYCE
and the
1ST MISSOURI INFANTRY, C.S.A.

Edited by

William C. Winter

MISSOURI HISTORY MUSEUM
ST. LOUIS
DISTRIBUTED BY UNIVERSITY OF MISSOURI PRESS

Library of Congress Cataloging-in-Publication Data

Boyce, Joseph, 1841-1928.
  Captain Joseph Boyce and the 1st Missouri Infantry, C.S.A. / edited by William C. Winter.
      p. cm.
  Includes bibliographical references and index.
  Summary: "Presents the story of the 1st Missouri Infantry, a Confederate regiment, through the words of Captain Joseph Boyce of Company D, the St. Louis Greys. Features an editor's introduction to each chapter, extensive endnotes, and other writings by Boyce"--Provided by publisher.
  ISBN 978-1-883982-70-6 (pbk. : alk. paper)
  1. Boyce, Joseph, 1841-1928. 2. Confederate States of America. Army. Missouri Infantry Regiment, 1st. 3. United States--History--Civil War, 1861-1865--Personal narratives, Confederate. 4. United States--History--Civil War, 1861-1865--Regimental histories. 5. United States--History--Civil War, 1861-1865--Campaigns. 6. Missouri--History--Civil War, 1861-1865--Personal narratives, Confederate. 7. Missouri--History--Civil War, 1861- 1865--Regimental histories. 8. Soldiers--Confederate States of America--Biography. 9. Soldiers--Missouri--Biography. 10. Saint Louis (Mo.)--Biography. I. Winter, William C., 1947- II. Title.
  E569.51st .B69 2011
  973.7'478--dc23

                              2011027863

Distributed by University of Missouri Press
Printed and bound in the United States by Sheridan Books

I am proud of my connection with the First Missouri Infantry,
and claim for it that it was
the best organized and disciplined volunteer regiment
the war produced.

Missourians,
whether they were for the North or South,
can take pride in the prowess of
the First Missouri.

We represented our state, and despite our failure,
we were Missourians,
and stood to our guns
from the first to the last.

—*Joseph Boyce*
Company D
1ˢᵗ Missouri Infantry
Confederate States of America

TABLE OF CONTENTS

Foreword
7

Introduction
9

Biographical Sketch
15

1. Getting Organized
JUNE–SEPTEMBER 1861
31

2. Camp Beauregard, Kentucky
OCTOBER–DECEMBER 1861
43

3. In Kentucky and Tennessee
JANUARY–MARCH 1862
51

4. Shiloh, Tennessee
APRIL 1862
59

5. Baton Rouge, Louisiana
MAY–SEPTEMBER 1862
75

6. Corinth, Mississippi
OCTOBER–DECEMBER 1862
83

7. In Defense of Vicksburg
JANUARY–MAY 1863
95

8. The Vicksburg Siege
MAY–JULY 1863
119

9. With Johnston's Army of Relief
MAY–JULY 1863
133

10. Rest and Reorganization
SEPTEMBER 1863–APRIL 1864
139

11. Defending Atlanta under Johnston
MAY–JUNE 1864
151

12. Defending Atlanta under Hood
JULY–SEPTEMBER 1864
163

13. North through Georgia
SEPTEMBER–OCTOBER 1864
177

14. Franklin, Tennessee
OCTOBER–DECEMBER 1864
189

15. The Last Battle
JANUARY–APRIL 1865
207

16. Prisoners of War
APRIL–MAY 1865
227

17. War Echoes
1887
241

Appendix
ROSTERS OF THE ST. LOUIS GREYS
249

Resources
253

Bibliography
255

Index
268

About the Author
272

FOREWORD

When William C. Winter suggested the idea of the Missouri History Museum publishing a history of a Confederate infantry regiment, I was intrigued. As we talked further about Joseph Boyce and the plan for Winter's book, the concept grew more and more attractive.

As a border state, where slaves and free citizens, slaveholders and abolitionists, states-rights advocates and stalwart supporters of the Union lived side by side in little more than an armed truce, Missouri has plenty of stories on all sides of the Civil War. Those who chose the Confederacy may have been the losers in the war, but their stories, each with its own values, its own lessons, and its own perceptions of right and wrong, belong to the legacy we have inherited. Within those stories we can discern hints of the future and suggestions for our own time.

The history of the 1st Missouri Infantry of the Confederate States Army is a saga of hard work, courage, and pride, admirable in its loyalty to duty and to a cause. Joseph Boyce's personal story is a chronicle of optimism— and not only in his war service. For more than thirty years he served the community as a director of the Missouri Historical Society (as the History Museum was known for many years), giving the Museum almost familial motivation in publishing the memoir. Furthermore—and this certainly endeared him to me—he sought to mend the rift between the North and the South that the war had, in essence, exacerbated. An organizer of the St. Louis chapter of Veterans of the Blue and Gray in 1896, he hoped to unite his fellow veterans in a move away from lingering animosity toward peace and community.

CAPTAIN JOSEPH BOYCE

At the same time, Boyce was determined that the service of his infantry would be remembered with respect. I believe he would concur with one of my favorite quotes from the great African American abolitionist Frederick Douglass. At an 1883 Emancipation Day festival in Rochester, New York, Douglass urged us to recall not just the gifts from the past but the burdens as well:

> You will already have perceived that I am not of that school of thinkers that teaches us to let bygones be bygones, to let the dead past bury its dead. In my view there are no bygones in the world and the past is not dead and cannot die. The evil as well as the good men do lives after them. The duty of keeping in memory the great deeds of the past, and of transmitting the same from generation to generation is implied in the mental and moral condition of men.

Despite the 150 years that separates us from this war of brothers, we in America still suffer from wounds inflicted by this sad and bloody conflict. As we commemorate the Civil War's 150th anniversary, as we read and retell the stories, we must remind ourselves that we who live together must make our peace with one another and with the past and that we must remember that which we dare not forget.

—ROBERT R. ARCHIBALD, PH.D.
PRESIDENT, MISSOURI HISTORY MUSEUM

INTRODUCTION

For too many readers, the role of the Missouri Confederate in the Civil War is that of the bushwhacker, typified in popular media by William Quantrill or a youthful Jesse James. These rebels create havoc within the state, warring at times with former neighbors, shooting soldiers and civilians alike, and—as I was once reminded impishly by a doyenne of the United Daughters of the Confederacy—burning antiques wherever they go. When the war ends, they fight on with no regard for consequences and no thought of reconciliation.

While there is some truth to the stereotype, there were other Missouri Confederates, soldiers who fought for the South at Shiloh and Corinth, from Vicksburg to Atlanta, in the assault at Franklin and in defense of Fort Blakely at Mobile in the war's last month. Published sources by these Missouri Confederates are few. Ephraim McDowell Anderson, a veteran of the 2nd Missouri Infantry, published *Memoirs: Historical and Personal; Including the Campaigns of the First Missouri Confederate Brigade* in 1868. Robert S. Bevier, an officer in the 5th Missouri Infantry, published *History of the First and Second Missouri Confederate Brigades, 1861–1865* in 1878. James Bradley, a veteran of the 3rd/5th Missouri Infantry, added a brief history of the brigade in 1894 when he published *The Confederate Mail Carrier*, with a lengthy subtitle that begins "Being an Account of the Battles, Marches and Hardships of the First and Second Brigades, Mo., C.S.A." Captain Joseph Boyce began publishing his serialized history of the 1st Missouri Infantry in 1883. It is presented here in full and as a continuous story for the first time.

CAPTAIN JOSEPH BOYCE

After the Camp Jackson massacre in St. Louis on May 10, 1861, the Missouri General Assembly quickly passed legislation to organize and support the Missouri State Guard. Former governor and freshly appointed major general Sterling Price commanded the new organization.[1] The Missouri State Guard would go on to fight at Boonville, Carthage, Oak Hills (Wilson's Creek), and Lexington before leaving the state for northwest Arkansas in the war's first winter. In December, after agreements between the Confederate states and the State of Missouri were in place, Price directed the process of enlisting new volunteers and re-enlisting members of the State Guard for the Confederate States Army.[2] Progress was slow. By mid-January 1862, only two infantry regiments, a cavalry regiment, and two artillery batteries had volunteered for the Confederate service. In April, after a defeat in February at Elkhorn Tavern (Pea Ridge), the Missourians were ordered east of the Mississippi River. That month, Price relinquished command of the Missouri State Guard and accepted an appointment as a major general in the Confederate army, encouraging others to follow his example and join the Confederate service.

To all of this, the 1st Missouri Infantry is the exception. After Camp Jackson, St. Louisan John Bowen traveled immediately to Richmond to obtain permission to raise a regiment of Missourians to fight for the Confederacy. Bowen, a graduate of the United States Military Academy and a colonel in the Missouri Volunteer Militia, was successful in his quest. He soon began collecting volunteers—predominantly from St. Louis and southeast Missouri—at Memphis, and his regiment became the 1st Missouri Infantry, C.S.A. With a few brief exceptions, these Missourians did not return to the western side of the Mississippi River for the duration of the war. A number of Confederate units claim to be "orphans," and the men of the 1st Missouri Infantry certainly share that dismal distinction. These Missourians were committed to the cause of their state, but from the beginning they were committed to the larger cause of Southern independence.

Captain Joseph Boyce, Company D, 1st Missouri Infantry, wrote his history of the regiment for presentation to the Southern Historical and Benevolent Society of St. Louis. After each presentation, his text appeared in the *Missouri Republican*, published in St. Louis and one of the state's leading

10

newspapers. As I first read these serialized accounts, leaning into a microfilm reader at the Missouri History Museum Library and Research Center, I recognized that Boyce had an important story to tell. His history of the 1st Missouri Infantry deserves as much attention from a modern audience as it received when he first wrote it. The value of Boyce's work is that he did not write a reminiscence or memoir. He worked to write an accurate history of his regiment, and for those events of which he did not have personal knowledge, he sought the resources of others. He was an amateur historian, but he wanted his story to stand the test of time. Boyce spent little time after the war with recriminations. He focused instead on reconciliation with the state and national government and on remembrance and support for those with whom he had served. His work as a historian was the principal way in which he assured that the hardships and heroism of these Confederates from Missouri would not be forgotten.

The articles from the *Missouri Republican* form the core of this work. The first installment of Boyce's story was published in November 1883. The last appeared in 1887. After his work was complete, Boyce mailed a set of clipped articles in scrapbook form to John Page Nicholson, a former Union officer. At the time, Nicholson was the recorder in chief for the Military Order of the Loyal Legion of the United States, an organization of Union veterans in which Nicholson's Pennsylvania commandery, as the state chapters were called, was the most prominent. Before he mailed the manuscript, Boyce made several revisions and corrections to the newspaper's text, and these revisions have been incorporated into this document. Boyce created four such compilations. The documents mailed by Boyce to Nicholson are now in the collections of the Huntington Library, San Marino, California.[3] Boyce gave his personal set of clippings to the Missouri Historical Society (now the Missouri History Museum Library and Research Center's Archives), where they would be "safely kept from fire and other destroying elements." He compiled another set for his son, John P. Boyce. Boyce sent the final set to the Prince de Joinville in Paris. De Joinville had served on the staff of Union general George McClellan.[4]

In the early years of the twentieth century, Boyce submitted portions of his history to *Confederate Veteran*, a periodical providing a forum for veterans seeking to preserve an accurate version of their history. In these articles, Boyce occasionally revised his original text, adding detail or making corrections that had come to his attention. On his own copies of *Confederate Veteran*, now in the collections of the Missouri History Museum, an aging Boyce penned a few minor corrections to these articles after they were published. These revisions, too, have been incorporated into this document. Boyce's letters, scrapbooks, collected papers, and other writings have been used to round out his history of the 1st Missouri Infantry.

Boyce wrote before the appearance of the U.S. War Department's compilation of the official records of the Union and Confederate armies, the cornerstone to research on the military aspects of the Civil War. The series began publication in 1881 but was not completed until 1901. Without this benchmark, Boyce is occasionally imprecise on dates, a circumstance I have attempted to correct. Within the text, corrections to the spelling of names and places are noted in brackets whenever they first occur. A second appearance is unmarked. Paragraph breaks have been added and modifications made to punctuation where needed for clarity, especially where material has been added to the core *Republican* account. With those exceptions, spelling and punctuation appear as they did in the original typeset text.

The initial audience for Boyce's history understood well the events of which he wrote. To assist the modern reader in maintaining an overall context for Boyce's story and to provide explanations of events that Boyce only briefly summarized, I have inserted short narratives to introduce each episode and bridge the topics in Boyce's account. Explanatory notes have been added throughout, with particular emphasis on the identification of individuals named within the text.

The task of identifying Boyce's fellow veterans was made significantly more bearable by the St. Louis County Library System, whose services include access to footnote.com, a site providing online access to the compiled service records of most of the soldiers of the Union and Confederate armies. My thanks are due particularly to the staff of the Eureka Hills branch library for their help and hospitality.

This narrative was improved throughout its development by the staff of the Missouri History Museum, particularly Dr. Robert R. Archibald and

INTRODUCTION

the Publications branch under the leadership of Victoria Monks. Associate archivist Dennis Northcott, curator Jeff Meyer, and associate archivist of photographs and prints Amanda Claunch each made specific contributions to this work. In particular, senior editor Lauren Mitchell has earned my sincere appreciation for her patience and professionalism in guiding this story to its final form.

To my friend, Marshall David Hier, I am indebted for his constructive criticism, freely and thoughtfully given, and for his continuous encouragement of my research. When he and I first met at the Civil War Round Table of St. Louis a few decades ago, we were in awe of the scholars and scholarship within the group. Now, with so many of our colleagues having crossed "over the river to rest in the shade of the trees," we find ourselves to be among the organization's veterans. My goal has been to maintain the standards of those who preceded me. Marshall will tell me whether I have succeeded.

To my father, William Earl Winter, I am indebted for leading me to love America's history. A veteran of the United States Army Air Corps during World War II, he had no hesitation in encouraging my younger brother and me to read biographies of American patriots. At the time, however, we were admittedly more excited by a box of lead soldiers from Wm. Britains than we were by a book when he returned to Union Station in St. Louis from a business trip. From him I learned how great a blessing it is to have a father who can truly stand up to the demands of being a role model.

To my wife, Judith Jane Johnson Winter, I am indebted for the daily encouragement and support necessary for the pursuit my avocation. She listens to my stories and almost always finds them interesting. Without her, none of this would have been possible.

—*William C. Winter*
Wildwood, Missouri

CAPTAIN JOSEPH BOYCE

Endnotes

1. The act "to provide for the organization, government, and support of the militia forces of the State of Missouri, was passed on May 14, 1861. It contained 216 sections and 48 articles of war. The Missouri State Guard replaced the Missouri Volunteer Militia. United States War Department, Record and Pension Office, *Organization and Status of Missouri Troops (Union and Confederate) in Service During the Civil War* (Washington, DC: Government Printing Office, 1902), 251.

2. Governor Claiborne Fox Jackson issued an address on December 13, 1861, encouraging enlistment in the Confederate service. U.S. War Department, *Organization and Status of Missouri Troops*, 292.

3. The Boyce clippings are to be found in the John Page Nicholson Collection (RB 47992), Rare Books, Henry E. Huntington Library. This document is hereafter referred to as Nicholson. The author is indebted to Mr. Alan Jutzi and Mr. Jean-Robert Durbin of the Huntington Library for assistance with this document.

4. Joseph Boyce to Isaac Fowler, May 10, 1913, Boyce Family Papers, Missouri History Museum Archives (hereafter MHM Archives).

CAPTAIN JOSEPH BOYCE
BIOGRAPHICAL SKETCH

On Tuesday, July 28, 1928, friends and family members stood by the graveside of Captain Joseph Boyce as he was laid to rest at Calvary Cemetery in St. Louis, but few Confederate veterans, his beloved "Camp Jackson boys," were there to grieve with them. Not that these compatriots would not have honored him had they been able, but at age eighty-seven, Captain Joe had simply outlived most of them.

Patrick M. and Sarah McLoone Boyce, his parents, had met in their native Donegal, Ireland, and married in 1835. They arrived in the United States in February 1841, and after a brief stay in New Orleans, they moved upriver to St. Louis to find their fortune. Joseph Boyce was born there on April 4, 1841. Between 1840 and 1850, the population of St. Louis increased from fewer than 15,000 citizens to more than 75,000. Immigration, especially from Ireland and from the German states of central Europe, was one of the most significant causes—or perhaps effects—of the region's prosperity. In this environment, it was not difficult for his parents to surround young Joseph with many things Irish. The first schools he attended were the Catholic church schools of St. Francis Xavier and St. Patrick. The Christian Brothers, still teaching in St. Louis today at the Christian Brothers College High School, conducted both of these schools.[1]

As Joe grew older, he attended classes at the St. Louis Cathedral, but to prepare more specifically for a livelihood in business, he also took classes at the Benton Night School and at Jones' Commercial College.[2] Boyce held his first job outside the home when he was thirteen, working as a "store boy" for one of the leading hatters in St. Louis. After three years in the haberdashery industry, he worked for two years as a clerk for an underwriter

15

before taking a job as a clerk with the wholesale grocery house of Ober, Norris & Co., a position he held until the eve of the Civil War.[3]

From an early age, Joseph Boyce demonstrated an interest in the military, an interest his parents clearly encouraged. At eleven, he was enrolled in the Black Plume Rifle Cadets and participated actively in the company until it disbanded two years later. The Rifle Cadets drilled in the same armory as the Continental Rangers, whose drillmaster was a former member of the British army and a veteran of the war with Mexico. The young Cadets were shocked when the drillmaster physically kicked one of the Rangers out of the ranks because he could not keep step, and they must have stood in stunned silence as the drillmaster boomed threats of similar treatment at the remaining recruits if their performance did not improve.[4]

At seventeen, Joe Boyce was ready to participate in the state militia, and he enlisted in the St. Louis Greys, Company A of the 1st Regiment, Missouri Volunteer Militia.[5] Of the numerous militia companies then active in St. Louis, the St. Louis Greys were the oldest and one of the most prestigious. Organized in 1832, the Greys conducted their first parade on January 8, 1833. For more than twenty-five years, they were a familiar sight to St. Louisans in their namesake uniforms, a single-breasted, swallow-tailed coat and pants of light gray cloth, trimmed in black and adorned with silver buttons and trimmings. The company was sufficiently prominent to have its own music, "The St. Louis Greys Quick Step."[6] After serving in the war with Mexico as the St. Louis Legion, the returning militia companies dwindled, became disorganized, and disbanded—all but the St. Louis Greys, considered by some to be the "Old Guard" of the Missouri Volunteer Militia.[7] The Greys became so popular that in 1853, the increased membership made it necessary to expand the unit to a battalion of seven companies, complete with a twenty-five-piece band.[8]

During the violence associated with the elections in St. Louis for the U.S. House of Representatives in August 1854, the militia was called out to help separate the immigrant Irish from the anti-immigrant populace. A voice for immigrant rights, former senator Thomas Hart Benton was defeated in the election, but four years later, St. Louisans by the thousands turned out to observe his funeral procession. The St. Louis Greys and other militia

BIOGRAPHICAL SKETCH

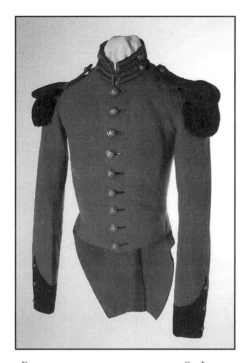

PRE-WAR UNIFORM COAT OF THE ST. LOUIS
GREYS, 1ST REGIMENT, MISSOURI VOLUNTEER
MILITIA.

companies marched with the casket to Bellefontaine Cemetery, then on the outskirts of the city.[9]

Citizens took pride in their militia companies, and friendly rivalries, measured by drill competitions, rifle matches, and elegant social events, were common. On the conclusion of the annual encampment in July 1860, the *Missouri Republican* proclaimed "with such a glorious band of soldiers ready to shoulder their muskets at a moment's notice in the course of freedom and the right, the city need not be afraid of facing an enemy, not matter whence or how he may come."[10]

In 1858, not long before Boyce joined the company, the uniform coat's black facings and gray epaulets had been changed to light blue, and the buttons and fittings were changed to gold. A small blue welt down the seam of the trousers replaced the black stripe of the earlier uniform. The company's military hat with visor had a black patent leather top and a black silk body. White crossbelts kept the black patent leather knapsack firmly in place on the soldier's back. When the Greys were on regimental duty with other companies of the 1ˢᵗ Regiment of the Missouri Volunteer Militia, they wore a dark blue frock coat with sky blue trousers during the winter months, white linen ones during the summer months. Because the members of the militia companies received only modest financial support, it seems likely that Boyce had some help from his family to serve in the Greys at the age of seventeen.[11]

Boyce's first experience with campaigning beyond the parks and streets of St. Louis came in the winter of 1860. On November 20, 1860, Governor Robert M. Stewart received a telegram from one of the militia's divisional inspectors advising him that James Montgomery and as many as three hundred men had invaded Vernon County in western Missouri, causing turmoil there and in neighboring Bates County. Additional alarum followed, and on November 23, 1860, Stewart called the St. Louis militia to active duty "to preserve the peace from the assaults of the Kansas jayhawkers."[12] The perceived incursion came nearly on the first anniversary of one-time Kansan John Brown's raid on Harpers Ferry, Virginia. After the numerous forays of Missouri's border ruffians into Kansas in the late 1850s, a retaliatory action by Montgomery was not difficult to imagine. Montgomery and Brown had conducted a "slave-liberating" raid into Missouri in 1858, and in 1859 Montgomery led an abortive mission to free Brown from prison after Brown's debacle at Harpers Ferry.[13]

Despite its distance from the scene, the St. Louis militia was summoned because it was the state's only sizable, effective military force. On Sunday, November 25, only two days after receiving the governor's call, 630 men left St. Louis on a special train to find and fight the invaders from Kansas. The brigade included the 1ˢᵗ Regiment of the Missouri Volunteer Militia, the Missouri Dragoons, the Engineer Battalion, and a battery of three six-pound guns.[14] General Daniel Marsh Frost, a graduate of the U.S. Military Academy, a former cavalry officer in the U.S. Army, and then a St. Louis businessman, commanded the Southwest Expedition, as the column was known. Boyce accompanied the expedition as a member of Company A, the St. Louis Greys' designation within the regiment, with the rank of fourth

BIOGRAPHICAL SKETCH

St. Louis Greys in formation. from the "St. Louis Greys Quick Step" sheet music, by J. W. Postlewaite, 10ᵀᴴ edition (originally published in 1852).

corporal.[15] "From this date [I] was continuously a soldier for four and a half years," Boyce observed years later.[16]

Frost and his men rode the rails for the next day and a half until reaching Smithton, the western terminus of the railroad, just east of Sedalia, Missouri. There, under "a heavy mist of rain," they unloaded their arms and equipment and prepared for an overland campaign.[17] For the first few days, the weather was beautiful, but the soldiers soon became acquainted with winter on the western plains. On December 3, snow began falling and the weather turned very cold. A series of marches brought the militia to the border with Kansas, but the raiders had yet to be seen. As the citizens of the area began to calm from the panic and as the governor received reports from more objective observers, it became apparent that launching the Southwest Expedition had been an overreaction. A small force of volunteer cavalry and artillery was left on the border under the command of Lieutenant Colonel John S. Bowen. General Frost and the bulk of the brigade returned to St. Louis.

Boyce and his comrades returned to a hero's welcome. Regardless of the necessity of the campaign, the St. Louis militia had performed admirably, and everyone but a few of the governor's critics seemed to be on hand when the train bearing the soldiers pulled into St. Louis on December 16. Boyce and the other soldiers of the St. Louis Greys formed as a company and marched to their unit's armory on Walnut Street between Third and Fourth streets in central St. Louis. From there, the Greys and their admirers were invited to the Everett House, where the soldiers were treated to "the richest and best" that the hotel could provide.[18]

Missouri's new governor, Claiborne Fox Jackson, was inaugurated on January 3, 1861. Governor Jackson was of pronounced states' rights sympathies, and as the secession crisis precipitated by South Carolina in December 1860 grew ever larger on the national scene, Jackson prepared Missouri as best he could for the course he saw ahead. On April 15, 1861, two days after the surrender of Fort Sumter to soldiers of the budding Confederacy, President Abraham Lincoln called for 75,000 militia "to maintain the honor, the integrity and existence of our national Union." Missouri was assigned a quota of four infantry regiments. Governor Jackson, believing Lincoln's call to be not only unconstitutional but also "inhuman and diabolical" in its intended purpose, declined the request and began more earnestly to render Missouri capable of defending itself. He sent two militia officers, Basil Duke and Colton Greene, to meet with President Jefferson Davis in Montgomery, Alabama, to ask for ordnance and other aid to protect Missouri's position.[19] He also began to direct the Missouri Volunteer Militia in ways that would enable his anticipated program of neutrality if not outright secession.[20]

On April 26, 1861, Captains Martin Burke and Joseph Kelly led Commissary Sergeant Boyce and other members of the St. Louis Greys and a sister company, the Washington Blues, to the powder magazine at Bissell's Point on the Mississippi River above St. Louis. During the night, the Greys and Blues moved the powder aboard the river steamers *Isabella* and *Augustus McDowell* and accompanied it up the Missouri River to Jefferson City, the state's capital. While they were on the river, a thunderstorm broke out that was, in Boyce's words, "simply fearful." The storm threatened the entire enterprise. "One stroke of lightning at that point would have carried sorrow into almost every family in St. Louis," he remembered.[21]

The St. Louis Greys and the Washington Blues delivered the powder to Jefferson City safely on April 28. Exhausted by their exertions, Boyce and his companions were relieved to see that someone in the state administration had arranged for convicts from the penitentiary to unload the powder and move it to its final destination. Governor Jackson arrived while the soldiers were still on the steamers to compliment them on "their faithful sense of duty." The command returned to St. Louis by railroad on April 29.[22]

On May 3, Sergeant Boyce was detailed to enlist recruits for the St. Louis Greys. Men of good character between the ages of eighteen and thirty-five were encouraged to join. As an inducement, the company would furnish uniforms and equipment.[23] The company's armory and drill hall were located on the third floor of a livery stable on the south side of Walnut Street between Third Street and Fourth Street in the St. Louis business district.[24]

Boyce and his comrades in the Missouri Volunteer Militia next assembled on May 6, 1861, in downtown St. Louis. The brigade of more than seven hundred men, two infantry regiments and their supporting units, had been summoned by Governor Jackson for its annual week of drill. Led by General Frost, the brigade marched west to make camp in a rolling, wooded area known as Lindell Grove. With tent rows and company streets neatly laid out by the engineers, the encampment was named Camp Jackson in honor of the governor.

The weeklong militia encampment was usually timed to coincide with Independence Day celebrations to assure that the militia was on hand to enliven the festivities. Given his refusal to support President Lincoln's call for troops, Governor Jackson's early call for the militia encampment was perceived by Federal authorities to have ominous portent. The arms and equipment of the United States Arsenal in St. Louis had long been discussed as the governor's objective. Throughout the South, seized Federal military property was being used to arm and equip the state militia.

CAPTAIN JOSEPH BOYCE

Anxious to assert Federal authority in St. Louis, Captain Nathaniel Lyon, 2nd U.S. Infantry, and Francis Preston Blair Jr., St. Louis's Republican congressman turned volunteer colonel, organized nearly ten regiments of Union volunteers, mostly immigrants from the Germanic kingdoms, principalities, or duchies of central Europe. On May 10, 1861, Lyon put most of them into motion to surround Camp Jackson and force the surrender of the Missouri Volunteer Militia encamped there. As the surrender proceeded, the crowd that had assembled to observe events became unruly, and someone fired a shot. Lyon's men fired in response into the crowd, their volleys killing guilty and innocent alike.

The soldiers of the Missouri Volunteer Militia, unarmed and under guard by Blair's regiment, could do no more than watch in horror. One of those soldiers was Joseph Boyce. Years later, he remembered the events:

> This capture was never forgiven and shall never be forgotten or condoned by those who were humiliated by this outrage. We were legally in our annual encampment by order of Gov. Claiborne F. Jackson as Missouri State troops and acting under the laws of the United States government. Our command at that time numbered about seven hundred muskets. Lyon and Blair surrounded our camp with over four thousand, and it was impossible to offer any resistance to their demand, so of course our commander, Gen. D. M. Frost, and his officers decided to comply with this shameful order. We were marched, guarded by our captors, to the St. Louis arsenal and held there until the next day, when we were paroled and set free. During the preliminaries [of the surrender] we were fired upon, and several of our comrades were killed and several wounded. Many citizens, lookers on, men, women, and children were shot down. A babe in its mother's arms was killed. Such a scene of brutality and murder resulted that to this day it is called the "Massacre of Camp Jackson."[25]

Not long after, twenty-year-old Joseph Boyce left St. Louis for Memphis, Tennessee, where he began his career in the 1st Missouri Infantry, C.S.A. During the next four years, the regiment would fight in many of the major

BIOGRAPHICAL SKETCH

CAPTAIN JOSEPH BOYCE, COMPANY D, 1ˢᵀ/4ᵀᴴ MISSOURI INFANTRY, C.S.A.
COLORED PHOTOGRAPH, 1865.

battles of the Confederacy in the western theater, from Shiloh to Vicksburg, from Atlanta to Franklin, surrendering at Fort Blakely in the defense of Mobile, Alabama, in April 1865. After Vicksburg's surrender until he fell in the attack at Franklin with his third wound of the war, Boyce served as the senior officer of his company.

After the war, Boyce returned to St. Louis where he persevered to become a success in business. Boyce worked briefly for his pre-war employer but soon became a traveling salesman in the wholesale tobacco business, covering Illinois, Wisconsin, Minnesota, and Missouri. In 1868, he entered into partnership with his brother, Anthony, to form Boyce Brothers, a tobacco manufacturer.

On June 17, 1868, Boyce married Miss Mary Elizabeth Casey, the youngest daughter of John and Juliette Casey of Carondelet, a southern suburb of St. Louis where the family had moved ten years before.[26] John Casey had made his fortune in lead mining around Potosi, Missouri, and was considered "a man of the most rigid integrity."[27] Joseph and Mary Elizabeth Boyce had five children: John P., William D., Sally M., Mary F., and Joseph Jr. All lived to maturity.

During the next three decades, Boyce Brothers suffered occasional financial reverses, but overall the enterprise was a success, expanding its trading area from the Midwest to Boston and Richmond. In 1903, Joseph Boyce formally added St. Louis real estate to his portfolio, an activity that greatly enhanced his fortune. His eldest son joined him in operating the Boyce Realty Company of St. Louis.

Throughout his life, Joseph Boyce was a participant in religious, civic, and military organizations, often in a leadership role. In 1857, he had become a member of the Young Men's Sodality of St. Xavier's Parish, and for several years he served as the president of the Holy Angels' St. Vincent de Paul Society. He was an organizer of the Society of Knights of St. Patrick and for two years served as secretary.[28] From 1901 until 1904, Boyce served as vice president of the St. Louis city council, and from this position he was actively involved in the planning for the Louisiana Purchase Exposition of 1904, the St. Louis World's Fair.[29]

Despite his commercial and civic involvements, it was through his postwar avocation rather than his professional dealings that Joseph Boyce made an enduring contribution. Twenty years after the events, Captain Boyce wrote his history of the 1st Missouri Infantry, C.S.A., for presentation to the Southern Historical and Benevolent Society of St. Louis. Boyce first presented his work as a series of lectures to an audience that included people who shared his experience of war. Rarely did he criticize, but he was equally careful and measured with his praise. Boyce was likely an entertaining presenter. His history is interrupted by anecdotes, often involving a fellow Irishman, and it is easy to imagine Boyce slipping into the entrancing

BIOGRAPHICAL SKETCH

brogue of his parents' Ireland. Captain Boyce has provided us with a factual, highly readable account of what is arguably one of the best regiments of the Confederate army and certainly one of the most interesting units in Missouri's military history. The Missouri Historical Society remembered him as "possessing a most accurate memory and delightful sense of humor, which was ever kind, [and] made him a much sought-after companion."[30]

On November 17, 1888, Boyce and eight others met at the Missouri Historical Society to form the Veteran Volunteer Fireman's Historical Society. In 1893, when the constitution and bylaws of the organization were published, an article was included that had been selected "as the most appropriate and best adapted to show the object of the Society." The article was written by Joseph Boyce. Membership was limited to veterans of the volunteer fire departments of St. Louis. By 1899, the social organization had eighty-four members, but membership was "steadily diminishing as there are no recruits."[31]

In 1896, Boyce and Union veteran Major Charles G. Warner organized a meeting of like-minded veterans at the Planter's House Hotel to form an association called "Veterans of the Blue and Gray." One of the primary purposes of the society was to "cultivate a feeling of friendship and fraternity between those who were once opposed in arms and to extinguish all animosities which were engendered by the late Civil War."[32] The society was a reflection of both Boyce's beliefs and the sentiments of St. Louis's veterans, Union or Confederate. As an indication of their interest in reconciliation, the society set the date of its annual meeting as February 12—Abraham Lincoln's birthday. In 1897 he completed a study entitled "Military Organizations Describing the Uniforms and the Action That These Organizations Took in the Civil War."[33] This typescript in the collections of the Missouri Historical Society is not only an invaluable compilation of information about the Missouri militia but also a personal account of Boyce's actions with the militia before the war.

In 1901, when Boyce was running for a position on the St. Louis City Council, a newspaper reminded its readers that "in the old times, before the war, Joe ran with the machine and was just about as good a volunteer fireman as ever handled a nozzle." "He may not be so young as he once was," the writer continued, "but mentally, morally and physically, he is the peer of any man in this great and glorious country of free men and beautiful women."[34]

Throughout this period, Boyce's greatest devotion was given to the Missouri Historical Society. Boyce joined the Society in 1881 and four years later, he was elected to the organization's board of directors, serving for more than thirty-four years and gaining a reputation as "one of the most active members" of the Society's board.[35] Founded in 1866, the Missouri Historical Society was viewed by many former Confederates as a repository for their history.[36] Among Boyce's donations to the Society are his uniform from the St. Louis Greys, a .31 caliber pocket pistol that he carried during the war, and a sword with the words "Shiloh" and "Vicksburg" engraved on the blade. The Society's library and archives also received his attention. Boyce had subscribed to *Confederate Veteran* since its first issue in 1893. Each year he had his copies of the magazine bound and presented to the Missouri Historical Society. On the shelves of the Society's library, Boyce wrote, "They are a treasure highly appreciated and frequently referred to by many who need information of their relatives who served in the Confederate army."[37] Boyce's devotion to the Society was legendary; after his death, a memorial from the Society claimed that he never, in thirty-four years as a director, "missed a meeting unless unavoidably prevented by illness or other cause." In 1904, he was elected vice president of the Society.[38]

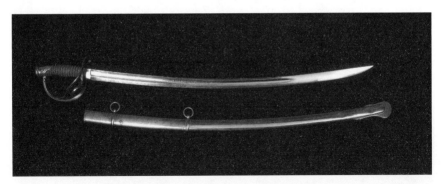

SWORD PRESENTED TO JOSEPH BOYCE, WITH THE SCABBARD INSCRIBED: "1861–1865/ JOSEPH BOYCE/CAPT. CO. 'D'/FIRST MO. INFTY./C.S.A./SHILOH/VICKSBURG/ BATON ROUGE/CORINTH/GEORGIA CAMPAIGN/UNDER GENLS. JOHNSTON & HOOD/ ALLATOONA [&] TILTON, GA./FRANKLIN, TENN./SELMA, ALA./UNDER GENL./N.B. FOREST [*sic*]." DATE UNKNOWN.

BIOGRAPHICAL SKETCH

Joseph Boyce succumbed to "the infirmities of age" on July 29, 1928.[39] He had retired from active participation in his business only two months before. "A brave and gallant soldier has passed to his reward," reported *Confederate Veteran*. A St. Louis newspaper pointed less to his military service and more to his accomplishments after the war. "Once the war was over he forgot internal strife and entered as eagerly into life of the reconstruction days as he had into that of the bloody days that preceded them." Boyce "became a patriot of his city, of his State and of his country, and so he remained to the end."[40]

The Missouri Historical Society recognized his many contributions and awarded him one of its highest honors. For the day of his funeral, the Society closed its doors.

THIS HEADSTONE IN CALVARY CEMETERY, ST. LOUIS, MISSOURI, MARKS THE FINAL RESTING PLACE OF CAPTAIN JOSEPH BOYCE, 1ST MISSOURI INFANTRY, C.S.A. PHOTO BY WILLIAM C. WINTER.

CAPTAIN JOSEPH BOYCE

ENDNOTES

1. The Christian Brothers College High School, a Roman Catholic college preparatory high school, was founded in St. Louis in 1850 by members of the De La Salle Christian Brothers, "serving youth through the ministry of education since 1680." www.cbchs.org.

2. An advertisement for Jones' Commercial College, founded by Jonathan Jones in 1841, appears in a city directory for 1857 and offers "a full course of instruction" in "double-entry bookkeeping" with "special instructions given in the art of detecting counterfeit money." Robert V. Kennedy, *Kennedy's Saint Louis City Directory for the Year 1857, Containing a General Directory of Citizens* (St. Louis: R.V. Kennedy, 1857), 18.

3. A city directory identifies Boyce as living with his widowed mother while working as a clerk for Ober, Norris & Co. Robert V. Kennedy, *Kennedy's Saint Louis City Directory for the Year 1859, Containing a General Directory of Citizens* (St. Louis: R.V. Kennedy, 1859), 65.

4. Joseph Boyce, "Military Organizations," in *Encyclopedia of the History of St. Louis: A Compendium of History and Biography for Ready Reference*, ed. William Hyde and Howard Louis Conard (New York: The Southern History Company, 1899), 1502–1503.

5. The details of Joseph Boyce's early life are based on the biographical entry "Boyce, Joseph" found in Hyde and Conard, *Encyclopedia of the History of St. Louis*, 203–205. It is likely that Boyce supplied these details personally, since he assisted the editors on other entries about St. Louis history. It is possible that he wrote the sketch himself.

6. "St. Louis Greys Quick Step," composed and dedicated to Captain George Knapp and the St. Louis Greys by J.W. Postlewaite, published by Balmer & Weber, St. Louis, MO.

7. M. Hopewell, M.D., *Camp Jackson: History of the Missouri Volunteer Militia of St. Louis* (St. Louis: George Knapp & Company, 1861), 15. Boyce, "Military Organizations," in *Encyclopedia of the History of St. Louis*, 1509.

8. Joseph Boyce, *Military Organizations, Describing the Uniforms and Actions That Those Organizations Took in the Civil War*, typescript, 1897, Missouri History Museum Archives, 8. An edited version of this work appears as the entry "Military Organizations" in Hyde and Conard, *Encyclopedia of the History of St. Louis*, 1489–1518.

9. "Irish Immigrants Fought Back in Nativist Riots of 1854," *St. Louis Post-Dispatch*, August 8, 2010, and "Many Mourned Death of Iconic Senator," *St. Louis Post-Dispatch*, April 18, 2010.

10. *Missouri Republican*, July 7, 1860.

11. Hopewell, *Camp Jackson*, 13, 16–17. Boyce, "Military Organizations," in *Encyclopedia of the History of St. Louis*, 1490.

12. *History of Vernon County, Missouri* (St. Louis: Brown & Co., 1887; reprint, Clinton, MO: The Printery, 1974), 255.

BIOGRAPHICAL SKETCH

13. Albert Castel, *Kansas: A Frontier State at War* (Lawrence: Kansas Heritage Press, 1958), 42.

14. *Missouri Democrat*, November 26, 1860. *History of Vernon County*, 256.

15. Hopewell, *Camp Jackson*, 26.

16. Boyce, *Military Organizations*, 93.

17. *Missouri Republican*, November 29, 1860.

18. *Missouri Democrat*, December 17, 1860.

19. Basil Wilson Duke, *The Civil War Reminiscences of General Basil W. Duke, C.S.A.* (Garden City, NY: Doubleday, Page, 1911; reprint, Cooper Square Press, 2001), 44.

20. Frederick A. Culmer. *A New History of Missouri* (Mexico, MO: The McIntyre Publishing Company, 1938), 365–366. Christopher Phillips, *Missouri's Confederate: Claiborne Fox Jackson and the Creation of Southern Identity in the Border West* (Columbia: University of Missouri Press, 2000), 242–245.

21. Boyce, *Military Organizations*, 73–74.

22. *Ibid.*

23. *Missouri Republican*, May 3, 1861.

24. "Volunteer Reviews History of the First Missouri Regiment," *St. Louis Republican*, July 26, 1908, in Camp Jackson Papers, MHM Archives.

25. Joseph Boyce, "What Flag Was This?" *Confederate Veteran* 27 (1919): 235.

26. Mary Casey was born in Old Mines, Missouri, on August 25, 1844. Her father, John, was born in Cork, Ireland. Her mother, Juliet Detchmendy, was a native of France. Missouri State Archives, Missouri Birth and Death Records Database, at http://www.sos.mo.gov/archives/resources/birthdeath.

27. William Hyde, "Gay and Festive Times in Old Carondelet," *Bulletin of the Missouri Historical Society* 6 (1950): 330.

28. Hyde and Conard, *Encyclopedia of the History of St. Louis*, 205. Entry for "Boyce, Joseph."

29. Missouri History Museum Archives, comp. Necrologies of Missouri Historical Society Members, Volume D, 78A. "Capt. Joseph Boyce," *St. Louis Post-Dispatch*, July 31, 1928.

30. Missouri Historical Society, Resolution Passed by the Officers and Members of the Board of Trustees, 1928, Boyce Family Papers, MHM Archives.

31. *Constitution and By-Laws of the Veteran Volunteer Fireman's Historical Society of the City of St. Louis, Mo.* (St. Louis: n.p., 1893). Hyde and Conard, *Encyclopedia of the History of St. Louis*, 2374. Boyce was a veteran of Union Fire Company No. 2. The company was in operation from 1832 to 1855.

32. Howard L. Conard, *Encyclopedia of the History of Missouri* (New York: The Southern History Company, 1901), 306.

33. Joseph Boyce, *Military Organizations*.

34. "Capt. Joe Boyce," *St. Louis Merchant*, March 31, 1901, Boyce Scrapbook, MHM Archives.

CAPTAIN JOSEPH BOYCE

35. "Funeral Services for Joseph Boyce to Be Held Tomorrow," *St. Louis Globe Democrat*, July 30, 1928, Boyce Family Papers, MHM Archives.
36. The former Missouri Historical Society now operates its two divisions in St. Louis as the Missouri History Museum and the Missouri History Museum Library and Research Center. It should not be confused with the State Historical Society of Missouri in Columbia.
37. Joseph Boyce, "In the Missouri Infantry," *Confederate Veteran* 33 (1925): 158.
38. Missouri Historical Society, Resolution Passed by the Officers and Members of the Board of Trustees, 1928, Boyce Family Papers, MHM Archives.
39. Mr. and Mrs. Boyce resided at 5812 Clemens Avenue in St. Louis. Mrs. Mary E. J. Casey Boyce died on March 30, 1932. As her husband had been, she was eighty-seven years old at the time of her death. Missouri Historical Society *Necrologies*, 79, unidentified clip, July 30, 1928. Missouri State Archives, Missouri Birth and Death Records Database, at www.sos.mo.gov/archives/resources/birthdeath.
40. *St. Louis Globe Democrat*, July 30, 1928, Boyce Family Papers, MHM Archives.

CHAPTER 1
GETTING ORGANIZED
JUNE–SEPTEMBER 1861

THE TERRIBLE EVENTS AT CAMP JACKSON ON MAY 10, 1861, SENT TREMORS THROUGH ST. LOUIS AND THE REST OF MISSOURI. WITH THE HELP OF MISSOURI'S GENERAL ASSEMBLY, GOVERNOR CLAIBORNE FOX JACKSON QUICKLY ESTABLISHED THE ADMINISTRATIVE MACHINERY TO CREATE THE MISSOURI STATE GUARD, A SUCCESSOR TO THE MISSOURI VOLUNTEER MILITIA. ON MAY 11, JACKSON WAS EMPOWERED "TO RAISE MONEY TO ARM THE STATE, REPEL INVASION, AND PROTECT THE LIVES AND PROPERTY OF MISSOURI." FORMER GOVERNOR STERLING PRICE WAS SOON APPOINTED MAJOR GENERAL AND COMMANDER OF THE MISSOURI STATE GUARD.[1]

SOUTHERN SYMPATHIZERS IN MID-MISSOURI AND IN THE FOUR CORNERS OF THE STATE NOW HAD AN OPPORTUNITY TO PROVIDE ARMED RESISTANCE TO FEDERAL AUTHORITY IF THEY SO CHOSE. IN ST. LOUIS, HOWEVER, REGIMENTS OF FEDERAL VOLUNTEERS PATROLLED THE STREETS AND GUARDED PUBLIC PROPERTY. UNABLE TO ENDURE THE PRESENCE OF FEDERAL AUTHORITY ON MISSOURI'S SOIL, MANY SOUTHERN SYMPATHIZERS OF MILITARY AGE TOOK ADVANTAGE OF THE CITY'S EASY ACCESS TO THE YOUNG CONFEDERACY AND WENT SOUTH TO ENLIST. JOSEPH BOYCE WAS AMONG THEM.

AT MEMPHIS, TENNESSEE, COLONEL JOHN BOWEN WAS BUSY ORGANIZING THE 1ST MISSOURI INFANTRY, C.S.A. BOWEN, A NATIVE OF GEORGIA, HAD BEEN ASSIGNED TO THE REGIMENT OF MOUNTED RIFLEMEN ON HIS GRADUATION FROM THE UNITED STATES MILITARY ACADEMY IN 1853. HIS FIRST POST

GETTING ORGANIZED

WAS THE JEFFERSON BARRACKS JUST SOUTH OF ST. LOUIS, AND IN 1854 HE MARRIED INTO A LARGE AND PROSPEROUS ST. LOUIS FAMILY. BOWEN LEFT THE ARMY IN 1856, AND AFTER A BRIEF STAY IN SAVANNAH, BOWEN AND HIS WIFE RETURNED TO ST. LOUIS TO MAKE THEIR HOME. BOWEN SOON BECAME ACTIVE IN THE MISSOURI VOLUNTEER MILITIA, FIRST AS A CAPTAIN AND COMPANY COMMANDER, THEN AS A STAFF OFFICER TO GENERAL DANIEL FROST AND FINALLY AS COLONEL, 2ND REGIMENT, MISSOURI VOLUNTEER MILITIA. AFTER HIS INVOLVEMENT IN THE CAMP JACKSON EVENTS, BOWEN WAS UNWILLING TO WAIT FOR THE MISSOURI STATE GUARD TO MATURE AND GO INTO ACTION. AFTER TRAVELING TO RICHMOND, BOWEN OBTAINED A COLONEL'S COMMISSION FROM THE CONFEDERATE WAR DEPARTMENT AND WITH IT PERMISSION TO RAISE MISSOURI'S FIRST REGIMENT FOR CONFEDERATE SERVICE. HE SOON BEGAN ASSEMBLING AND ORGANIZING RECRUITS FROM MISSOURI IN MEMPHIS.

JOSEPH BOYCE JOINED FOR DUTY AND ENROLLED IN THE 1ST MISSOURI INFANTRY AT MEMPHIS ON JULY 11, 1861. LATER THAT MONTH, BOYCE WROTE TO FRIENDS IN ST. LOUIS TO TELL HOW IMPRESSED HE WAS WITH THE WAR EFFORT IN MEMPHIS. AT ONE FACTORY, "THEY TURN OUT COMPLETE THREE (BRASS 6 POUNDERS) CANNONS PER WEEK MOUNTED AND READY FOR USE, ALSO SWORDS THREE DOZEN A DAY DONE UP IN THE MOST IMPROVED STYLE.... TO SEE THE SHOT THEY HAVE AROUND THE WORKS WOULD ASTONISH YOU," HE ASSERTED. CONCERNING PERSONAL NEWS, BOYCE ADDED WITH YOUTHFUL CONFIDENCE THAT THE ELECTION OF OFFICERS HAD NOT YET BEEN HELD, BUT "THE BOYS SAY THAT I MUST BE FIRST LIEUT. OR THEY WILL LEAVE THE CORPS. THEY WILL NOT SERVE UNDER ANY COUNTRY JAKE IN WAR TIMES AS THEY DO NOT UNDERSTAND THE DRILL."[2]

WHEN THE REGIMENT COMPLETED ITS ORGANIZATION IN AUGUST, JOSEPH BOYCE HELD THE POSITION OF SECOND LIEUTENANT IN COMPANY D. HE WAS TWENTY-ONE YEARS OLD.

Immediately after the capture of Camp Jackson, May 10, 1861, Col. John S. Bowen, commanding the Second Regiment, M.V.M.,[3] or better known as

JOHN S. BOWEN OF CARONDELET, MISSOURI,
WAS THE ORGANIZER AND FIRST COLONEL OF THE
1ST MISSOURI INFANTRY. DATE UNKNOWN.

the "Minute Men," left for Richmond, Va., via Louisville, Ky., and arrived safely, when he at once called upon President Davis, who received him very cordially, immediately commissioned him Colonel, and authorized him to raise a regiment of Missouri infantry.[4] Col. Bowen, without delay, proceeded to Memphis, Tenn., and issued his call to the Camp Jackson prisoners, who had been released on parole and were awaiting a decision whether their parole was binding or not.[5] This is a point the writer will not discuss or enlarge upon, as the paroled prisoners were shortly after exchanged by Gen. Sterling Price for the prisoners captured by him at Lexington, Mo., under command of Col. Mulligan, thereby relieving us of any responsibility attached to our parole.[6]

The information spread quickly throughout the city of St. Louis that Col. Bowen wanted us at Memphis. At once the men began leaving in squads of five, ten, fifteen and less. It was hard work to run the blockade at Cairo, Ill., and Louisville, Ky., but it was successfully done, however, by several hundred of the old 1st Missouri infantry and the Second regiment mentioned above.[7] The men were place in camps on the Pigeon Roost road, about two miles east of Memphis, and the organization started.

The regiment remained at this point about two months, when it was ordered to Fort Pillow.[8]

There were plenty of boats lying at the wharf, but no hands to man them. This was soon overcome, as we had a company—B, Captain Robert J. Duffy—that was almost made up entirely of boatmen; this company took charge of three boats and made the detail of pilots, engineers, etc., and the day after we received our orders, much to the satisfaction of Gen. Leonidas Polk, they had us underway for Fort Pillow with all our baggage and every man on board.[9] We reached this point in due time, but had hardly gotten into camp when we were ordered up to New Madrid, Mo.[10] This news was received with every evidence of pleasure by the command. Again Company B took charge of the boats, and landed us safely the next night about 10 o'clock at our destination. Again we were in Missouri. As we marched ashore we made the woods ring with our cheers for the old state.

The regimental colors were two large silk flags, one the regulation Stars and Bars, presented to the regiment by the ladies of Memphis, Tenn., the day the command left for New Madrid, Mo., about August 15, 1861. The other one was of rich dark blue silk, heavily bordered with gold fringe. On one side handsomely painted was the seal of the State of Missouri; the reverse bore a picture of a large tigress in the jungle, lying on the grass, with her young cubs at play about her. Beneath this scene on a gilded scroll was in large letters the word BEWARE.

This flag, a beautiful work of St. Louis artists, originally was the colors of the Second Missouri Infantry organized by Col. Jno. S. Bowen and known as "The Missouri Minute Men."[11] It was formed about a year before the breaking out of the war. This regiment was captured at Camp Jackson with its brigade, May 10, 1861. The flag, however, was taken away before the final surrender by Mrs. Bowen and later carried through the federal lines at Cairo, Ill., about her body. Upon her arrival at Memphis, she presented it to our regiment and the name "Second" changed to "First Missouri Confederate Infantry."[12]

We were placed in camp about half a mile back of the town, and a few weeks after, or about the 1st of September, the organization was completed as follows:

JOHN S. BOWEN	COLONEL
LUCIUS L. RICH	LIEUTENANT COLONEL
CHAS. C. CAMPBELL	MAJOR
LEWIS H. KENNERLY	ADJUTANT
WILLIAM F. HAINES	CAPTAIN AND QUARTERMASTER
JAMES M. QUINL[A]N	CAPTAIN AND COMMISSARY
CARY N. HAWES	SURGEON
JOSEPH REYNOLDS	ASSISTANT SURGEON
FRANK SHAW	HOSPITAL STEWARD
CHARLES CORWIN	QUARTERMASTER SERGEANT
JAMES KERR	COMMISSARY SERGEANT
TIM HEALY	SERGEANT MAJOR
WILLIAM BUCKLEY	ORDNANCE SERGEANT
JAMES KENNERLY	BAND MASTER
JAMES LALOR	ARTIFICER
JOHN MCINTOSH, PATRICK MARR	SERGEANTS, COLOR BEARERS
REV. MR. UNGERER	CHAPLAIN
ARTHUR MCCOY	CAPTAIN, MASTER OF TRANSPORTATION
WILLIAM CANNON	ASSISTANT MASTER OF TRANSPORTATION

COMPANY A: PARGOUD VOLUNTEERS, NEW ORLEANS[13]

    CAPT. J. KEMP SPRAGUE

    LIEUTS. [HENRY H.] WALSH, JOSEPH [H.] BASS, AND DUDLEY [A.] WALSH

GETTING ORGANIZED

COMPANY B: WADE GUARDS, ST. LOUIS

CAPT. ROBERT J. DUFFY

LIEUTS. WILLIAM [J.] MCARTHUR, GREGORY BYRNE, AND [AUGUSTA] "GUS" GALBAUGH

COMPANY C: SOUTH ST. LOUIS GUARDS, CARONDELET

CAPT. DAVID HIRSCH

LIEUTS. JOHN [M.] MUSE, DAVID WALKER, AND GUY [P.] SMITH

COMPANY D: ST. LOUIS GREYS

CAPT. MARTIN BURKE

LIEUTS. LEWIS H. KENNERLY, W. C. P. CARRINGTON, AND JOSEPH BOYCE

COMPANY E: ST. LOUIS MINUTE MEN

CAPT. OLIN F. RICE

LIEUTS. JAMES PRITCHARD, JOSEPH DEANE, AND L[LOYD] A. HAYNES

COMPANY F: ST. LOUIS SOUTHERN GUARDS

CAPT. HUGH A. GARLAND

LIEUTS. JOHN [C.] DOUGLASS, R[ANDOLPH] R. HUTCHINSON, AND SMITH N. HAWES.

COMPANY G: NEW MADRID GUARDS, NEW MADRID COUNTY

CAPT. [THOMAS J.] PHILLIPS

LIEUT. A. C. R[ILE]Y, WASH. DAWSON, AND JOSEPH T. HARG[ETT]

COMPANY H: PEMISCOTT RIFLES, PEMISCOTT COUNTY

CAPT. [JOHN A.] GORDON

LIEUTS. [GEORGE C.] GORDON, JAMES [H.] MCFARLAND, AND [GEORGE W.] YERG[IN]

COMPANY I: MISSOURI GUARDS, NEW MADRID COUNTY

    CAPT. [TILFORD] HOGAN

    LIEUTS. [BRADFORD] KEITH, GOAH [W.] STEWART, AND SAM[UEL A.] KENNERLY

COMPANY K: MISSOURI GREYS, NEW MADRID COUNTY

    CAPT. [JOHN C.] AVER[ILL]

    LIEUTS. CHARLES L. EDMONDSON, [GEORGE C.] KNIGHT, AND JAMES [M.] DAUGHT[ERS][14]

CHRIS SCHAFFER	SUTLER
JABEZ MULHOLLAND	SUTLER'S CLERK
MORDECAI MILLER, ISAAC FOWLER, MICHAEL GARDNER	CLERKS AT HEADQUARTERS

The enlisted men, exclusive of officers, numbered at least 1,000 the day after the regiment was organized. It was reported for duty, every officer and man present. Not one on the sick list. Everybody present and for duty. This was so remarkable in a regiment so large that Gen. Pillow (for we were assigned to his brigade) had us formed and complimented Col. Bowen and the command.[15]

The drilling and the discipline now began in earnest; first, the officers were called upon and examined; all had to have a good English education and a natural talent for their position; if not, they had to resign at once to make way for better material. The above named list of officers passed a satisfactory examination and were commissioned at once.

All the officers were formed into a company and put through the manual of arms and company movements daily by our field officers. Later on a school was established and Hardee's *Tactics* and *Army Regulations* took the place of all the other reading matter about camp.[16]

We had a large blackboard, like those used in schools, and we had to step up and make our movements with chalk, give the proper commands and show how the company or regiment would be placed after certain movements; in fact, we received such instruction of this kind as is given at the Military Academy at West Point.

GETTING ORGANIZED

It was absolutely necessary that an officer of this regiment should be able not only to drill his company, but to take command of the regiment and manoeuvre it.

Many a time a line officer, when least expected, would be called on to take charge of the regiment, and woe be to him if he blundered. This soon made the officers feel they had no easy job before them. To their credit be it said, they were generally equal to the occasion.

We were very fortunate in our selection for field officers, as they all were graduates of the West Point Military Academy, while several of our line officers were from the same institute and the Kentucky and Virginia military schools.[17] Almost all the officers had experience as such in the St. Louis military companies for several years prior to the war.[18]

While at New Madrid the regiment was drilled several hours during the day in battalion movements, mostly at the double-quick. We had encamped near us the Memphis Light Dragoons, a fine body of men that afterwards formed a part of the famous Forrest's cavalry.[19] For the benefit of visitors from Memphis and the surrounding country of New Madrid we would be ordered out for drill—the command would form squares at a double quick to resist cavalry, then the Memphis cavalry would charge us with flashing blades and charging steeds; they would come at us with a rush, but no amount of urging and spurring could induce the horses to face the bayonets; they would come nearly up, but they would be forced to wheel about and form again.[20]

This company found this experience of vast advantage to them afterwards when they charged the enemy in earnest. It gave the regiment great confidence in the bayonet, and our favorite movement was double quick and charge bayonets.

After six weeks' hard drilling we were ordered up to Columbus, Ky., and encamped on one of the high bluffs just north of the town.[21] The only thing worthy of mention in regard to the enemy while encamped here was the shelling of our camp one afternoon by the gun-boats *Conestoga* and *Lexington*. These boats would come down the river almost every day from Cairo and give us a little artillery practice. With the exception of one day, their shells always fell short of the camp.[22]

I wish to state that while here Gen. Albert Sidney Johnston took command of the army and he reviewed us. He was so well pleased with the bearing and movements of the command that he ever afterward called for the First Missouri when he wanted a thoroughly reliable regiment. He was well acquainted with Col. Bowen in the old army and our Lt. Col. Rich was with him on the Salt Lake or Utah campaign.[23]

GETTING ORGANIZED

ENDNOTES

1. U.S. War Department, Organization and Status of Missouri Troops, 251.

2. Joseph Boyce to Messrs. Keogh & Dowell, July 20, 1861, Boyce Family Papers, MHM Archives.

3. The M.V.M. is the Missouri Volunteer Militia, the designation of the pre-war state militia. The organization should not be confused with the Missouri State Guard, as the pro-Confederate state forces were known after May 1861.

4. In the turbulent months of late 1860 and early 1861, Republican supporters in St. Louis organized the "Wide Awakes" to assist with political parades and demonstrations. In response, supporters of the Democratic ticket formed groups called "Minute Men." In the early months of 1861, a special effort was made to recruit these "Minute Men" into companies for the Missouri Volunteer Militia. Several were organized, and when they were combined with other militia companies, they were sufficient to create the Second Regiment of the Missouri Volunteer Militia. Robert J. Rombauer, *The Union Cause in St. Louis in 1861* (St. Louis: Nixon-Jones Publishing Co., 1909), 53.

5. Parole, in Civil War terminology, was a promise made by a captured soldier not to bear arms until "exchanged" for an enemy soldier who had also been given parole. In return for this promise, the parolee remained free. The parole system was based on the word of honor of the participants, and early in the war, at least, treated with formality. Mark M. Boatner III, *The Civil War Dictionary* (New York: David McKay Company, 1959), 619–620.

6. On September 20, 1861, Colonel James Adelbert Mulligan and 2,800 soldiers surrendered to Price and the Missouri State Guard after an intermittent ten-day siege at Lexington, Missouri. Jay Monaghan, *Civil War on the Western Border, 1854–1865* (Lincoln: University of Nebraska Press, 1955), 187–194.

7. The "old First Missouri Infantry," the senior regiment of the Missouri Volunteer Militia in the St. Louis district, should not be confused with the 1st Missouri Infantry, C.S.A. The 1st Infantry, M.V.M., was commanded at Camp Jackson by Lieutenant Colonel John Knapp. Knapp and others of his regiment served creditably in the Union army. Hopewell, *Camp Jackson*, 11.

8. The regiment left the Memphis area for Fort Pillow, Tennessee, in mid-July. Jane B. Hewitt, Noah Andre Trudeau, and Bryce A. Suderow, eds., *Supplement to the Official Records of the Union and Confederate Armies* (Wilmington, NC: Broadfoot, 1994), vol. 38, 379 (hereafter *OR Supplement*).

9. Leonidas Polk, a graduate of the United States Military Academy, an Episcopal bishop, and a close friend of President Jefferson Davis, commanded the Mississippi River defenses in 1861. Ezra J. Warner, *Generals in Gray: Lives of the Confederate Commanders* (Baton Rouge: Louisiana State University Press, 1959), 242–243.

10. The incomplete regiment returned to Missouri in late August 1861. At Camp Reynolds near New Madrid, Companies F, C, D, and E were mustered

into service on consecutive days beginning on August 24. *OR Supplement,* vol. 38, 382–386.

11. Boyce's reference is to the 2nd Regiment, Missouri Volunteer Militia, Missouri's pre-war militia.

12. This description of the regimental flags is added from a handwritten account by Boyce, "The Flags of the First Missouri Confederate Infantry," in Boyce Family Papers, MHM Archives.

13. The company names and their geographic origin are added from "Roster of Field and Line Officers, First Missouri Confederate Infantry, Organization Completed New Madrid, Mo. Sept. 1861," typescript, Boyce Family Papers, MHM Archives. A handwritten correction to this typescript identifies the Louisianans of Company A as the Suchet Guards, but reports by the State of Louisiana identify the company as the Pargoud Volunteers raised in Orleans Parish (New Orleans).

14. The corrections and completions to names are based on *OR Supplement,* vol. 38, 373–378, which is in turn based on an examination of unit rolls and reports. In Nicholson, Boyce deleted the name of Lieutenant John W. Brownell in Company K, replacing him with Lieutenant Knight.

15. Gideon Johnson Pillow was a law partner of future president James K. Polk before being appointed a brigadier general of volunteers in 1846 for service in the war with Mexico. He was appointed brigadier general in the Confederate army on July 9, 1861. Warner, *Generals in Gray,* 241.

16. The work known as "Hardee's *Tactics*" was a standard drill manual for both Union and Confederate soldiers. Under the direction of Secretary of War Jefferson Davis, William J. Hardee produced the two-volume *Rifle and Light Infantry Tactics* in 1855. Grady McWhiney and Perry D. Jamieson, *Attack and Die: Civil War Military Tactics and the Southern Heritage* (Tuscaloosa: University of Alabama Press, 1982), 49.

17. Bowen and Rich were cadets together at the West Point, both graduating in the class of 1853. Major Charles Carroll Campbell and Captain Olin F. Rice, commander of Company E, were both members of the class of 1861, resigning from the U.S. Army immediately after graduation. George W. Cullum, *Biographical Register of the Officers and Graduates of the U.S. Military Academy at West Point, N.Y.* (New York: D. Van Nostrand, 1868), vol. 2, 342–343, 365. Mary Elizabeth Sergent, *They Lie Forgotten: The United States Military Academy, 1856–1861* (Middleton, NY: Prior King Press, 1986), 122, 174.

18. Of the ten captains now commanding companies in the 1st Missouri, Martin Burke and Hugh Garland had recently been captains in the Missouri Volunteer Militia. Regimental commissary James Quinlan and surgeon Cary Hawes had held these positions under Bowen in the 2nd Regiment, M.V.M. Lieutenants Lewis H. Kennerly (Co. B), David Walker (Co. C), W. C. P. Carrington (Co. D), P. R. Hutchinson (Co. F), and Wash. Dawson (Co. G) had previously served as lieutenants in the Missouri militia. In 1861, Boyce

GETTING ORGANIZED

was fourth corporal in the St. Louis Greys, Company A, 1st Regiment, M.V.M. Hopewell, *Camp Jackson*, 11–13, 16–25.

Writing fifty years later, when asked about Carrington, Boyce answered, "I never speak or think of him without a pang of sorrow. He was my good friend." Carrington was killed at Champion Hill (Baker's Creek) in May 1863. Joseph Boyce to Isaac J. Fowler, May 10, 1913, Boyce Family Papers, MHM Archives.

19. The Memphis Light Dragoons were organized in 1860 as cavalry in the Tennessee militia. The company was mustered in for Confederate service on May 16, 1861, and served initially in the 6th Tennessee Cavalry Battalion. In April 1862 the Memphis Light Dragoons became Company A of the 7th Tennessee Cavalry Regiment. Civil War Centennial Commission, *Tennesseans in the Civil War* (Nashville: n.p., 1964) vol. 1, 27, 68–69.

20. The European tactical infantry maneuver of forming squares as a defense against cavalry was rarely practiced in American armies during the Civil War. A British historian suggests that "the day of the cavalry charge had passed; that the rifled musket's improved firepower had given a new security to infantry." Paddy Griffith, *Battle Tactics of the Civil War* (New Haven: Yale University Press, 1987), 180.

21. The 1st Missouri embarked for Columbus on September 1, 1861. Hewitt, *OR Supplement*, vol. 38, 379.

22. *Conestoga*, *Lexington*, and a sister ship, *Tyler*, began their military careers in Cincinnati as side-wheel steamboats, three stories tall. Their superstructure was cut down, the interiors of the hulls lined with oak plank, the boilers lowered and placed between the engines, and the decks cleared for action. After being floated to Cairo, Illinois, *Conestoga* was equipped with three 32-pound guns. *Lexington* received four 64-pounder broadside guns and two 32-pounders. James M. Merrill, *Battle Flags South: The Story of the Civil War Navies on Western Waters* (Rutherford, NJ: Farleigh Dickinson University Press, 1970), 27–31.

23. As a second lieutenant in the 5th United States Infantry, Rich served in the Utah Expedition led by Johnston in 1857 and 1858. According to Captain Jesse Gove of the 10th Infantry, Rich served as acting assistant quartermaster on Johnston's staff and was one of the "gentlemen in his mess." Otis G. Hammond, ed., *The Utah Expedition, 1857–1858: Letters of Capt. Jesse A. Gove, 10th Inf., U.S.A. of Concord, N.H.* (Concord: New Hampshire Historical Society, 1928), 273.

CHAPTER 2
CAMP BEAUREGARD, KENTUCKY

OCTOBER–DECEMBER 1861

On August 31, 1861, Albert Sidney Johnston was promoted to the rank of full general in the Confederate army and given command of the vast Western Department, encompassing all of the Confederacy from west of the Allegheny Mountains to the Mississippi River. President Davis held the experienced Johnston in high regard, matched only by Davis's expectations in the sprawling western Confederacy. On September 3, before Johnston could arrive to coordinate his new subordinates, Confederate forces under Brigadier General Gideon J. Pillow and Major General Leonidas Polk moved from Tennessee into Kentucky despite the state's attempts to maintain neutrality. On the following day, they occupied Columbus, Kentucky, on the Mississippi River. The high bluffs above and below the town were ideal positions on which to position artillery to counter the growing Federal threat in southeast Missouri and to control movement on the Mississippi River. Polk's move, "a political blunder of the first order," relieved Federal forces from the stigma of being first to violate Kentucky's neutrality.[1]

On the same day that Polk seized Columbus, Brigadier General Ulysses S. Grant arrived in Cairo, Illinois, to take command of the Federal District of Southeast Missouri, including southern Illinois and western Kentucky.[2] Seeing the opportunity created by Polk's move, late on September 5 Grant put two Illinois infantry regiments and

CAMP BEAUREGARD, KENTUCKY

ARTILLERY ON THREE RIVER STEAMERS AND, ACCOMPANIED BY TWO GUNBOATS, ARRIVED IN PADUCAH, KENTUCKY, THE NEXT MORNING. ON THE SOUTHERN BANK OF THE OHIO RIVER AND JUST WEST OF WHERE IT IS JOINED BY THE TENNESSEE RIVER, PADUCAH WAS ALSO THE NORTHERN TERMINUS OF THE NEW ORLEANS AND OHIO RAILROAD. GRANT OCCUPIED PADUCAH WITHOUT FIRING A SHOT.

AS PART OF THEIR RESPONSE TO THIS MOVE, CONFEDERATE AUTHORITIES SENT COLONEL JOHN BOWEN, THE 1ST MISSOURI INFANTRY, AND OTHER UNITS TO ESTABLISH A DEFENSIVE POSITION NEAR MAYFIELD, ABOUT THIRTY MILES SOUTH OF PADUCAH ALONG THE RAILROAD. BOWEN CHOSE A RIDGE LINE FIFTEEN MILES SOUTH OF MAYFIELD AND TWO MILES EAST OF WATER VALLEY, AND HE NAMED THE POSITION CAMP BEAUREGARD.[3] BY OCTOBER, BOWEN HAD MORE THAN 3,300 SOLDIERS UNDER HIS COMMAND. AT THE END OF NOVEMBER, MORE THAN 4,200 MEN WERE IN THE CAMP, ORGANIZED IN A DIVISION OF TWO BRIGADES.[4] MORE THAN 6,000 TROOPS MAY HAVE BEEN AT CAMP BEAUREGARD AT SOME TIME DURING THAT WINTER.

MANY OF THE MEN ARRIVING AT CAMP BEAUREGARD HAD RECENTLY SURVIVED MEASLES, A COMMON MALADY IN THE WAR'S EARLY DAYS, AND WITH THE ONSET OF COLD AND RAINY WEATHER, THEY WERE ALREADY WEAKENED WHEN PNEUMONIA AND TYPHOID ARRIVED. LIEUTENANT COLONEL S. S. FORD OF THE 10TH ARKANSAS INFANTRY WROTE FROM CAMP BEAUREGARD AT THE END OF OCTOBER ABOUT THE MEN'S WANT OF CLOTHING AND THE IMPACT OF DISEASES, EXPLAINING THAT ALTHOUGH MEASLES WAS THE MOST PREVALENT, "THE TYPHOID FEVER AND PNEUMONIA ARE COMMITTING ALMOST DAILY RAVAGES AMONG OUR MEN."[5] GEORGE WASHINGTON DAWSON, A LIEUTENANT IN THE 1ST MISSOURI, WROTE HOME IN EARLY NOVEMBER THAT THE STRENGTH OF HIS COMPANY HAD "FALLEN OFF VERY MUCH FROM SICKNESS AND DISCHARGES ON ACCOUNT OF DISABILITY."[6] SURGEON G. C. PHILLIPS OF THE 22ND MISSISSIPPI INFANTRY REMEMBERED THAT DURING ONE MONTH, HE HAD MORE THAN 75 CASES OF TYPHOID FEVER AND PNEUMONIA IN HIS CARE. MENINGITIS, HOWEVER,

WAS THE MOST DREADED THREAT, "KILLING NEARLY EVERY CASE ATTACKED AND FREQUENTLY IN A FEW HOURS." PHILLIPS DESCRIBED THE IMPACT OF THESE CONDITIONS AS "WORSE THAN A BATTLE." WRITING YEARS AFTER THE WAR, PHILLIPS REMEMBERED THE FEARFUL CONDITIONS IN THE CAMP: "THE MEN BECAME DEPRESSED AND GLOOMY; EACH ONE FEARED THAT HE WOULD BE THE NEXT ONE TAKEN AND IF SO IT MEANT DEATH." IN THE CAMP'S FIVE-MONTH EXISTENCE, BETWEEN 1,200 AND 1,500 SOLDIERS DIED THERE.[7]

THE MEN AT CAMP BEAUREGARD SAW LITTLE OF THE ENEMY. ON NOVEMBER 10, ELEMENTS OF THE 1ST MISSOURI AND THREE OTHER UNITS LEFT TO PURSUE A FEDERAL INCURSION FROM PADUCAH. THE UNION COLUMN REACHED MILBURN, ABOUT HALFWAY BETWEEN MAYFIELD TO THE EAST AND COLUMBUS TO THE WEST. THE COLUMN'S GOAL WAS TO CREATE A DIVERSION WHILE GRANT ATTACKED AT BELMONT, MISSOURI, UPRIVER OF COLUMBUS. THE UNION COLUMN RETREATED THROUGH MAYFIELD, BUT THE PURSUING CONFEDERATES MADE NO CONTACT. IN A LETTER HOME A FEW DAYS LATER, A DISAPPOINTED LIEUTENANT A. C. RILEY OF THE 1ST MISSOURI LAMENTED THAT HAD THEY STARTED THE PURSUIT SOONER "WE CERTAINLY WOULD HAVE HAD A FIGHT."[8]

ON DECEMBER 28, A SMALL BODY OF UNION CAVALRY LEFT PADUCAH TO DETERMINE WHETHER THE CONFEDERATES STILL OCCUPIED THE CAMP. THE 1ST MISSOURI INFANTRY HAD LEFT CAMP BEAUREGARD FOR BOWLING GREEN A FEW DAYS BEFORE, BUT SUFFICIENT FORCE REMAINED TO CAUSE A FEDERAL PICKET TO REPORT WITH ALARM THE PRESENCE OF A "A HEAVY FORCE OF INFANTRY AND CAVALRY."[9] CAMP BEAUREGARD REMAINED IN OPERATION FOR ANOTHER TWO MONTHS. ON FEBRUARY 21, 1862, AFTER A STOCKPILE OF PROVISIONS AND SOME WAGONS HAD BEEN REMOVED, CAMP BEAUREGARD AND ITS FORTIFICATIONS WERE BURNED AND ABANDONED.[10]

BOYCE ACCORDS HIS REGIMENT'S TIME AT CAMP BEAUREGARD LITTLE MORE THAN A PASSING MENTION, PERHAPS WANTING TO DIMINISH THE MEMORY OF ONE OF THE WORST PERIODS IN ITS HISTORY.

CAMP BEAUREGARD, KENTUCKY

Early in October the regiment was ordered to a point near Mayfield, Ky., about thirty miles southwest of Columbus, and went into camp at a place we called Camp Beauregard. There we kept up the drilling and the discipline to such an extent that the regiment became so proficient that it was christened "The Regulars."

The command was brought to this perfection by Lieut. Col. Rich, who made nearly all his movements at the "double quick" time, so the men named him "Double Quick," which was a term of respect, for the men loved him dearly as an officer. I do believe he had hardly an equal in the entire army as a tactician or an officer. He was devoted to his command, and it was returned by all who had the good fortune to serve under him in any capacity. He became our colonel while here, Col. Bowen having received his commission as a brigadier-general.[11]

Our band or drum corps in charge of Bandmaster James Kennerly, an accomplished musician and soldier, consisted of ten drummers and an equal number of fifers, with one large or bass drum.[12] This band was made up of boys from 14 to 16 years of age. They were drilled in movements usual to regimental field bands and practised daily. All our calls were the same as those used in the United States regular army. Our colors were two flags, one the regulation stars and bars that was presented to the regiment by the ladies of Memphis; it was a beautiful silk flag with gilt stars in a field of blue. The other was the flag of the Second Regiment, presented by the ladies of St. Louis and saved after the capture of Camp Jackson.[13] This flag was carried safely through the enemy's lines by Mrs. Gen. Bowen, who joined her husband early in August 1861, and acted as a mother to many of us while we were sick or wounded. She will always be gratefully and kindly remembered while any of the members of this regiment lives.[14]

While the First Missouri Confederate infantry was encamped at Camp Beauregard, Graves County, Ky., in the fall and winter of 1861, Father Arthur J. Durbin visited the camp three times to look after the spiritual welfare of the many Catholics in the regiment. This good priest used to ride on horseback from Shawneetown, Ill., sixty miles distant. At this time he was 63 years of age; nevertheless he made us monthly visits. We were at the above camp three months. His coming was hailed with delight by the command, and it was a beautiful sight to see this worthy man escorted into camp by the men. He remained about three days at each visit. He was always the guest of our colonel, L. L. Rich.[15]

We had quite a number of deaths while we were there, but I can recall only one of the St. Louis men—E. S. Carter of Co. B. He was a member of a distinguished St. Louis family and I believe, but I am not positive, that later his remains were removed to St. Louis.[16]

After several marches to Mayfield, Ky., with the hope of meeting the Eighth Missouri (federal) regiment, Col. Johnny McDonald, and a demonstration made towards Paducah, on Christmas Eve, 1861, orders were received by General Bowen to move his brigade to Bowling Green, Ky., and report to Gen. Albert Sidney Johnston.[17] Early Christmas morning we were marched to State Line Station, on the Mobile and Ohio Railroad, about twenty miles distant, where we took the cars.[18]

CAMP BEAUREGARD, KENTUCKY

ENDNOTES

1. Nathaniel Cheairs Hughes Jr., *The Battle of Belmont: Grant Strikes South* (Chapel Hill: University of North Carolina Press, 1991), 4.
2. Steven E. Woodworth, *Nothing but Victory: The Army of the Tennessee, 1861–1865* (New York: Alfred A. Knopf, 2005), 32.
3. For the history of Camp Beauregard, we are indebted to the efforts of Mrs. George T. Fuller of Graves County, Kentucky, who in 1909 was moved to begin efforts to commemorate the camp. In 1916, news of her efforts reached Joseph Boyce, and he corresponded with Mrs. Fuller on several occasions, providing information similar to that included in his history of the 1st Missouri. Mrs. Fuller's correspondence with veterans of Camp Beauregard is included in Tilghman–Beauregard Camp No. 1460, Sons of Confederate Veterans, *A History of Camp Beauregard, Graves County, Kentucky* (Mayfield, KY: privately printed, 1988).
4. Abstract from returns, Camp Beauregard, Colonel John S. Bowen commanding, October and November 1861. United States War Department, *The War of the Rebellion: A Compilation of the Official Records of the Union and Confederate Armies* (Washington, DC, 1881–1901), ser. 1, vol. 4, 494, and vol. 7, 728. (Hereafter *OR*. References are to Series 1 unless otherwise noted.)
5. James Willis, *Arkansas Confederates in the Western Theater* (Dayton, OH: Morningside, 1998) 87.
6. H. Riley Bock, ed., "One Year at War: Letters of Capt. Geo. W. Dawson, C.S.A.," *Missouri Historical Review* 73 (1979): 175.
7. Tilghman–Beauregard Camp No. 1460, *A History of Camp Beauregard*, 21, 3.
8. H. Riley Bock, ed., "Confederate Col. A. C. Riley, His Reports and Letters, Part I," *Missouri Historical Review* 85 (1991): 170–171.
9. Report of Brigadier General Lewis Wallace, January 1, 1862. *OR*, vol. 7, 66.
10. Report of Lieutenant Colonel T. H. Lockwood, February 21, 1862. *OR*, vol. 7, 898.
11. Lucius L. Rich graduated from the United States Military Academy in July 1853 and served as an officer in the 5th Infantry until he resigned on May 13, 1861, to join Bowen and the 1st Missouri Infantry, C.S.A. Boyce has confused Bowen's command of the brigade with Bowen's promotion to brigadier general. Colonel Bowen commanded the troops that wintered at Camp Beauregard in 1861–1862. These responsibilities would have removed him from the day-to-day management of the 1st Missouri, duties assumed by Lieutenant Colonel Rich. Bowen was not promoted to brigadier general until March 14, 1862. Cullum, *Biographical Register*, 365. Tilghman–Beauregard Camp No. 1460, *A History of Camp Beauregard*, 5–6.
12. James Amadee Kennerly was eighteen when he enlisted in June 1861. After serving as drum major, he was promoted to lieutenant in Company G in 1862. Kennerly served through the war, commanding Company A of the 1st/4th Missouri Infantry when he was captured at Fort Blakely, Alabama,

in April 1865. Kearny–Kennerly Scrapbook, 22, MHM Archives. National Archives and Records Administration, Publication No. M320, *Compiled Service Records of Confederate Soldiers Who Served in the Organizations from the State of Missouri* (hereafter *CSR—Confederate, Missouri*).

13. Boyce's reference is to the 2nd Regiment, Missouri Volunteer Militia.

14. While stationed at Jefferson Barracks with the Regiment of Mounted Riflemen in 1854, then lieutenant Bowen married Mary Lucretia Preston Kennerly of a large and well-known St. Louis family. Born in 1834, Mary Bowen hardly seems old enough to have been considered "Mother Bowen" to Boyce and his compatriots; perhaps the fact that Mrs. Bowen was living when Boyce wrote this history influenced his choice of words. Mrs. General Bowen, as she was known throughout the postwar years, died in 1904. Stella M. Drumm, "The Kennerlys of Virginia," *Missouri Historical Society Collections* 6 (1928): 112–113.

15. Boyce wrote this paragraph in response to Father Durbin's obituary. "The Soldier's Friend" and "one of the oldest and best known priests in the West" died at Shelbyville, Kentucky, in March 1887. His age at death was reported as eighty-eight. Joseph Boyce, "He was the Soldier's Friend," *Missouri Republican*, March 26, 1887.

16. Joseph Boyce to Mrs. Geo. T. Fuller, March 15, 1916, in Tilghman–Beauregard Camp No. 1460, Sons of Confederate Veterans, *A History of Camp Beauregard*, 26.

Edward (or Edwin) Carter was thirty-four years old when he joined Company B on July 1, 1861, at Camp Calhoun near Memphis. Carter died at Camp Beauregard on November 18 later that year. *CSR—Confederate, Missouri.*

17. John McDonald was a passenger agent for steamboat companies in St. Louis in the 1850s prior to owning and operating his own passenger and freight service on the Missouri River. In 1861, McDonald encouraged sufficient enlistments to create the 8th Missouri Infantry, U.S.A., and was subsequently promoted to brigadier general. At the time of Boyce's writing, McDonald was perhaps better known for his involvement in the Whiskey Ring scandal of 1875, a plan that defrauded the government of tax revenue while it helped build up Republican election funds. Convicted and sentenced to three years in the state penitentiary, McDonald was pardoned by President Grant on his last day in office. Mary E. Seematter, "McDonald, John," in Lawrence O. Christensen et al., eds., *Dictionary of Missouri Biography* (Columbia: University of Missouri Press, 1999), 534–535.

18. At this point in *Nicholson*, Boyce inserted a tantalizing note: "This paper was much fuller in description and had many anecdotes, etc. The editor cut it up considerably, but I hope in my last paper to insert some of the matter he omitted. J. B."

CHAPTER 3
IN KENTUCKY AND TENNESSEE

JANUARY–MARCH 1862

SIMON BOLIVAR BUCKNER HAD SEEN MANY OF THE MEN OF THE 1ST MISSOURI INFANTRY BEFORE AND IN MORE PLEASANT TIMES. BUCKNER, AS COMMANDER OF THE KENTUCKY STATE GUARD, WAS ONE OF THE DIGNITARIES WELCOMED AT CAMP LEWIS IN ST. LOUIS FOR THE FOURTH OF JULY CELEBRATION IN 1860. THE 1ST BRIGADE OF THE MISSOURI VOLUNTEER MILITIA BEGAN ITS WEEKLONG ENCAMPMENT ON JUNE 30 TO ASSURE THE UNITS WERE OUT IN FULL FORCE FOR THE PARADES AND FESTIVITIES ON JULY 4, AND BUCKNER WAS AMONG THOSE WHO REVIEWED THE TROOPS IN THE FINAL HOURS OF THE ENCAMPMENT.[1]

IN SEPTEMBER 1861, NOW A CONFEDERATE BRIGADIER GENERAL, BUCKNER AND HIS MEN OCCUPIED BOWLING GREEN, KENTUCKY, AS A DEFENSIVE MEASURE AGAINST THE FORCES OF "NORTHERN DESPOTISM."[2] IN LATE DECEMBER AND EARLY JANUARY, TROOPS INCLUDING THE 1ST MISSOURI INFANTRY WERE MOVED FROM CAMP BEAUREGARD TO REINFORCE THOSE COLLECTED AT BOWLING GREEN. NOT LONG AFTER, A FEDERAL OFFENSIVE CAUSED THE CONFEDERATE POSITION IN WESTERN KENTUCKY TO COLLAPSE, CAUSING A RETREAT INTO TENNESSEE.

ON FEBRUARY 6, 1862, FORT HENRY ON THE TENNESSEE RIVER FELL TO UNION FORCES COMMANDED BY GRANT AND FLAG OFFICER ANDREW H. FOOTE, FOOTE'S GUNBOATS HAVING POUNDED THE POORLY POSITIONED FORT'S LIGHTER GUNS INTO SUBMISSION. THE NEXT DAY, AS PART OF HIS RESPONSE TO THIS UNEXPECTED MOVE, JOHNSTON SENT ORDERS TO EVACUATE BOWLING GREEN TO MAJOR GENERAL WILLIAM J. HARDEE, NOW IN COMMAND THERE.

IN KENTUCKY AND TENNESSEE

HARDEE'S 14,000 TROOPS BEGAN THE SIXTY-FIVE-MILE TRIP TO NASHVILLE, TENNESSEE, IN FREEZING WEATHER ON FEBRUARY 11. THE EVACUATION WAS COMPLETE BY FEBRUARY 13.[3]

ON FEBRUARY 12, FOLLOWING UP THE VICTORY AT FORT HENRY ON THE TENNESSEE RIVER, UNION GROUND FORCES BEGAN INVESTING FORT DONELSON ON THE NEARBY CUMBERLAND RIVER AND AWAITED THE ARRIVAL OF FOOTE'S SQUADRON. THE GUNS IN FORT DONELSON REPULSED AN ATTACK BY FOOTE'S IRONCLADS AND GUNBOATS ON FEBRUARY 14. THE NEXT DAY, THE CONFEDERATES CONDUCTED A SUCCESSFUL SALLY FROM THE FORT, BUT THEIR LEADERSHIP DESPAIRED OF CREATING A BREAKOUT AND RECALLED THE TROOPS INTO THE WORKS. THAT NIGHT, FORMER U.S. SECRETARY OF WAR GENERAL JOHN BUCHANAN FLOYD, FEARING RETALIATION FOR HIS PRE-WAR ACTIONS AS A FEDERAL OFFICIAL, AND GENERAL PILLOW ABANDONED FORT DONELSON AND ESCAPED UP THE CUMBERLAND RIVER TO NASHVILLE WITH 3,000 OF PILLOW'S TROOPS. BUCKNER, SENT TO FORT DONELSON EARLIER WITH REINFORCEMENTS, REMAINED BEHIND TO SURRENDER TO GRANT.

HARDEE'S COLUMN FROM BOWLING GREEN BEGAN ARRIVING IN NASHVILLE ON SUNDAY, FEBRUARY 16, 1862. THE STEAMBOAT FROM FORT DONELSON CARRYING PILLOW, FLOYD, AND FLOYD'S MEN ARRIVED THERE SOON AFTER. JOHNSTON PUT FLOYD IN CHARGE OF NASHVILLE'S SECURITY, AND FLOYD PUT THE 1ST MISSOURI ON POLICE DUTY, BACKED BY CAVALRY UNDER JOHN HUNT MORGAN. TWO DAYS LATER, NATHAN BEDFORD FORREST ARRIVED AND TOOK OVER THE DIRECTION OF THE REMOVAL OF STORES AND MACHINERY FROM THE CITY.[4]

The day after Christmas we took the cars at State Line Station, on the Mobile and Ohio railroad, and started for Bowling Green, Kentucky. All were in good spirits, and the best of feeling prevailed. The following evening we reached Clarksville, Tenn., where we were delayed a day.

During this time the men roamed about the town putting in the time quietly and awaiting the time for our train to proceed. While doing this

Company B spied an undertaker's establishment with some very handsome metallic caskets in stock, "just the thing for mess chests, boys, just the thing." That night when we left, Billy Conklin, Bill McConlogue and Jerry Lewis, while some of the other members engaged the undertaker in conversation, quietly slipped out with one of the coveted caskets and away with it to the train. "Just the thing, all nicely padded and a glass front to see that everything is packed away in good shape."[5]

While this was going on "Texas" and some more of his messmates of the same company got away with the hotel gong, so they would have something better than a drum to call this high-toned mess to their meals. They did not enjoy their spoils long, for upon our arrival at Bowling Green Col. Rich had the property returned.[6]

Gen. Bowen had preceded us several days to arrange for camping ground, etc. One day while at Gen. Albert Sidney Johnston's headquarters, General Bowen was bantered by Gen. Breckinridge to drill the First Missouri against the Second Kentucky, Col. Hanson commanding, the prize to be a stand of colors. At once Gen. Bowen accepted the wager. Gen. Johnston cautioned Gen. Breckinridge at the time, for he had seen the First Missouri manoeuvre often while he was at Columbus, Kentucky.[7]

Upon our arrival a few days later, January 1, 1862, the men were informed of the wager when formed into line at the railroad depot. The line of march was taken up for camp, about a mile north of town. Everybody was out to see the Missourians, and as our regiment (1,000 strong) wheeled into the main street, company front, and our band of twenty musicians struck up "Dixie," we were greeted with cheers and a regular old Kentucky welcome.

Just before we left Camp Beauregard, near Mayfield, Graves County, Ky., the command had received new muskets, overcoats, and caps, and presented a very soldierly appearance as it passed in review before Generals Johnston, Breckinridge, Hardee, Bowen and their staffs, and General Breckinridge remarked good-naturedly, and by way of the highest compliment he could pay Gen. Bowen and his regiment. "Do you expect me to back the Second Kentucky against your old 'regulars' who deserted from Jefferson Barracks and followed you here? No, no, Bowen, I shan't fall into any such trap." Gen. Bowen replied: "There are no old regulars there, general. That regiment is composed entirely of volunteers and it has the best blood of Missouri in it." So ended the challenge against the First Missouri.[8]

The command was given charge of Bowling Green and furnished guards and patrols to keep the town cleared of stragglers and night prowlers. The daily guard mounting at General Johnston's headquarters was the great attraction of the place. This duty lasted until the 12th of February, 1862, when Bowling Green was abandoned. The rest of the army had been withdrawn some days before this, but the First Missouri had been left in charge to see that all the public property was safely placed in the cars and wagon trains and under way for Nashville.

The line of march was taken up for the last named place, where we arrived after a week's march. During the last day of our journey we heard of the battle of Fort Donelson. First the news was that the enemy had been badly defeated and that he was flying in hot haste for Paducah. The next morning the news was just the reverse of this, and our army was doing the flying. A few hours later we marched across the suspension bridge and entered the city.

The battle of Fort Donelson had been fought, most of our troops had been captured, and those who escaped (of whom there were several thousand) were for the most part a demoralized band of fugitives. The railroad depots were crowded with wounded. The citizens were panic-stricken; many were about the depots seeking the opportunity for flight, and between panic-stricken people and ungoverned fugitive soldiers the wounded suffered greatly. The most demoralized of the soldiers were demanding food and liquor, taking possession of cars and having things their own way generally. That was the condition of affairs when we arrived. Gen. A. S. Johnston then ordered our regiment to restore order.

It required but the announcement that the First Missouri had been ordered to clear the city. A great many of those characters who bring disgrace on an army had felt the treatment this regiment knew so well how to administer, and remembering how quiet and orderly Bowling Green was kept left very suddenly, and the roads leading southward were soon black with the crowd of fugitives and stragglers seeking their commands, which had left several days previous for Murfreesboro. In one day order was restored, and despite the fact that our troops were falling back before the enemy, the citizens felt they had been delivered from an awful danger, as they feared the city would be fired by the stragglers and fugitives and ransacked.

The week the regiment remained was one of hard work and care, little or no rest of any kind, as boats and cars had to be loaded with supplies of all kinds and the wounded cared for and sent off in the direction of Murfreesboro. At last the task was over. In this we were ably assisted by Morgan's cavalry and Capt. Basil Duke of this command, formerly a captain in the Second Missouri, captured at Camp Jackson.[9]

The last order was issued, "destroy the bridges." Axes were procured and the wire cables of the suspension bridge were cut and it fell into the Cumberland river with a roar and a crash that sounded to us like a hideous cry that we were leaving the city to the enemy. The railroad bridge was fired at the same time and destroyed, Lieutenant David Walker of Company A in charge of the work.[10] Almost immediately after this several boats and warehouses at the landing were set on fire, and this dreadful destruction was continued during the entire night. When daylight came the regiment was drawn up in the public square, and a few moments later we marched away, sad at heart on leaving the hospitable citizens of Nashville, to rejoin our brigade at Murfreesboro.[11]

During this service Generals Pillow and Floyd, who escaped from Fort Donelson, were frequently at our headquarters in the courthouse with our colonel. They commended his actions and often spoke in praise of the discipline and activity of his men in the arduous work they were doing, and especially praised the fearlessness of the vigourous manner of handling the stragglers, and this without killing or injuring any of them.[12]

The railroad managers, who were helpless before our arrival, were well pleased with the regiment. Fortunately for them, quite a number of the regiment were railroad men, and with their help the trains were soon running on fairly good time, considering the deplorable condition of affairs.

Gen. Bowen and Col. Rich were thanked by Gen. Johnston and the regiment kindly remembered for its successful and difficult task.

IN KENTUCKY AND TENNESSEE

ENDNOTES

1. Undated newspaper clip, "The Military Encampment—Camp Lewis Deserted—Homeward March," ca. July 6, 1860, in William R. Babcock Scrapbook, MHM Archives. The newspaper reports "On marching out of the camp the Brigade was reviewed by Major General Simeon B. Buckerer, commanding the Kentucky State Guard...."

2. Report of S. B. Buckner to S. Cooper, Adjutant General, September 18, 1861. *OR*, vol. 4, 413.

3. Stanley F. Horn, *The Army of Tennessee* (Norman: University of Oklahoma Press, 1952), 99.

4. Horn, *The Army of Tennessee*, 102–103.

5. William Conklin and William McConlogue joined for duty on July 1, 1861, and mustered in to Company B at Memphis, McConlogue as a musician. The discipline of army life apparently suited neither, as both deserted from Camp Price in June 1862 near the expiration of their initial one-year enlistment. Conklin was returned to service, and in September 1862, he was part of a detail guarding barrels of hospital whiskey. The temptation proved too strong. Later that month, a military court sentenced him to receive thirty-nine lashes, have his head shaved, and be drummed out of the regiment in front of the entire brigade for breaking into a whiskey barrel, distributing its contents to other soldiers, and leaving his post. Lewis has not been identified. *CSR— Confederate, Missouri.*

6. The 1ˢᵗ Missouri arrived at Bowling Green on December 30, 1861. *OR*, vol. 7, 810.

7. John Cabell Breckinridge was elected to the Kentucky legislature in 1849 and to the U.S. House of Representatives in 1851 before he became the vice president of the United States, serving President James Buchanan, in 1856. He resigned this position in 1859 to take a seat in the U.S. Senate representing Kentucky. Then becoming a brigadier general in the Confederate army, Breckinridge commanded the five Kentucky infantry regiments of the First Kentucky Brigade. Warner, *Generals in Gray*, 34–35.

Roger Weightman Hanson, a Mexican War veteran and later a politician, was commissioned a colonel in the Confederate army on August 19, 1861. He assumed command of the 2ⁿᵈ Kentucky the following month. William C. Davis, *The Orphan Brigade: The Kentucky Confederates Who Couldn't Go Home* (Garden City, NY: Doubleday & Co., 1980), 39–40.

8. The Jefferson Barracks was established in St. Louis, Missouri, in 1826. Before the war with Mexico, it was one of the U.S. Army's largest posts. A number of the former U.S. Army officers serving the Confederacy had been stationed there during their military careers. William C. Winter, *The Civil War in St. Louis: A Guided Tour* (St. Louis: Missouri Historical Society Press, 1994), 4–7.

Of this event, a modern historian writes: "Learning how good the Missourians were, [Breckinridge] wisely backed out." Davis, *The Orphan Brigade,* 56.

9. Future Confederate cavalry general and noted raider John Hunt Morgan had not yet ridden to prominence. At this time, he commanded the Kentucky Cavalry Squadron, which would later be reorganized into the 2nd Kentucky Cavalry Regiment. Joseph H. Crute, *Units of the Confederate States Army* (Midlothian, VA: Derwent Books, 1987), 129.

"Captured at Camp Jackson" refers to the Second Regiment, Missouri Volunteer Militia, not to Basil Duke. Just before the outbreak of war, Basil Wilson Duke was an attorney in St. Louis and captain of Company C of the Second Regiment. Duke was not present at Camp Jackson on May 10, 1861. He had left the camp the previous day for Jefferson City, Missouri, to report to Governor Claiborne Jackson concerning Duke's recent visit to President Jefferson Davis in Montgomery, Alabama, as Jackson's emissary. Duke, *Reminiscences,* 50–51.

10. David Walker entered Confederate service on June 22, 1861. He was promoted to second lieutenant of Company A in May of the following year. In August 1864, unit records indicate that he was absent from the unit with "Hill's Scouts" on orders from General John B. Hood. He survived the war to surrender and be paroled. *CSR—Confederate, Missouri.*

Over the protests of Nashville's citizens, the bridges were dropped into the Cumberland River on the night of February 19 as a matter of military necessity. Horn, *The Army of Tennessee,* 103.

11. Floyd and his command left Nashville for Murfreesboro on the afternoon of February 20, 1862. *OR,* vol. 7, 429.

12. After their perfidy at Fort Donelson became known, Pillow and Floyd were never again trusted with significant assignments. President Davis relieved Floyd from command on March 11, 1862. He later received a command in Virginia, serving until his death by illness in August 1863. Pillow, too, was relieved from duty. Late in the war he worked in the conscript bureau for Tennessee and as commissary general for prisoners. Warner, *Generals in Gray,* 90, 241.

CHAPTER 4
SHILOH, TENNESSEE

APRIL 1862

AFTER THE FALL OF FORTS HENRY AND DONELSON AND THE OCCUPATION OF NASHVILLE, GRANT AND HIS ARMY OF THE TENNESSEE FOLLOWED THE TENNESSEE RIVER SOUTH WHILE GENERAL DON CARLOS BUELL MOVED SOUTHWEST FROM NASHVILLE WITH THE SMALLER ARMY OF THE OHIO.

JOHNSTON AND GENERAL P. G. T. BEAUREGARD, HIS SECOND IN COMMAND, CONCENTRATED THE CONFEDERATE ARMY AT CORINTH, A RAIL JUNCTION IN NORTHERN MISSISSIPPI, AFTER THE LOSS OF MIDDLE TENNESSEE. GENERAL BRAXTON BRAGG COMMANDED TROOPS IN DEFENSE OF THE CONFEDERACY FROM PENSACOLA, FLORIDA, TO MOBILE, ALABAMA, WHEN HE WAS SUMMONED TO REINFORCE JOHNSTON'S COMMAND AT CORINTH. HE SOON ARRIVED FROM ALABAMA WITH TEN THOUSAND SOLDIERS. GENERAL DANIEL RUGGLES BROUGHT FIVE THOUSAND MORE FROM LOUISIANA. BRAGG HELPED MAKE SIGNIFICANT IMPROVEMENTS IN THE MANAGEMENT OF THE DISORGANIZED FORCES AT CORINTH AND DID MUCH TO RESTORE DISCIPLINE TO JOHNSTON'S ARMY AFTER ITS RECENT REVERSES. JOHNSTON AND BEAUREGARD COMBINED THESE FORCES WITH THEIR OWN FROM KENTUCKY AND TENNESSEE TO CREATE THE CONFEDERATE ARMY OF MISSISSIPPI.[1]

THE ARMY OF MISSISSIPPI WAS ORGANIZED INTO THREE CORPS AND A RESERVE CORPS. BRAGG, POLK, AND HARDEE EACH COMMANDED A CORPS. BRECKINRIDGE LED THE RESERVE CORPS, IN REALITY A SMALL DIVISION. HIS THREE BRIGADES WERE COMMANDED BY COLONEL ROBERT P. TRABUE, COLONEL W. S. STATHAM, AND BRIGADIER GENERAL BOWEN. BOWEN'S BRIGADE INCLUDED THE 1ST

SHILOH, TENNESSEE

Missouri, 2ND Confederate, 9TH Arkansas, and 10TH Arkansas infantry regiments and Hudson's Mississippi artillery battery. The 1ST Missouri infantry was the only regiment from the state in Johnston's army.

Grant used the mobility offered by the Tennessee River to advance General William T. Sherman's division to Pittsburg Landing, Tennessee, in mid-March 1862. Sherman moved a few miles from the landing before encamping in the vicinity of Shiloh Church, a log meetinghouse on the road that led to Corinth. He was soon joined by the other divisions of Grant's army.

The battle at Shiloh on April 6 and 7 was the regiment's first significant experience of combat, and the men would soon recognize the benefits of their training and discipline. Leaders fell and commands were separated, but the regiment retained its cohesion and served effectively in the attack on April 6 and the withdrawal on April 7, becoming part of the rear guard. Major A. C. Riley, the regiment's senior surviving officer, described the action of April 7: "The enemy having outflanked us, Colonel Martin ordered us to retreat which we did losing First Lieutenant J. T. Hargett, Co. I, killed, soon after retreating and Lieutenant Boyce wounded."[2] Joseph Boyce, severely wounded in the left hip, was one of the last Confederates to become a casualty at Shiloh. He was moved to Memphis for recuperation.[3]

After a short rest at Murfreesboro the march was renewed, after the troops under the gallant but unfortunate Zollicoffer had been reorganized at this place.[4] After several weeks' march the junction of Johnston's and Beauregard's troops was effected at Corinth, Miss., during the last of March.[5] We had hardly arrived there when we were hurried off to Iuka and after a tedious march through the rain and mud arrived early next morning just about daylight, when we found the enemy's cavalry had fallen back. About noon we were moved again in the direction of Corinth, where we arrived during the night.

Early the following morning we were called again for extra duty. The roads leading to Shiloh that our division (Breckinridge's) had to pass over were in a dreadful condition from the rains, and had to be repaired at once; this work was cheerfully done, as we knew we were soon to meet the enemy. After putting the roads in good order we joined the brigade (Bowen's) the next day. Saturday, during the day, we saw a great many of Bragg's troops passing to take their position in line of battle.[6] These troops were well drilled and thoroughly disciplined. They presented a very soldierly appearance, well uniformed and armed. This command was composed principally of troops from Louisiana, Mississippi, and Alabama. We also noticed a very fine battery from Georgia and a regiment of infantry from Florida.[7]

A little time before dark we were in motion and passed to the front, where we took our position in line with the reserve corps; our division (Breckinridge's) formed this line. Gen. Johnston's address to the troops was read to us by candlelight and all felt that the morrow would give us the day so long looked for by the men of the regiment to avenge Camp Jackson.

We bivouacked on this line; no fires were allowed and all unnecessary talk or noise of any kind prohibited. Soon all was silence. Nothing disturbed the quiet and it was hard to realize that we were part of 40,000 men lying in those woods. Sleep stole upon us rapidly, and we were tired after the labor and excitement of the day.

Just before the dawn we were quietly awakened, overcoats and knapsacks were piled and a small guard detailed to watch the property. We never saw our overcoats, etc., again.[8] At last day began to show through the trees, and just at this moment the crack of the rifles announced that the enemy was attacked. A few heavy volleys of musketry in our front, then on the right, the left, again the centre, and the whole army moved forward with a rush. A wild yell broke forth and we saw every thing in our front disappear. The surprise was complete. It was hard to hold our division in hand; the regiments wanted to charge at once. Slowly we were moved forward through the enemy's camp. The dead and wounded seemed everywhere. The firing along the line grew fainter, as it was pushing the enemy towards the Tennessee river. We felt that the reserve had been slighted, and that a great battle had been fought without our help. All this time we were moving, very slowly to

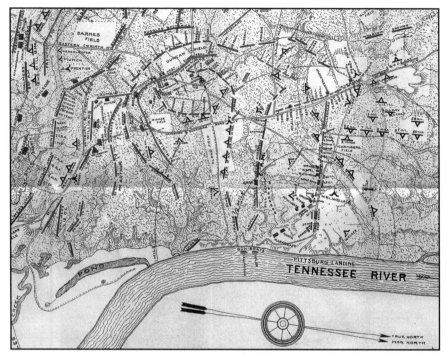

DETAIL OF SHILOH BATTLEFIELD, SOUTHWEST. FROM *Ohio at Shiloh: Report of the Commission*, BY T. J. LINDSEY, 1903.

the front, then the firing grew louder and more distinct. Soon the batteries opened, and the thunder of the guns were received with cheers by all of us. It was inspiriting. At last some of the Kentucky troops in our division were moved forward, then another detachment of the same troops was ordered to the front; this left our brigade alone. In a short time the Second Confederate and the Ninth and Tenth Arkansas left us for the front, and the First Missouri was left alone. We were all that remained of the reserve corps. Then the growling commenced, and to add to it a detail was made from the writer's company to help fill out our brigade's battery (Hudson's), that needed some cannoneers who had served in Guibor's battery in Missouri, and who had joined us at Camp Beauregard.[9]

At last the men began to murmur, "Does Gen. Johnston think we have left the service?" "What about getting even on this Camp Jackson business?" During this bantering everybody was buoyant and happy and despite their impatience waited like veterans the command that would send them to the front.

About half-past 9 a staff officer from Gen. Beauregard came dashing up and instructed Col. Rich to move his regiment rapidly to the front. Away we went at "double quick." About half a mile down the road we came upon the hero of Manassas, Gen. Beauregard and his staff. He was instantly recognized by the men, who saw him there for the first time. He was standing on a log and, as we came up, he saluted us and pointed towards our line of battle down the road. At once three times three and a tiger for Gen. Beauregard was called out by Sergt. Johnny Corkery of "D" Company and it was given with a will.[10] The general and his staff were surprised at this, but laughed heartily and waved their caps at us as we rushed to the front.

When we arrived on the battlefield we found Bragg's troops hotly engaged and we had to move to the right by fours front and continued this for almost a mile, moving all the time to the right under fire of musketry and shell. This fire was extremely annoying as we could not respond to it. However, the regiment received the fire all along this line, and as the enemy was very stubborn here, it taxed our patience and discipline very much. It was the first fire the regiment was ever under and did not agree with our idea of a battle at all. At last we cleared the line in our front and found our loss had been quite small. We found Gen. Johnston and several of his staff a little to our right and front, and as our line of march carried us towards them we were compelled to force our way through a swampy place, which interfered very much with our double-quick movement. In this place we found great numbers of the enemy's dead. We thought he sought refuge here. If so, it was a fatal mistake as his loss at this point was dreadful.

At last we got through and came upon solid ground. The firing in our front was very light, like a few skirmishers would deliver. We moved forward slowly, but steadily, and did not reply as we were told to be careful as some of our troops had fired into each other during the early part of the day. One of my company—Scott Elder—asked Col. Rich for permission to run over and see if they were our men. I mention this because it raised a laugh and showed the indifference the men had of fear.[11] While this was going on the enemy was concentrating in our front and his actions were hidden by the timber. Suddenly we discovered him and the command from Col. Rich, "Charge him boys! Charge him!" We dashed upon him, but he received us with a volley; it was his last; we rushed upon him with the bayonet, and with the cry of "Remember Camp Jackson." The line in our front gave way and we sent a sharp fire after it that was very destructive. We captured a great many prisoners and then became aware of the fact that they were Missouri troops and a part of Prentiss' division. The regiments some of the prisoners belonged to were the queerest Missourians we ever saw. They were nearly all Germans, spoke English very poorly, but informed us they were nearly all from Belleville, Ill. However, we took them in and sent them to the rear.[12]

We now reformed. The fire had passed from our front, but was increasing on our left. We hurried over to this point and found the battle raging. We could see that the enemy was harassed by the way he was giving ground. Col. Rich took in the situation at once. He commands: "Cease firing! Right shoulder, shift arms, double quick, march," and away we went. We cleared the line on our left about 150 yards.[13] "Battalion, left wheel—charge bayonets." This was the grandest move made that bloody day. We received their fire without replying while wheeling battalion front. That grand regiment was from Missouri; they were "regulars," and as it swept round it closed the only escape for Prentiss. It burst on his left flank with the yell of "Remember Camp Jackson, boys, remember Camp Jackson."[14]

The cheers of the troops that we had left as they discovered our movements were deafening. They could hardly realize that a division of the enemy was captured. It was so, nevertheless, and as Prentiss and his division threw down their arms we found many that assisted in our capture at Camp Jackson. The prisoners were hurried off towards Corinth and no time lost in moving to the front. I should judge this was about 3 o'clock p.m.[15] As all commands were forward we were again soon under fire. The enemy by this time had been driven well towards the Tennessee river. He began making a stand and gave up no ground that he did not fight for. The position in our front seemed very strong; the ground did not admit of charging; as it was considerably broken up by ravines and gullies, it was well adapted to an advance, as the broken condition gave us a great deal of protection. We forced the fighting at every point and pushed the enemy fiercely all along the line. Gen. Johnston rode up and urged us forward. It was gratifying to all of us to see him and hear his kindly expressions. Every man in the regiment knew him and loved him.

While the battle raged the thorough instruction was evident in an amusing manner. Many of the men were observed under a deadly fire standing bolt upright with every faculty devoted to loading and firing "by numbers," tearing cartridge, drawing rammer, ramming cartridge, etc., precisely as if their captains were calling the numbers. Their thorough drill actually caused them to forget the dead and wounded lying around.

The battle grew hotter as we forced our way forward. Some artillery was brought to bear on us, but the officer in charge evidently did not know his business, as he opened on us with solid shot. Probably he was out of everything else. At all events the guns were not handled very well, and except the noise of the round shot, did us no harm.[16]

It was in this deadly stand-up fight that Gen. Johnston was killed.[17] A regiment next to us on our left—I think it was the Ninth Arkansas—broke front and "bunched up" behind trees at a critical time. The line could not continue the advance very well until this was remedied, and many of the officers of the First Missouri left their companies and hurried over to this regiment and assisted in re-forming it. The men were simply demoralized, but showed no disposition to fall back. Order was soon restored and the line advanced. This kind of fighting and advancing continued until nearly dark, when we found we had forced the enemy to the river bank. Here he had concentrated his artillery and improvised a breastwork of timber, but mostly of bales of hay. I must say it was rather formidable. Besides, he had got his gunboats into position, and they were adding very much to the dreadful noise, for it was nothing but noise.[18] We never lost a man from the time we occupied this position, at least two hours. Until we left it the fire of the enemy was simply wild. Now and then a branch would be knocked from a tree and fall among the men, but it did no harm. One vigorous charge at any time from 5 o'clock until 7 would have sent every one of Grant's army into the Tennessee river or made prisoners of them. We waited for the command to charge. It was not given, and about 8 o'clock we were withdrawn about a quarter of a mile back and took possession of the camp of the Seventy-first Ohio. Judging from all the good things they abandoned they were a most excellent regiment and composed of good fellows, as they had everything to comfort a soldier, and after a hard day's fight without much breakfast we sat down to enjoy all that our friends at the river bank left for us when they broke up house-keeping so early that morning.[19]

We found everything to comfort the soldier in the camp of the Seventy-first Ohio and, notwithstanding our loss was heavy in killed and wounded, the feeling of exultation that we occupied and were to sleep in the camp of the enemy in a great measure restored our spirits and allayed for the time being the sorrow that prevailed for the loss of our comrades.

Camp chests were soon ransacked and all eatables quickly discovered, with several jugs of good whiskey and packages of white sugar. Tom Dwyer of the writer's company called the boys around him and proposed that they have, as a starter, a bucket of punch, and that they "drink the health of the 'poor divils' who had left such good whiskey behind them." Some one told Tom that they could not get any water to make the punch. "Niver mind, me boy; let the Siventy-first keep all the wather in the Tianissee river, we have the best part of the punch anyway, we have the whiskey and the sugar, and we'll make it a bit stronger."[20] Care was taken by the officers that too much punch was not indulged in by the companies and shortly after 9 o'clock the men were ordered to the tents, where they made themselves comfortable and soon dropped off to sleep.

The enemy kept up the fire during the night from the heavy pieces on the gunboats, but we were so tired that the noise from the guns and shells that passed over the camp could not keep us awake. The shells were thrown far above us and bursted some distance in the rear, judging from the sound of the explosions.

Gen. Hardee remained with the regiment during the night and at the first approach of day had the command aroused and formed in line of battle.

Details were made to cook breakfast and a hurried meal prepared from the abundance in our possession. We expected an attack, as couriers reported frequently during the night that the enemy was crossing in force. About 6 o'clock the enemy's skirmishers opened fire. They were Buell's troops and appeared a little to our front and right, and came into action quite vigorously.[21] Our skirmishers were so long in replying that we feared they had been captured, but Gen. Hardee passed along the line and cautioned us to be quiet, as he desired to know the strength of the force in our front. At last our skirmishers opened fire, and the enemy, thinking so small a line in his front of no consequence, moved out from the timber quite rapidly, in two lines of battle. The Georgia battery had been placed in position on our left masked by branches of trees thrown over and in front of the guns. Our skirmishers were ordered to rally on the regiment and they came in on the run, hotly pursued by the enemy. As he came closer he raised a cheer. At this moment the battery opened and we sprang forward at the charge bayonets. The enemy was astounded at his reception and broke and fled in confusion towards the river, followed by our line until he finally disappeared.

The command was halted and all the canteens filled from a stream near by. Shortly after this, heavy firing on our left told us too plainly that our rest was over. Away we went at the "double quick" and were soon engaged. The battle raged hotly for several hours. The enemy fought well, but we had him at a disadvantage. We were fresh from our night's sleep, while he was worn and badly used up by his disastrous defeat of the previous day. Buell's troops were not fresh; they had made a forced march on the day before and were kept awake during the night by crossing the river and taking up their position to attack us at daylight. It is true they outnumbered us, but our strength had been renewed by sleep and our great victory of Sunday had made us almost invincible.

About 3 o'clock the battle assumed a most desperate state of affairs for our side. The enemy had massed in front of the "Crescent" regiment and the fifth company of the Washington artillery, both of New Orleans.[22] Their position was very exposed and the enemy in such force that they could not possibly withstand his assault. The "Crescents" were forced back and the guns of the Washington artillery captured. We were brought up at the "double quick" just as this was taking place in our front. We took advantage of a ridge of ground about 100 yards in rear of the engagement. The situation was very alarming and the excitement all along the line was very great. It appeared to us we were about to be annihilated, but

Gen. Hardee and Col. Wm. Kearny of his staff passed in front of us and told us to be firm, all would be well.[23] If it were not for the discipline of the First Missouri and for the firmness displayed by the regiment at this critical time our forces would have been driven from the field. This was the turning point of the second day's battle. To add to this deplorable state of affairs the "Crescents" came running over us, for we were lying down and hugging the ground, while they rapidly formed in our rear. The artillerists came back with the sponge-staffs, hand-spikes and lanyards in their hands, imploring us to save their guns. Still another horror awaited us; the Georgia battery and the Mobile light artillery came up at the gallop and went into battery immediately in our rear on a slight elevation and opened a terrific fire from their twelve guns.[24] The pieces at the first two or three rounds were so much depressed and the gunners so excited that the shells burst and tore through our ranks, killing and wounding our men dreadfully. It's remarkable what effect discipline has upon men. Despite this dreadful state of affairs the men kept their position and called upon the "Crescents" to fall in with them and we would rescue the guns. Corporal John O'Neil of the writer's regiment, seeing the faces of the men assuming such grave looks and notwithstanding the gravity of the situation, raised a laugh by saying: "Yesterday mornin' you were afeared you would nivir get into this battle, and I'm —— if I aint afeard we'll niver get out av it. Faith, there's no dress parade about this bisness."[25]

Gen. Hardee took his place in front of the regiment, ordered the charge and led it in person. He was the bravest man I ever saw in my four years' experience in the war, "the bravest of the brave."[26] We followed him with a yell at the charge bayonets and drove back the enemy from the guns and restored them to the grateful Louisianians, and they never forgot it for they always referred to it when we met afterwards "way down in Georgia." It was a sad sight that awaited us when we rescued the battery; the poor fellows were lying dead all about, some holding on to the spokes of the wheels in their dead grasp, while the wounded crawled up and cried out, "God bless you Missourians." The air rang with cheers of "Louisiana and Missouri forever."[27] We repaid Louisiana that day for the glorious work the Third Louisiana rendered our boys at Oak Hill, Mo., a few months previous.[28]

Our old friends at New Madrid, the Memphis Light Dragoons, dashed by, led by a former St. Louisan, Maj. Tom Sheridan, and as they passed to the front they cheered us: "Well done Missouri, you have saved the guns." The battle was over, our line re-established, and after waiting for about an hour and hearing no firing anywhere we were marched by the right flank to one of the main roads and took our position again about three miles south of the battle-field. There was no confusion that I saw, and not until the following morning did we know that we were going to fall back to Corinth.

About daylight, in the midst of a pouring rain, the line of march was taken up for Corinth.[29] The roads—well, the best way to describe the roads is to say there were none left; they were simply rivers of mud. Fences were thrown down, and the command marched back across fields, and arrived at camp about 3 o'clock that afternoon.

Our loss in killed, wounded and missing, as I recollect, was: killed, 48; wounded, 130; missing, 29; total, 207.[30] We carried into action about 850 muskets. Among the officers killed I recall the names of Col. Lucius L. Rich, Capt. J. Kemp Sprague, Lieuts. Jos. Har[gett], James Daughtry, and Jos. Deane. Wounded: Maj. Chas. C. Campbell, Capts. James M. Quinlan, Robert J. Duffy, Lieuts. Lewis H. Kennerly, W. C. P. Carrington, Smith N. Hawes and Jos. Boyce. Among the enlisted men I remember the names of— killed: Commissary—Sergt. James Kerr, Sergts. Ben White, Wm. Hodnett, Wm. Smith, Patrick Madden, Wm. Gallagher, Privates Wm. Dawson, Ed Murray, Jack Drought, Parker Dunnica, John Conners, Wm. Cook, Malcom McDonald; wounded: Andy Byrnes, Joseph T. Donovan, Joseph Smith, Ed Brennan, Michael Reardon, James Boyd, Frank Fisher, Alfred Sutton, Jno. Slocumb and P. S. Thompson.[31]

The wounded were sent by rail from Corinth to Memphis, where many died of gangrene. Those that recovered rejoined the regiment as soon as possible. They were all kindly received by the ladies of Memphis, who had established the Southern Mothers' association, and the kindness and attention of those good women will never be forgotten by the members of the old First Missouri.[32] We received much more attention than the other troops, as we had no chance of going to our own homes. I remember the kindness of Mrs. Sam Tate, the wife of Col. Sam Tate, president of the

Memphis and Charleston railroad. This excellent lady at all times was doing something good for the Missourians. She turned her home into an hospital, and I really believe that the exertion and fatigue she underwent shortened her days, for she died shortly after Memphis was occupied by the federal forces. May the sod rest lightly on her.[33]

APRIL 1862

ENDNOTES

1. Grady McWhiney, *Braxton Bragg and Confederate Defeat, Volume I* (Tuscaloosa: The University of Alabama Press, 1969), 212–217.

2. Bock, "Confederate Col. A. C. Riley, His Reports and Letters, Part I," 180.

Joseph T. Hargett, a native of Christian County, Kentucky, was an attorney living in New Madrid, Missouri, when he joined the 1st Missouri Infantry in June 1861 to serve as a brevet second lieutenant. He was promoted to full rank by election in October and promoted to first lieutenant four days before his death on April 7, 1862. *CSR—Confederate, Missouri.*

3. *CSR—Confederate, Missouri.*

4. Brigadier General Felix Kirk Zollicoffer, a former Tennessee congressman, was killed at the battle of Mill Springs, Kentucky, on January 19, 1862, when he mistakenly rode toward a Union regiment believing it was one of his own. Warner, *Generals in Gray*, 350.

5. Johnston's army began arriving at Corinth, Mississippi, on March 18. Hardee's troops were not all in Corinth until a week later. Horn, *The Army of Tennessee*, 109.

6. Saturday, April 5, 1862.

7. Captain I. P. Girardey's Georgia battery and Major T. A. McDonnell's 1st Florida Battalion were the only units in Bragg's command representing these states. "The Opposing Forces at Shiloh," in Robert Underwood Johnson and Clarence Clough Buel, ed., *Battles and Leaders of the Civil War* (1887; reprint, New York: Thomas Yoseloff, 1956), vol. 1, 539.

8. Knapsacks were sometimes made of leather but heavy cloth, treated with enamel or rubber for durability, was much more common. Carried on the back by means of straps, knapsacks carried extra socks, underwear, shirts and any personal items the soldier may have brought from home. In the Confederate army, knapsacks fell out of favor by early 1862 as the realities of movement and combat began to set in. Veterans learned to roll any essentials inside a blanket, tie the ends together, cover it with oilcloth and wear the blanket around the body hanging from left shoulder to right hip. Bell Irvin Wiley, *The Life of Johnny Reb: The Common Soldier of the Confederacy* (Baton Rouge: Louisiana State University Press, 1943, 1978 edition), 306.

9. Captain Alfred Hudson's Mississippi battery, also known as the Pettus Flying Artillery, was recruited largely from Hinds County, Mississippi. Crute, *Units of the Confederate States Army*, 192.

Boyce and Henry Guibor had marched together in 1860 as members of the St. Louis Greys. Guibor commanded a battery in the Missouri Volunteer Militia from December 1860 through May 1861. Undated clip, "Members of the St. Louis Grays," ca. June 1860, Babcock Scrapbook, MHM Archives. Winter, *The Civil War in St. Louis*, 137.

10. John J. Corkery, born in Martinsburg, Virginia, was brought to St. Louis as a child. In his youth, he joined the St. Louis Greys, serving with Boyce.

Corkery was on detached service in Jefferson City, Missouri, at the time of Camp Jackson and subsequently joined the Missouri State Guard. Wounded at Wilson's Creek, Corkery left the Missouri State Guard to recuperate and enlisted in the 1st Missouri Infantry in December 1861. John C. Moore, *Confederate Military History Extended Edition, Volume XII: Missouri* (n.p.: Confederate Publishing Company, 1899; reprint, Wilmington, NC, Broadfoot Publishing Company, 1988), 264–265.

11. John Scott Elder, twenty, was born in Baltimore but living in St. Louis at the time of his enlistment in Confederate service in July 1861, identifying his pre-war occupation as "gentleman." In August 1862, during the brigade's advance to Baton Rouge, Elder crossed into Federal lines, took the loyalty oath and returned to St. Louis. *CSR—Confederate, Missouri.*

12. Brigadier General Benjamin Mayberry Prentiss commanded the Sixth Division in Grant's army. The division included the 18th, 21st, 23rd, and 25th Missouri Infantry regiments, none of which was distinctly German. Belleville, Illinois, east of St. Louis, was a destination for immigrants from the German states of central Europe. Several German American companies from Illinois enrolled in Missouri units raised in St. Louis, a city with a significant German population. Report of Brig. Gen. B. M. Prentiss, November 17, 1962, *OR*, vol. 10, pt. 2, 277–280. William L. Burton, *Melting Pot Soldiers: The Union's Ethnic Regiments* (Ames: Iowa State University Press, 1988), 3–9.

13. In *Nicholson*, Boyce corrects "50 feet" to "150 yards."

14. Prentiss chose a defensive position "behind a dense thicket on the crest of a hill" that was "almost perfectly protected by the conformation of the ground, and by logs and other rude and hastily prepared defenses." The "Hornet's Nest," as the position became known, was instrumental in breaking the impetus of the Confederate assault and in saving Grant's army. William Preston Johnson, *The Life of General Albert Sidney Johnston* (1879; reprint, New York: DaCapo Press, 1997), 604–605.

15. In *Nicholson*, Boyce corrects "11 o'clock a.m." to be "3 o'clock p.m."

16. Field artillery of the era used four types of ammunition. Solid shot, commonly called "cannon balls," was the least effective against infantry or cavalry, hence Boyce's derision of the Union artillerymen using it. Shell, a hollow projectile filled with black powder and designed to break into ragged fragments, would have been more effective. Canister, a container of iron balls not unlike a very large shotgun shell, was reserved for anti-personnel work at close range. Case shot or "shrapnel" was similar to canister but with a time fuse. Dean S. Thomas, *Cannons: An Introduction to Civil War Artillery* (Arendtsville, PA: Thomas Publications, 1985), 16–17.

17. The 1st Missouri's brigade commander, John Bowen, was seriously wounded about this time, further contributing to the deterioration in command and control. Report of Col. John D. Martin, April 14, 1862, *OR*, vol. 10, pt. 1, 622.

18. The Union gunboats were *Tyler* and *Lexington*.
19. The 71st Ohio Infantry was the largest of the three regiments in the Second Brigade of Brigadier General William T. Sherman's 5th Division. More than four decades after the war, a state historian was still unforgiving of the regiment's conduct: "This regiment has been severely censured for its conduct in the battle of Shiloh; and so far as Colonel [Rodney] Mason is concerned, deserved the severest condemnation. At the first appearance of the enemy, Colonel Mason put spurs to his horse, basely deserting his men." Ohio Battlefield Commission, *Ohio at Shiloh* (Cincinnati: C. J. Krehbiel & Co., 1903), 37–38.
20. A native of Tipperary, Ireland, Thomas Dwyer was twenty-eight years old and a drayman in St. Louis when he enrolled in Confederate service on July 21, 1861. Shortly before the battle of Shiloh, he was promoted to corporal in Company D, and after the battle he was promoted to sergeant. In May 1863, following the battle at Baker's Creek (Champion Hill), Mississippi, Dwyer was initially listed as missing in action. It was subsequently determined that he had been killed. *CSR—Confederate, Missouri*.
21. Major General Don Carlos Buell led the four divisions of the Army of the Ohio. His command arrived behind Grant's lines during the night of April 6–7, enabling Grant's setback on April 6 to be turned into victory the next day.
22. The 24th Louisiana Infantry was known as the "Crescent" regiment because it was raised in New Orleans, the "Crescent City." Nathaniel Cheairs Hughes, Jr., *The Pride of the Confederate Artillery: The Washington Artillery in the Army of Tennessee* (Baton Rouge: Louisiana State University Press, 1997), 5, 12.
23. William Kearny, the son of General Stephen Watts Kearny, joined Hardee's staff in Arkansas in August of 1861 in the rank of colonel and role of assistant inspector general, a position he held until June 1862. His rank was not confirmed, and he was assigned as a first lieutenant to rank from March 16, 1861. In mid-1863, he joined the staff of John Bankhead Magruder in Texas and served there for the remainder of the war. National Archives and Records Administration, Publication No. M331, *Compiled Service Records of Confederate General and Staff Officers and Nonregimental Enlisted Men*.
24. The Mobile Light Artillery was also known as Captain William H. Ketchum's Alabama battery. Crute, *Units of the Confederate States Army*, 38. "The Opposing Forces at Shiloh" in Johnson and Buel, eds., *Battles and Leaders of the Civil War*, vol. 1, 539.
25. John O'Neil (also presented in his company's records as "John Neil") entered Confederate service in New Orleans in June 1861 as a member of the Pargoud Volunteers. On reaching Memphis, his unit helped fill out the 1st Missouri, becoming Company A when the regiment was formed. On May 2, 1863, Neil was left behind among the sick when Grand Gulf was evacuated. On May 19, he was captured near the Big Black River and was eventually imprisoned at Alton, Illinois. *CSR—Confederate, Missouri*.

26. The "bravest of the brave" was the appellation given by the Emperor Napoleon to Marshal of France Michel Ney for his heroics in commanding the rear guard of the French army during the retreat from Moscow in 1812. Peter Young, *Napoleon's Marshals* (New York: Hippocrene Books, 1973), 111.
27. Hughes, *The Pride of the Confederate Artillery: The Washington Artillery in the Army of Tennessee*, makes no mention of the role of the 1st Missouri in saving the 5th Company, Washington Artillery.
28. The 3rd Louisiana Infantry was part of the Confederate force under General Ben McCulloch which teamed with the Missouri State Guard under General Sterling Price to defeat Union forces at the battle of Oak Hills (Wilson's Creek), Missouri, on August 10, 1861.
29. April 8, 1862.
30. Major Amos C. Riley, commander of the 1st Missouri after Lieutenant Colonel Rich was mortally wounded, tallied 135 killed and wounded when he wrote his after-action report on April 14, 1862. H. Riley Bock, "Confederate Col. A. C. Riley, His Reports and Letters, Part I," *Missouri Historical Review* LXXXV, no. 2 (1991): 180.
31. In *Nicholson*, Boyce added P. S. Thompson to the listed of wounded enlisted men.
32. The Association of Ladies of the City of Memphis formed the Southern Mothers' Association in May 1861, and under the leadership of its president, Mrs. S. A. Law, the ladies quickly established a hospital. The female members of the association performed nursing duties, and Dr. G. W. Currey served as surgeon. Memphis *Daily Appeal*, May 30 and June 13, 1861.
33. Since 1854, Colonel Sam Tate had been president of the Memphis & Charleston Railroad, the last link in a chain of railroads connecting the Mississippi River to the Atlantic coast. From Chattanooga, trains could reach Virginia or Georgia. Colonel Tate is listed among the benefactors of the hospital operated by the Southern Mothers' Association, and Mrs. Tate was active in its operation. J. M. Keating, *History of the City of Memphis, Tennessee* (Syracuse, NY: D. Mason & Co., 1888), 343. *The Tennessee Encyclopedia of History and Culture* accessed at http://tennesseeencyclopedia.net, entry for Memphis & Charleston Railroad. Memphis *Daily Appeal*, June 13 and August 4, 1861.

CHAPTER 5
BATON ROUGE, LOUISIANA
⚬⟩⟨⚬
MAY–SEPTEMBER 1862

Lieutenant Colonel Lucius L. Rich had been struck in the head on April 6 while leading the 1ˢᵀ Missouri in the battle at Shiloh. His wound was immediately recognized to be mortal, but Rich lingered until August 9, when he died at Okolona, Mississippi.[1] On Rich's death, Major Amos C. Riley assumed command of the regiment.[2] Under Riley's leadership, the 1ˢᵀ Missouri experienced its first summer in the Deep South as it moved from place to place in support of the defense of Vicksburg.

After the battle at Shiloh, General Beauregard regrouped the Confederate army at Corinth, Mississippi. Generals Earl Van Dorn and Sterling Price arrived with their Army of the West, fresh from defeat at the battle of Pea Ridge (Elkhorn Tavern), Arkansas. Among the troops brought with them from across the Mississippi River were several regiments and batteries of Missouri Confederates, former members of the Missouri State Guard. Beauregard and his army evacuated Corinth on May 29, 1862, retiring without challenge to Tupelo, Mississippi. When Beauregard went on sick leave in mid-June, President Davis replaced him with Braxton Bragg, one of Beauregard's corps commanders.

Bragg completed the reorganization of the army begun by Beauregard. Breckinridge's division was enlarged to four brigades, adding one to the three composing his Reserve Corps at Shiloh. The

BATON ROUGE, LOUISIANA

COLONEL AMOS C. RILEY LED THE 1ST/4TH
MISSOURI FOR MORE THAN TWO YEARS UNTIL
HE WAS KILLED IN ACTION AT NEW HOPE
CHURCH ON MAY 30, 1864.

1ST MISSOURI REMAINED IN THE 1ST BRIGADE UNDER BOWEN WITH THE 9TH
ARKANSAS, 10TH ARKANSAS, 6TH MISSISSIPPI, AND 2ND CONFEDERATE INFANTRY
REGIMENTS AND WATSON'S LOUISIANA BATTERY.[3] THE DIVISION, HOWEVER, WAS
TRANSFERRED TO THE COMMAND OF GENERAL VAN DORN, NOW CHARGED WITH
THE DEFENSE OF VICKSBURG.

BRECKINRIDGE AND HIS BRIGADES LEFT GRENADA, MISSISSIPPI, FOR
VICKSBURG ON JUNE 23, 1862.[4] AS THEY NEARED THE RIVER BASTION, VAN DORN
ASSIGNED THEM THE ROLE OF THE MOBILE FORCE IN HIS PLAN FOR VICKSBURG'S
DEFENSE. ON JUNE 30, BOWEN'S BRIGADE MARCHED NORTH OF VICKSBURG TO
DEFENSIVE POSITIONS ALONG THE BLUFFS OVERLOOKING THE YAZOO RIVER.
THERE, THE 1ST MISSOURI AND ITS SISTER REGIMENTS REMAINED FOR ANOTHER
MONTH. ON JULY 4, 1862, JOSEPH BOYCE WAS PROMOTED TO THE RANK OF
FIRST LIEUTENANT.[5]

MAY–SEPTEMBER 1862

VAN DORN DECIDED THAT ONE WAY TO PROTECT VICKSBURG WOULD BE TO EXPEL THE FEDERAL FORCES FROM BATON ROUGE, LOUISIANA, WHICH IN TURN WOULD HELP SECURE ACCESS TO THE RED RIVER AND CONSEQUENTLY TO SUPPLIES FROM THE CONFEDERACY WEST OF THE MISSISSIPPI RIVER. ON JULY 25, HE ORDERED BRECKINRIDGE AND HIS SMALL DIVISION TO ATTACK BATON ROUGE. ALTHOUGH HEAT AND BAD WATER, WHEN WATER WAS AVAILABLE, DROPPED MEN FROM THE RANKS IN SCORES, THE CONFEDERATES REACHED THE COMITE RIVER ABOUT TEN MILES EAST OF BATON ROUGE ON AUGUST 3. BRECKINRIDGE DELAYED THE ATTACK UNTIL AUGUST 5 IN THE HOPE THAT THE CSS *ARKANSAS*, WORKING ITS WAY DOWNRIVER FROM VICKSBURG, COULD PARTICIPATE. THE ATTACK WAS INITIALLY SUCCESSFUL, BUT THE UNION FORCES RALLIED, AND BRECKINRIDGE WAS DRIVEN BACK WITH NO RESULT. THE ENGINES OF THE CSS *ARKANSAS* FAILED, CAUSING IT TO BE BLOWN UP BY ITS CREW TO PREVENT ITS CAPTURE.[6]

THE 1ST MISSOURI INFANTRY AND THE OTHER REGIMENTS OF BOWEN'S BRIGADE WERE NOT INVOLVED IN THE ATTACK. HAVING FARTHER TO TRAVEL, THEY HAD TRAILED THEIR DIVISION SOUTH, AND THE BRIGADE ARRIVED AT BRECKINRIDGE'S FORMER POSITION ON THE COMITE RIVER AS BRECKINRIDGE MOVED THE OTHER ELEMENTS OF HIS COMMAND TO PORT HUDSON, A HEALTHIER AND MORE DEFENSIBLE POSITION. FROM ITS POST ON THE COMITE RIVER, THE 1ST MISSOURI AND ITS SISTER REGIMENTS WERE "TO OBSERVE BATON ROUGE FROM THAT QUARTER, TO PROTECT OUR HOSPITALS, AND TO COVER THE LINES OF COMMUNICATION BETWEEN CLINTON AND CAMP MOORE (LOUISIANA)."[7] AFTER TWO WEEKS OF THIS HOT, DRY, DUSTY DUTY, THE BRIGADE MOVED TO JACKSON, MISSISSIPPI. THE REGIMENTS RESTED FOR A FEW DAYS BEFORE MOVING AGAIN, THIS TIME TO DAVIS' MILL NORTH OF HOLLY SPRINGS, MISSISSIPPI, NEAR THE TENNESSEE BORDER, ARRIVING THERE ON SEPTEMBER 6.[8]

ONE OF PRICE'S OFFICERS, AS YET UNAWARE OF THE OUTCOME OF THE CAMPAIGN, RECORDED IN HIS DIARY WHAT MANY OFFICERS IN VAN DORN'S COMMAND MUST HAVE BEEN THINKING: "I FEAR THERE WILL BE SOME RASH

BATON ROUGE, LOUISIANA

The regiment was kept constantly on duty at Corinth, and during the advance of the federal troops under Halleck, was in all the engagements until the final evacuation of the place, when it was sent with its brigade (Bowen's) to Camp Price, one of the defences of Vicksburg, about twelve [miles] north of it and near the Yazoo river.

Just before Memphis was abandoned the regiment was called on to furnish a detail of pilots and engineers for the gunboat service under Commodore Edward Montgomery, an old St. Louis steamboat captain. Nearly all of the pilots and engineers in the regiment responded, and we had quite a number of them, too, in Companies B and D. I well remember the citizens giving coal to the service, as the gunboats were short of fuel. It was well understood by all that there was going to be a gunboat fight in front of the city. The large bluff overlooking the river was crowded from day to day with convalescent soldiers and citizens to see the fight. After several daily visits, one morning early the city was startled by the heavy boom of a cannon and all repaired to the bluffs. The most interested of all that gathered there were the members of the First Missouri. We hobbled down on crutches to see how our comrades on the gunboats would share. The federal fleet soon came in sight, but kept close to the Arkansas shore. We thought they were going to pass the city and avoid our fleet. In this we were mistaken, for they soon turned and came up stream. Commodore Montgomery advanced at once to the attack, but he had no show against such boats as the enemy had. The *Little Rebel* fired a shot and then every boat dashed forward, selecting such as the commander thought he was able for.

It was soon over. The iron-clads made quick work of our boats, and the poor fellows of the regiment had to swim for it. The sharp-shooters on the federal boats had no mercy on them, for they fired at our men in the water and killed several while making their way to shore. Those who escaped rejoined the command at Camp Price and said they would do their fighting hereafter on the land, where a fellow had a chance to run somewhere, even if he was whipped.[10]

About the last of July we were ordered into Vicksburg. After a pleasant march we arrived during the night and bivouacked on the levee. At daylight we were aroused by the cheers of the men who, upon awaking, saw the Mississippi river for the first time since we left it at Columbus, Ky., about a year before. "Here's the old Mississippi, all the way from our homes in Missouri," with a yell almost everybody threw off their clothes and dashed into the river. The citizens hurried down to see what caused the excitement, but soon returned laughing at the capers of the men in the water and on the shore.

The next morning we were placed on board the cars and sent to Tangipahoa station on the Jackson railroad about 60 miles north of New Orleans.[11] Our division (Breckinridge's) had preceded us about a week on its way to Baton Rouge about forty miles west of Tangipahoa.[12] The weather was extremely hot and we were marched during the night and rested through the day. We were hurried forward to assist in the attack on the federal troops under command of Gen. Ben Butler.[13] Gen. Breckinridge, however, made the attack the day before we arrived, driving the federal forces through the town and under the river bank where they were protected by their gunboats.

This attack was made to prevent Butler reinforcing Port Hudson.[14] This place was taken possession of by some of our division and fortified.[15] After this was accomplished, we remained about a week longer in the vicinity of Baton Rouge when the line of march was taken up and we returned to Tangipahoa station and took the cars for Jackson, Miss.[16] After a stay at this place of two or three weeks we were sent by rail to Holly Springs.[17]

Here Gen. Breckinridge and nearly all of the Kentucky troops were ordered to Bragg's army in Tennessee. We saw them leave with sad hearts, as we were from the first up to this time a part of Breckinridge's division. Gen. Breckinridge was much moved in taking leave of us.[18]

BATON ROUGE, LOUISIANA

ENDNOTES

1. H. Riley Bock, "Confederate Col. A. C. Riley, His Reports and Letters, Part II," *Missouri Historical Review* 85 (1991): 266.

2. Amos Camden Riley was a native of Kentucky, one of thirteen children. The family moved to New Madrid County, Missouri, in 1844 when he was seven. At fourteen, Riley entered the Kentucky Military Institute. After graduation in 1855, he took up farming near Island No. 10 in New Madrid County. At the outbreak of the war, Riley helped form a company in New Madrid and was elected first lieutenant, later advancing to captain. C. N. Riley to A. R. Taylor, June 27, 1886, Boyce Family Papers, MHM Archives. C. N. Riley was a brother of A. C. Riley. *CSR—Confederate, Missouri.*

3. The brigades in the division were numbered on July 10, 1862. *OR*, vol. 15, 1121.

4. *OR*, vol. 15, 1120.

5. *CSR—Confederate, Missouri.*

6. Robert G. Hartje, *Van Dorn: The Life and Times of a Confederate General* (Nashville: Vanderbilt University Press, 1967), 205–207. William C. Davis, *Breckinridge: Statesman, Soldier, Symbol* (Baton Rouge: Louisiana State University Press, 1974), 318–323.

7. Report of Maj. Gen. John C. Breckinridge, September 30, 1862, *OR*, vol. 15, 80–81.

8. H. Grady Howell, Jr., *Going to Meet the Yankees: A History of the 'Bloody Sixth' Mississippi Infantry, C.S.A.* (Jackson, MS: Chickasaw Bayou Press, 1981, 2002), 123–124.

9. Albert Castel, ed., "The Diary of General Henry Little, C.S.A., *Civil War Times Illustrated* (October 1972): 44. Diary entry for August 6, 1862.

10. Not long after sunrise on May 10, 1862, Commodore and Captain James Edward Montgomery, aboard his flagship *Little Rebel*, led a flotilla of eight cottonclad rams against the *Cincinnati*, the lone Union gunboat guarding a group of moored mortar boats. *Cincinnati* was rescued by the arrival of the heavily armed and armored *Benton, Carondelet, St. Louis,* and *Mound City*. After an engagement of ten minutes, the Confederate flotilla withdrew to the protection of Fort Pillow, high on the Mississippi River's left bank at a bend in the river. James M. Merrill, *Battle Flags South: The Story of the Civil War Navies on Western Waters* (Rutherford, NJ: Fairleigh Dickinson University Press, 1970), 137–138, 191–194.

11. Bowen's regiments boarded the railroad at Vicksburg, traveling east to Jackson on the Southern Railroad of Mississippi before turning south on the New Orleans, Jackson & Great Northern Railroad. James Willis, *Arkansas Confederates in the Western Theater* (Dayton, OH: Morningside House, 1998), 250. Warren E. Grabau, *Ninety-Eight Days: A Geographer's View of the Vicksburg Campaign* (Knoxville: University of Tennessee Press, 2000), Map 5: The Core Region.

12. Breckinridge and his other three brigades left the Vicksburg area for Baton Rouge on July 27, 1862. Willis, *Arkansas Confederates*, 250. Report of Maj. Gen. John C. Breckinridge, September 30, 1862, *OR*, vol. 15, 76.

13. On May 1, 1862, General Benjamin Franklin Butler took possession of New Orleans following the reduction of the city's defenses by Admiral David Farragut and the U.S. Navy. Butler had been a Democrat in the Massachusetts House of Representatives before becoming a brigadier general in the Massachusetts militia at the start of the war. For marching to the defense of Washington, D.C., with the 8th Massachusetts, he was rewarded with Lincoln's first appointment of a volunteer major general. Ezra J. Warner, *Generals in Blue: Lives of the Union Commanders* (Baton Rouge: Louisiana State University Press, 1964), 60–61.

14. Bowen's brigade arrived to occupy Breckinridge's former position on the Comite River near Baton Rouge while Breckinridge moved the other elements of his command to Port Hudson, a healthier and more defensible position. From their post on the Comite River, the 1st Missouri and its sister regiments were "to observe Baton Rouge from that quarter, to protect our hospitals, and to cover the lines of communication between Clinton and Camp Moore [Louisiana]." Report of Maj. Gen. John C. Breckinridge, September 30, 1862, September 30, 1862, *OR*, vol. 15, 80–81.

15. Ironically, but in compliance with his orders, Breckinridge had bypassed Port Hudson, a much more defensible position and one which also helped secure the Red River, on his way to attack Baton Rouge. On August 12, his troops took Port Hudson unopposed. It was soon fortified and would remain in Confederate hands until the fall of Vicksburg. Davis, *Breckinridge*, 324.

16. Bowen's troops arrived at Camp Moore on August 24, 1862, and boarded the railroad for Jackson, Mississippi, where they arrived the next day. Howell, *Going to Meet the Yankees*, 123.

17. The Missourians remained at Jackson until September 6 when they moved to Davis' Mill, arriving the next day. Howell, *Going to Meet the Yankees*, 124.

18. Breckinridge and his division, less Bowen's brigade, moved north on September 19, 1862, to join Bragg for the invasion of Kentucky. *OR*, vol. 17, pt. 2, 899.

CHAPTER 6
CORINTH, MISSISSIPPI

OCTOBER–DECEMBER 1862

THE BRIGADE'S MOVEMENT WAS PROMPTED BY VAN DORN'S PREPARATIONS FOR AN INITIATIVE TO RECAPTURE THE IMPORTANT RAIL JUNCTION AT CORINTH, MISSISSIPPI. AS PART OF HIS PREPARATION, VAN DORN REORGANIZED HIS COMMAND CONSISTENT WITH WAR DEPARTMENT GUIDELINES TO FORM BRIGADES OF REGIMENTS FROM THE SAME STATE WHEREVER POSSIBLE. CONSEQUENTLY, THE 1ST MISSOURI WAS SEPARATED ON THE EVE OF THE CAMPAIGN FROM SEVERAL OF THE REGIMENTS WITH WHICH IT HAD CAMPAIGNED ALL SUMMER. THE 1ST MISSOURI, 6TH MISSISSIPPI, AND WATSON'S BATTERY WERE JOINED BY THE 15TH MISSISSIPPI AND 22ND MISSISSIPPI INFANTRY REGIMENTS AND CARUTHERS'S MISSISSIPPI BATTALION. THE ARKANSAS REGIMENTS WERE MOVED TO OTHER BRIGADES. BOWEN'S REORGANIZED BRIGADE JOINED THOSE LED BY GENERALS JOHN VILLEPIGUE AND ALBERT RUST IN A NEW DIVISION COMMANDED BY GENERAL MANSFIELD LOVELL.

GENERAL LOVELL JOINED VAN DORN'S ARMY FROM NEW ORLEANS, RECENTLY SURRENDERED TO THE UNION ARMY AND NAVY.[1] LOVELL, A WEST POINT GRADUATE AND VETERAN OF THE WAR WITH MEXICO, WAS APPOINTED A MAJOR GENERAL IN THE CONFEDERATE SERVICE IN OCTOBER 1861 AND ASSIGNED TO DIRECT THE DEFENSES OF NEW ORLEANS. UNABLE TO PREVENT THE CITY'S LOSS, LOVELL NOW SERVED UNDER A CLOUD OF DISGRACE, LATER ONLY SLIGHTLY DISSIPATED BY THE FINDINGS OF A COURT OF INQUIRY.[2]

VAN DORN NOW REPORTED TO GENERAL BRAXTON BRAGG. IN SEPTEMBER 1862, BRAGG WAS BUSY EXECUTING HIS PLAN TO RECAPTURE TENNESSEE AND

CORINTH, MISSISSIPPI

KENTUCKY FOR THE CONFEDERACY. VAN DORN REMAINED AT VICKSBURG WHILE STERLING PRICE AND HIS ARMY DEFENDED NORTHERN MISSISSIPPI. AS BRAGG AND HIS ARMY MOVED NORTH, VAN DORN AND PRICE WERE TO COORDINATE THEIR MOVEMENTS TO THWART ANY FEDERAL OFFENSIVE. UNSURE OF THEIR ORDERS AND UNCERTAIN OF THEIR COMMAND RELATIONSHIP, VAN DORN AND PRICE FOUND IT DIFFICULT TO COOPERATE. ALTHOUGH VAN DORN WAS SENIOR IN RANK TO PRICE, HE DID NOT HAVE THE AUTHORITY TO COMMAND PRICE AS BOTH REPORTED TO BRAGG, AT LEAST UNTIL THEIR FORCES WERE UNITED ON THE SAME FIELD.[3]

IN RESPONSE TO BRAGG'S MOVEMENTS, PRICE BEGAN MOVING NORTH IN THE SECOND WEEK OF SEPTEMBER. ON THE AFTERNOON OF SEPTEMBER 19, PRICE AND HIS CORPS WERE SURPRISED AT IUKA, MISSISSIPPI, BY TWO INFANTRY DIVISIONS AND CAVALRY UNDER MAJOR GENERAL WILLIAM S. ROSECRANS. A COUNTERATTACK BY PRICE'S MISSOURIANS HELPED HOLD THE FIELD, ALLOWING PRICE'S ARMY TO RETREAT DURING THE NIGHT. THE ARMY RETREATED SOUTHWEST UNTIL IT REACHED RIPLEY, MISSISSIPPI, ON SEPTEMBER 23. AFTER A SHORT REST, PRICE RESUMED THE MARCH TO THE NORTHWEST, LINKING UP WITH VAN DORN AT BALDWYN, MISSISSIPPI.[4]

ALTHOUGH VAN DORN WAS BY THEN IN COMMAND, PRICE WAS RESPONSIBLE FOR TWO-THIRDS OF THE ARMY THAT VAN DORN PROPOSED TO USE TO ATTACK THE FEDERAL FORCES AT CORINTH. PRICE'S ARMY OF THE WEST WAS COMPOSED OF TWO INFANTRY DIVISIONS, ONE COMMANDED BY DABNEY MAURY AND THE SECOND BY LOUIS HEBERT, ALTHOUGH MISSOURIAN MARTIN GREEN COMMANDED THE DIVISION DURING THE UPCOMING BATTLE. LOVELL COMMANDED VAN DORN'S THIRD DIVISION.

The army now was reorganized and we became a part of Lovell's division.[5]

About this time Gen. Van Dorn commenced his move against Corinth. He ordered our division to La Grange, Tenn., and it was one of the hottest Sundays we ever felt.[6] We were pushed forward rapidly and soon found the enemy, under Gen. Ord, on the retreat.[7] As we came up to the wells on the way we found the enemy had filled them with fence rails and branches of trees, so that it was impossible to get a bucket down for water. We suffered terribly. It was really water, water, everywhere, but not a drop to drink. Towards sundown he made a stand at the river, but we rattled him out of that in a hurry. It was water we wanted, and if he had been in twice the strength he was we would have driven him. We were desperate with thirst.[8]

The next morning the only tidings we could get of him were that he had made his way to Bolivar, about twelve miles distant.

We returned in a few days to the neighborhood of La Grange, cooked three days' rations and performed the usual army feat of eating them in one day. We took up the line of march for Corinth.

The battle of Iuka had been fought while we were operating near La Grange, Tenn.[9] Price and Van Dorn arranged to concentrate their forces and attack Corinth as soon as possible. About the last days of September both forces were on the march. The junction of the troops was effected October 3, about five miles west of Corinth.

Our division (Lovell's) arrived at the point selected about two hours before Price. We were moved off of the main road, "stacked arms" and quietly awaited the arrival of the heroes of Wilson Creek, Lexington, etc. "Here they come, boys!" and we rushed to the road to welcome them.[10] Many old friends met who had parted at Camp Jackson, and our pleasure was great, indeed, to meet so many friends and former comrades. They presented a very soldierly appearance, marching and moving like veterans. They were well armed but indifferently uniformed.[11]

As soon as the last of Price's command passed we moved down the same road a short distance, when we entered the timber to the right of the road and took our position just in rear of Vill[e]pigue's brigade of our division. I may say here that our command (Lovell's) was composed of Villepigue's, Bowen's and Rust's brigades of infantry, several batteries of artillery and a squadron of cavalry.[12]

The day was drawing to a close, and it appeared we were to have no opposition to our advance from the enemy. Suddenly, however, a sharp fire from Villepigue's brigade broke the silence, and the hissing bullets about our heads informed us the enemy was on the alert.

CORINTH, MISSISSIPPI

Our brigade at once moved quickly to the right of Villepigue's, while Rust marched in the rear as a reserve.

After clearing the brigade in our front we moved up to our line and skirmishers were thrown out by the regiments, the firing soon ceased and after a march of half a mile, we came upon a deserted camp of a cavalry brigade. It was evidently abandoned hurriedly, as the ovens were filled with bread just nicely baked, coffee and soup, hot and ready for consumers. It was a treat we enjoyed, but our hosts gave a very rude reception to their guests—no doubt we were the unbidden guests.[13]

For the first time we saw desiccated food. The command which abandoned their camp left great quantities of provisions of all kinds, but more especially the desiccated vegetables, consisting of potatoes, carrots, turnips, cabbage, etc., etc., packed in large square tins of one hundred pounds each. This was a revelation to us, such food and so nicely kept. I am sure there was at least twenty wagon loads of it, and we secured all of it and sent it to the rear by order of Gen. Bowen. It was by this means saved, and was issued to us for several weeks after we arrived at Holly Springs.[14]

Bob Louden, the famous spy and scout, had been sworn into the service in the writer's company at our camp near La Grange.[15] He was ordered to report daily at Bowen's headquarters, and continued with us until after the fall of Vicksburg, coming and going at his pleasure. About one hour after dark Bob was sent off to Van Dorn's headquarters, and shortly after 9 o'clock came back to the company. It was useless to ask him any questions. He had the closest mouth of any man in the entire army. If you were to ask him a question about anything concerning his business you would never do so the second time. A look and a laugh that conveyed, "attend to your own affairs," so clearly prevented any talk with Louden on army affairs. Towards midnight he passed through the line of skirmishers and just before day returned and repaired at once to Lovell's headquarters in company with Gen. Bowen. He had been in Corinth and carried the desired information to his superiors. The entire line in our front had been examined by him and, as we learned afterwards, the strength of the enemy's position and the heavy abatis that he had placed in front of his works was clearly explained by Louden. This information was most valuable, as it saved our division from destruction, for it was the intention to assault the works at daylight. If we had done so the same fate that befell Price's division on our left would have been ours.

At day-light the battle opened with a roar on our left.[16] The guns in Battery Robinette opened fire on Price, while the guns in our front, I think it was Battery Williams, were silent. The musketry fire on our left was very slack until 9 o'clock, when it became awful. We knew by the yell that reached us that Price was charging.[17] The fire of our skirmishers was increased, but our line kept its place, not moving at all. This continued until about 11 o'clock, when Bowen ordered up our battery (Watson's) under command of Capt. A. A. Bursley and Lieut. W. P. Barlow. This famous battery from Louisiana came up on the gallop and went into battery like a flash. They were grand fellows. They opened on Fort Williams and the Tishomingo house and fired about sixty rounds so rapidly that we could hardly believe that amount of ammunition had been expended.[18]

The first round from this battery caused a response from Fort Williams that opened our eyes. The large 32-pounders replied quickly and silenced one of Barlow's pieces by tearing the axle away. The air seemed filled with iron and flying branches from the trees about us. Still we suffered no loss, and lying down behind a ridge of ground in our front, enjoyed the noise without any danger. Heavy bodies of troops could be seen hurrying along the line of works in our front and taking position to resist our expected attack.[19]

In the meantime Price had been defeated and had fallen back, retreating by the main or Chewalla road on our left. This placed us in a bad position, and a desperate one had Rosecrans followed immediately. He delayed doing so, thus enabling Lovell and Bowen to withdraw the division and gain the main road.

The First Missouri, under command of Col. Riley, was left behind to cover the retreat. The entire regiment was thrown out as skirmishers, the centre resting on the road. We were moved forward quickly and the skirmishers of the Fifteenth Mississippi and our own recalled by Maj. Robt. Duffy of our regiment.[20] After getting affairs in pretty good shape and finding the enemy had not followed up his success, the commands were assembled and moved rapidly down the road to rejoin Bowen and the rest of the brigade at the Little Hatchie river. The writer and his company was left behind to cover his retreat, with instructions from Bowen and Riley to remain on the field until dark and then fall back quickly to the river. If in the meantime we found we had been flanked to make our way out the best we could.

In less than an hour we found that we had been flanked. Rosecrans' troops moved on a road parallel with the one we were on about half a mile to our left. The writer got his information from a planter who had just left the other road as the enemy commenced to pass. We soon abandoned any idea of being captured and hurried after the regiment, which we overtook about 5 o'clock. We were warmly welcomed. The First Missouri and the Fifteenth Mississippi, under command of Col. Michael Farrell, an old St. Louisan, and the Watson battery occupying a ridge well adapted for a defensive position.[21]

Gen. Bowen had selected this place to make a stand and save the army that had passed on the pontoon bridge over the Little Hatchie river just at our rear.[22] Shortly after our arrival the enemy appeared in heavy force on our left and front. The bend of the river was in our favor, and the position itself an excellent one and easily held by determined men. Despite the fact that we kept perfectly quiet and would not respond to his occasional fire, he felt that danger lurked at this point. Two guns on our left under the direction of Lieut. T[o]lledano were masked by branches of trees being thrown in front of them, so that it was almost impossible to discover any indications of a force at this point.[23] As darkness began to close around us the enemy determined to assault the position in force. After listening to every command, and hearing him move his line of battle up to his skirmish line at the foot of the hill, he started up with a rush just about dark. We rose in four ranks deep, the two regiments as close together as we could press, and delivered our fire right in his face. The two guns opened with canister at the same instant, and those that escaped that dreadful fire rushed down the hill, terror-stricken at the reception. Not a word was spoken. We faced to the right and quietly marched down to the pontoon bridge. The stillness was only broken by the quiet tread of the men. It was unnecessary to command silence. The gravity of the situation was felt by all. We had heard nothing of Price and Van Dorn, and really we did not know whether we were going to escape or not. We were fully aware of the great disaster that befell our army that day, and we knew we left a force at Bolivar, Tenn., that could be brought against the fleeing army.

About 9 o'clock we bivouacked on the side of the road, and at midnight Barlow and Toledano came up with their pieces. We then felt easier when they told us they had destroyed the bridge by cutting the boats loose, and telling us the loss of life by the enemy was fearful.

Just at dawn we moved again, but the enemy had replaced his loss by other troops, and they followed in hot pursuit. We would form line of battle with the Fifteenth Mississippi, then the Twenty-second Mississippi, and Ninth and Tenth Arkansas, would pass to the rear about two miles, and when they had formed we would fall back in the rear of their line.[24] This kind of retreat was continued all the day. It has a very harassing effect on troops, but it was our only chance in case we were attacked.

The firing at Big Hatchie river was awful. Price and Van Dorn were trying to effect their escape, which they fortunately accomplished late in the afternoon. We were followed closely until we reached Ripley, when the enemy gave up the chase, not before he wounded two of our men just as we entered the town. We were pressed so hard and were so certain of being attacked every instant that we carried our guns at the "right shoulder shift" and at a "full cock." There was no excitement or unnecessary hurry. The discipline and order was excellent, and we were determined to make a bitter fight before we would surrender. We arrived at Holly Springs the following afternoon, where we found Price's command. Notwithstanding the dreadful loss they sustained at Corinth and Hatchie they bore their losses quietly and philosophically. It is true, our division had effected in a great measure the salvation of the army, and more especially this had been done by Gen. Bowen. They were very glad to see us safe among them. The defeat was really appalling.[25]

CORINTH, MISSISSIPPI

ENDNOTES

1. Archer Jones, *Confederate Strategy from Shiloh to Vicksburg* (Baton Rouge: Louisiana State University Press, 1961, rev. ed. 1991), 57–65.

2. Warner, *Generals in Gray*, 194–195.

3. Ben Earl Kitchens, *Rosecrans Meets Price: The Battle of Iuka, Mississippi* (Florence, AL: Thornwood Publishers, 1985), 22–23.

4. Albert Castel, *General Sterling Price and the Civil War in the West* (Baton Rouge: Louisiana State University Press, 1968), 104.

5. Mansfield Lovell, a West Point graduate and veteran of the Mexican War, was appointed a major general in the Confederate service in October 1861 and assigned to direct the defenses of New Orleans. Unable to prevent the city's loss to the Union army and navy, Lovell served under a cloud of disgrace only slightly dissipated by the findings of a court of inquiry. Warner, *Generals in Gray*, 194–195.

6. On Sunday, September 28, 1862, Van Dorn issued orders to his command to cook three days' rations and to prepare to march at a moment's notice. Lovell's division led Van Dorn's army north from Ripley, Mississippi, leaving camp on the afternoon of September 29. Robert G. Hartje, *Van Dorn: The Life and Times of a Confederate General* (Nashville: Vanderbilt University Press, 1967), 215–216. Monroe F. Cockrell, ed., *The Lost Account of the Battle of Corinth and the Court Martial of Gen. Van Dorn* (McCowat-Mercer Press, 1955; reprint, Wilmington, NC: Broadfoot Publishing Company, 1987), 19.

7. Major General Edward Otho Cresap Ord commanded the Federal 3rd Division in the District of Jackson, Tennessee, from September 24 until October 5, 1862. Frederick H. Dyer, *Compendium of the War of the Rebellion* (1908, reprint, Dayton, OH: Press of Morningside Bookshop, 1978), 482.

8. The events described occurred on Thursday, October 2, 1862. Hartje, *Van Dorn*, 219.

9. On September 19, 1862, Price and the Army of the West were surprised and nearly enveloped by Major General William S. Rosecrans and the Union Army of the Mississippi at Iuka, Mississippi. Price's Missouri infantry played a key role in extricating the Confederates. Thomas L. Snead, "With Price East of the Mississippi," in *Battles and Leaders of the Civil War*, ed. Johnson and Buel, vol. 2, 731–733.

10. On August 10, 1861, Price and the Missouri State Guard, aided by Confederate units under General Ben McCulloch, repulsed an attack by Brigadier General Nathaniel Lyon at Wilson's Creek (Oak Hills), near Springfield, Missouri. Six weeks later, the Missouri State Guard was at its peak strength when it lay siege to Union forces in Lexington, Missouri, capturing the garrison of 3,600 men on September 20. E. B. Long and Barbara Long, *The Civil War Day by Day: An Almanac* (Garden City, NY: Doubleday & Company, 1971), 117–120.

11. Price's command included the 2nd, 3rd, 4th, 5th and 6th Missouri Infantry, the 1st and 3rd Missouri Cavalry (both serving dismounted), the 2nd Missouri Cavalry, and the five Missouri artillery batteries of William Wade, William E. Dawson, Samuel Churchill Clark (Houston King), Henry Guibor, and John C. Landis. *OR*, vol. 17, pt. 1, 374–375.

12. Brigadier General John Bordenave Villepigue led the 2nd Brigade of Mississippi troops. Brigadier General Albert Rust led the 1st Brigade, consisting of troops from Alabama, Arkansas, and Kentucky. Lovell's 3rd Brigade under Bowen included the 1st Missouri Infantry; the 6th, 15th, and 22nd Mississippi Infantry regiments; Caruthers's Mississippi Battalion; and Watson's Louisiana Battery. "Organization of the Confederate Army of West Tennessee," *OR*, vol. 17, pt. 1, 375.

13. Lovell's division struck the left flank of the Federal army in their first defensive line outside Corinth around 10:00 a.m. on October 3, 1862, and encountered only light opposition. The Federals withdrew into their fortifications nearer Corinth, and resistance stiffened. By 3:00 p.m., Lovell's attack had lost its momentum, and his division stalled for the remainder of the day. Peter Cozzens, *The Darkest Days of the War: The Battles of Iuka and Corinth* (Chapel Hill: University of North Carolina Press, 1997), 167, 174.

14. "Desiccated compressed mixed vegetables," as they were specified in Union army regulations, were only relative blessings. "Desecrated vegetables," as they were commonly known, were an assortment of turnips, carrots, beets, onions, and string beans. Issued in hard cakes, the compound was to be soaked in water. The result, observed one Union officer, was a soup that looked like "a dirty brook with all the dead leaves floating around promiscuously." Desiccated vegetables did have their admirers, especially when the alternative was no vegetables at all. Bell Irwin Wiley, *The Life of Billy Yank: The Common Soldier of the Union* (Baton Rouge: Louisiana State University Press, 1952), 242.

15. Robert Louden was an associate of former steamboat pilot Absalom Grimes in the "grapevine enterprise" of carrying mail to and from Confederate Missouri. In 1864, Louden was captured, held in the Gratiot Street prison in St. Louis, and sentenced to be hanged. While being transferred by steamer to the prison in Alton, Illinois, he shed his iron cuffs and escaped. He survived the war. M. M. Quaife, ed., *Absalom Grimes: Confederate Mail Runner* (New Haven: Yale University Press, 1926), 63, 188–191.

In *Nicholson*, Boyce notes: "Louden was from Philadelphia and at one time a member of the Franklin Engine Co. He was a desperate man. I believe his proper name was Deal(s). JB."

16. On October 3, Van Dorn's army, with Lovell's division on the right and Price's two divisions in the center and on the left, rapidly drove in the Union advance lines, forcing them to a second line about one mile from Corinth.

The Confederates regrouped and, around 4:00 p.m., launched another attack that forced the Federals back into their third, and most heavily fortified, line of works. Cockrell, *The Lost Account*, 25–27.

17. The Union line was anchored by Battery Powell on its right. Battery Robinette marked its center. Battery Williams, the largest of the Union fortifications, stood only a quarter-mile south of Battery Robinette. Battery Williams stood in the projected path of the left of Lovell's division. James M. McPherson, *The Atlas of the Civil War* (New York: Macmillan, 1994), 89.

The shabby two-story brick Tishomingo Hotel faced the Memphis & Charleston Railroad tracks that gave importance to Corinth. Cozzens, *The Darkest Days of the War*, 22.

18. Louisiana planter Augustus C. Watson organized and equipped the Watson Flying Battery, complete with six guns and one hundred white horses, at his own expense in July 1861, recruiting the cannoneers from the finest families of New Orleans. The battery was all but destroyed at the battle at Belmont, Missouri, on November 7, 1861, losing all of its guns and nearly half of its horses. Allen Bursley commanded the unit at Corinth. Don Troiani, *Don Troiani's Regiments and Uniforms of the Civil War* (Mechanicsburg, PA: Stackpole Books, 2002), 220–221.

William P. Barlow, a Missourian, began his military service with the artillery of the Missouri State Guard, seeing action at Carthage, Missouri, in July 1861. In December of that year, he transferred to become a second lieutenant in the Watson battery. He finished the war serving as captain of his own battery serving in the Trans-Mississippi region. *CSR—Confederate, Missouri*.

19. Bowen, anxious to advance while Price's corps was heavily engaged, ordered a "reconnaissance by fire" to be conducted by Watson's battery. "[Bowen] drew such a terrific cannonade that he knew that he had no chance of success." Cockrell, *The Lost Account of the Battle of Corinth*, 69.

20. Robert J. Duffy was the captain of Company B when it was officially organized near Memphis on July 23, 1861. He was subsequently promoted to major, but in November 1862, after the consolidation of the 1st and 4th Missouri regiments, he was relieved from duty to perform recruiting duty in the Trans-Mississippi region. There he served on the staff of Generals William L. Cabell and Joseph O. Shelby. *CSR—Confederate, Missouri*.

21. Michael Farrell, a veteran of the U.S. Army, had made his living in St. Louis as a brick mason before the war. He served in the Missouri Volunteer Militia in 1859 and 1860 as second lieutenant in the St. Louis company known as the Montgomery Guards. He moved to Yalobusha County, Mississippi, not long before the outbreak of hostilities, and in June 1861, he was chosen to command Company E, 15th Mississippi. In April of the following year, the "brave and impulsive" Irish immigrant was advanced to the position of lieutenant colonel, frequently commanding the regiment. Farrell's

OCTOBER–DECEMBER 1862

"booming voice and thick accent were a source of both amusement and respect" to the men of the 15th Mississippi. Ben Wynne, *A Hard Trip: A History of the 15th Mississippi Infantry, C.S.A.* (Macon, GA: Mercer University Press, 2003), 47, 82–83. Joseph Boyce, "Military Organizations," in *Encyclopedia of the History of St. Louis*, Hyde and Conard, 1513.

In the battle at Franklin, Tennessee, in November 1864, Farrell was severely wounded and removed to the McGavock residence. He died from his wounds on March 17, 1865. Joseph Boyce, "Military Organizations," typescript, MHM Archives, 96.

22. This rearguard action was conducted on October 5, 1862. The Confederates held a position on the east side of the Tuscumbia River defending the crossing at Young's Bridge. Crossing the Tuscumbia in good order, Bowen's men burned the bridge and attempted to obstruct a nearby ford. Report of Brig. Gen. John S. Bowen, October 12, 1862, *OR*, vol. 17, pt. 1, 413.

23. First Lieutenant Edmund A. Toledano was living in New Orleans when he enlisted in Watson's Flying Battery. He was captured on July 9, 1863, at Port Hudson and was held as a prisoner of war at Johnson's Island, Ohio, until June 11, 1865. Thomas C. Carwell, 1st Louisiana Cavalry Regiment, C.S.A., to author, February 4, 2004.

24. In *Nicholson*, Boyce replaces "First Missouri" with "Fifteenth Mississippi" in this sentence.

25. Bowen's brigade caught up with the other brigades of the division on the evening of October 5. Report of Brig. Gen. John S. Bowen, *OR*, vol. 17, pt. 1, 413.

1

CHAPTER 7
IN DEFENSE OF VICKSBURG
JANUARY–MAY 1863

THE CONFEDERATE COMMAND STRUCTURE IN MISSISSIPPI WAS REORGANIZED IN THE FALL OF 1862 IN AN ATTEMPT TO CORRECT THE DEFICIENCIES IT HAD DISPLAYED IN THE RECENT CAMPAIGN. ON OCTOBER 12, 1862, JOHN CLIFFORD PEMBERTON WAS PROMOTED TO LIEUTENANT GENERAL TO COMMAND THE DEPARTMENT OF MISSISSIPPI AND EAST LOUISIANA. PEMBERTON GRADUATED FROM THE UNITED STATES MILITARY ACADEMY IN 1837, AND HE SERVED IN THE UNITED STATES ARMY CONTINUOUSLY UNTIL RESIGNING IN 1861 TO JOIN THE CONFEDERACY. PEMBERTON'S PROMOTION WAS NECESSARY TO MAKE HIM SENIOR TO VAN DORN AND LOVELL, BOTH OF WHOM HAD BEEN SENIOR TO HIM AS MAJOR GENERALS. MOST OF THE TROOPS OF PEMBERTON'S DEPARTMENT WERE CONCENTRATED NEAR VICKSBURG AND REMAINED UNDER VAN DORN'S COMMAND.[1]

VAN DORN IN TURN BEGAN A REORGANIZATION OF HIS BRIGADES AND DIVISIONS. THE 1ST MISSOURI JOINED FIVE OTHER MISSOURI INFANTRY REGIMENTS IN A BRIGADE COMMANDED BY BRIGADIER GENERAL MARTIN E. GREEN. BOWEN, THE 1ST MISSOURI'S FORMER BRIGADE COMMANDER, WAS ADVANCED TO LEAD A DIVISION CONTAINING GREEN'S BRIGADE AND TWO OTHERS CONSISTING PRIMARILY OF ARKANSAS TROOPS. ON OCTOBER 22, 1862, BOWEN RATIONALIZED HIS COMMAND INTO TWO BRIGADES, ONE OF MISSOURI AND ONE OF ARKANSAS TROOPS.[2]

THE CASUALTIES OF CAMPAIGNING WERE INCREASINGLY DIFFICULT TO OFFSET WITH REINFORCEMENTS FROM MISSOURI AS THE UNION ARMY AND NAVY

IN DEFENSE OF VICKSBURG

GRADUALLY GAINED CONTROL OF THE MISSISSIPPI RIVER. ON NOVEMBER 1, 1862, THE 1ST MISSOURI INFANTRY WAS CONSOLIDATED WITH THE SMALLER 4TH MISSOURI INFANTRY. THE COMBINED REGIMENT WOULD CORRECTLY BE KNOWN AS THE 1ST/4TH MISSOURI INFANTRY CONSOLIDATED, BUT THE VETERANS OFTEN CONTINUED TO REFER TO THE REGIMENTS INDIVIDUALLY. THE 4TH MISSOURI INFANTRY WAS ONE OF SEVERAL INFANTRY REGIMENTS FORMED FROM THE TRANSITION OF THE MISSOURI STATE GUARD FROM STATE SERVICE TO CONFEDERATE SERVICE IN DECEMBER 1861.

1ST/4TH MISSOURI	FORMER ORGANIZATION
Company A	1st Missouri, Co. A
Company B	4th Missouri, Co. A, F, G
Company C	4th Missouri, Co. B, C
Company D	1st Missouri, Co. B, D
Company E	4th Missouri, Co. E, H
Company F	1st Missouri, Co. E, F, H
Company G	1st Missouri, Co. C, G
Company H	4th Missouri, Co. K
Company I	4th Missouri, Co. D, I
Company K	1st Missouri, Co. I, K

TO REDUCE CONFLICT AND TO PROVIDE SOME SENSE OF CONTINUITY OF THE REGIMENTAL ORGANIZATION, CONSOLIDATION WAS ACCOMPLISHED BY MERGING COMPANIES FROM THE SAME REGIMENT RATHER THAN MERGING COMPANY A OF THE 1ST MISSOURI WITH COMPANY A OF THE 4TH MISSOURI.[3] BOYCE RETAINED HIS POSITION AS A FIRST LIEUTENANT IN COMPANY D. SEVERAL OF THE OFFICERS WHO LOST POSITIONS IN THE CONSOLIDATION WERE ORDERED TO MISSOURI TO RECRUIT.

INITIALLY, PEMBERTON WAS WILLING TO ALLOW THE MISSOURI AND ARKANSAS TROOPS OF PRICE'S COMMAND TO BE TRANSFERRED WEST OF THE MISSISSIPPI RIVER IF "THEIR PLACE [WERE] SUPPLIED BY AN EQUAL NUMBER OF TROOPS."[4] AFTER CONDUCTING A REVIEW OF THE TROOPS, HOWEVER, HE QUICKLY CHANGED HIS MIND. TO THE SECRETARY OF WAR HE WROTE: "I WISH

JANUARY–MAY 1863

TO WITHDRAW MY RECOMMENDATION AS TO EXCHANGE OF GENERAL PRICE'S TROOPS. I HAVE JUST WITNESSED A REVIEW AND AM MUCH PLEASED WITH THEM."[5] HE WOULD REMAIN MUCH PLEASED WITH THEM THROUGHOUT THE VICKSBURG CAMPAIGN.

IN EARLY DECEMBER, PEMBERTON FINALIZED THE ORGANIZATION OF THE ARMY OF THE DEPARTMENT OF MISSISSIPPI AND EAST LOUISIANA.[6] ON DECEMBER 9, DIVISION COMMANDER BOWEN HELD A REVIEW OF HIS TWO BRIGADES, AT WHICH TIME THE ORDER WAS READ TO THE $1^{ST}/4^{TH}$ MISSOURI AND THE OTHER REGIMENTS OF HIS COMMAND.[7] THE DIVISION REMAINED IN THE IMMEDIATE VICINITY OF VICKSBURG UNTIL THE SECOND WEEK OF MARCH, WHEN THE TWO BRIGADES MOVED TO GRAND GULF, MISSISSIPPI. ALONG THE MARCH, LIEUTENANT COLONEL FINLEY HUBBELL OF THE 3RD MISSOURI INFANTRY RECORDED IN HIS DIARY: "BEAUTIFUL TIME OF YEAR, TREES BUDDING OUT AND ALL NATURE SEEMS TO BE PUTTING ON HER BLANDEST SMILES. WHAT A SHAME IT IS THAT A WHOLE NATION, BOASTING MORE ENLIGHTMENT THAN ANY OTHER, SHOULD BE EXHAUSTING ALL ITS ENERGIES IN THIS RELENTLESS, UNHAPPY AND UNNATURAL WAR."[8]

GRAND GULF SITS JUST SOUTH OF THE ENTRY OF THE BIG BLACK RIVER INTO THE MISSISSIPPI RIVER. IT WAS GRANT'S FIRST CHOICE FOR A CROSSING PLACE, AND ON APRIL 29, SIX UNION GUNBOATS HAMMERED BOWEN'S POSITION WHILE TRANSPORTS LOADED WITH INFANTRY AWAITED THE OUTCOME. THE BOMBARDMENT FAILED, AND THE FEDERALS SOUGHT A CROSSING FARTHER DOWNSTREAM. FINDING ONE AT BRUINSBURG, GRANT AND HIS ARMY BEGAN CROSSING THE RIVER THE NEXT DAY. BOWEN, UNCERTAIN WHETHER THE LANDING AT BRUINSBURG WAS A FEINT, LEFT THE 2ND MISSOURI INFANTRY NORTH OF GRAND GULF TO GUARD THE CROSSING ON THE BIG BLACK RIVER AND SENT THE 1ST MISSOURI INFANTRY SOUTHWEST TO FORESTALL A POTENTIAL FEDERAL CROSSING OF BAYOU PIERRE. THE REMAINING UNITS OF HIS TWO SMALL BRIGADES MARCHED SOUTH TOWARD PORT GIBSON AND THEN EAST TO DELAY ELEMENTS OF TWO UNION CORPS. GRANT WAS ACROSS THE RIVER IN FORCE.

IN DEFENSE OF VICKSBURG

The work of reorganizing the army was set about at once. Our regiment a few days later was withdrawn from our old friends, the Mississippians and Arkansans. Gen. Bowen was given a brigade in the Missouri troops, and we were consolidated with the Fourth Missouri infantry, Col. Archie M[a]cFarlan[e] of St. Louis becoming the colonel.[9] Owing to Col. MacFarlane's wound, received at Corinth, this arrangement could not be carried out.[10] Col. A. C. Riley became colonel, Hugh A. Garland, lieutenant colonel, and Martin Burke, major.[11] A great many of our officers left us here at the consolidation and went over to the trans-Mississippi department, where they took service under Marmaduke and Joe Shelby.[12]

Shortly after the reorganization was effected we fell back to Abbeville, and again to Grenada, Miss.[13]

While at Grenada we were visited by President Davis, and a grand review held Christmas eve. President Davis reviewed us, surrounded by Gens. Jos. E. Johnston, Price, Bowen, etc. He said: "It is hard to realize that troops that met with such disaster a few weeks ago have been so quickly reorganized and recovered to the service. Such men are rarely seen, and show a very high order of intelligence." He complimented Gens. Price and Bowen, and desired that his commendations be conveyed to the troops.[14]

During our stay at Grenada the officers of the First Missouri gave a grand dinner and invited the officers of the division to attend. The invitations were promptly accepted, healths were drunk, speeches made and the best of feeling prevailed. We felt we needed the acquaintance of our fellow officers, and many friendships were formed that day that continue until the present time. The federal forces were not idle all this time. Grant had determined upon the reduction of Vicksburg. The Yazoo river route and the attack on Haines' Bluff had met with disaster, but this did not deter him from making another move.[15]

Gen. Price had in the meantime gone to Richmond, Va., to confer with the authorities, and while there we learned with great sorrow that we were to lose him. He had determined to go to the trans-Mississippi department, and took his leave for his new field of operations. In his address he spoke to us like a father. We had an affection for him that only his good heart could attract. It was not at all surprising the love we had for him. He was always in the midst of the battle where it raged the fiercest, and he never ordered men to go where he would not go himself. He said: "When it is possible I will send for you."[16]

Gen. Bowen was placed in command of the division, and early in January 1863, the troops were ordered to Jackson, Miss., where we remained several weeks.[17] While here Maj. Martin Burke and the writer found in the guardhouse among the officers captured, Col. Thomas C. Fletcher, Lieut. Van Dor[e]n and several other Missourians of the federal army who had been captured at Ha[yne]s' Bluff a short time before our arrival at Jackson.[18] Col. Fletcher afterwards became governor of the state of Missouri, and he always remembered the kind treatment bestowed on him by the officers of the First Regiment. We got him and his fellow officers the liberty of the town, and as for tobacco and "pine-top" they were not allowed to suffer.[19]

BOYCE MET FUTURE GOVERNOR THOMAS C. FLETCHER,
THEN COMMANDING THE 31ST MISSOURI INFANTRY,
U.S.A., AFTER FLETCHER'S CAPTURE NEAR VICKSBURG
IN LATE 1862.

IN DEFENSE OF VICKSBURG

The winter was about over when we were ordered to Big Black river. Our stay at this place was short. We proceeded to Port Gibson and Grand Gulf, arriving after a pleasant march of a few days.[20]

Nearly all of the infantry were located at Port Gibson, while the batteries were sent to Grand Gulf. Works were thrown up at a point commanding the river from above and below the position strengthened in every way. Rifle

UNIFORM OF PRIVATE JOHN T. APPLER, COMPANY H, 1ST MISSOURI INFANTRY. WEAK FROM THE EFFECTS OF TYPHOID FEVER, APPLER RETURNED TO CLAYTON, MISSOURI, IN LATE 1863.

pits and lines of defence for the infantry added to the works, making the place almost impregnable.[21]

Gen. Bowen grasped the situation at once. He felt sure, the moment he arrived with his forces, that Grant would attempt to cross the Mississippi in this neighborhood. His force was entirely too small to cover his line of defence, and his appeals to headquarters at Jackson met with very little encouragement. Gen. Pemberton did not forward his reserve forces to this point, as Bowen desired. If he had, and allowed Gen. Bowen to conduct the defense, Grant would have been attacked with his forces divided when he crossed at Bruinsburg below us and his repulse accomplished.

Our regiment was sent over to Louisiana with the Second Missouri, and two pieces of artillery from Guibor's battery in charge of Lieut. Wm. Corkery, to reconnoiter and keep a watch on the movements of the enemy.[22] The detachment was placed under command of Col. F. M. Cockrell.[23] This duty was anything but pleasant. A great deal of it was done in boats, as the water was very high. The federal forces were very near, and we could hear their drums distinctly.[24]

After several days of this work we were hurriedly recalled to Grand Gulf, as the federal gunboats put in an appearance, and in a short time came down the river, in grand style, opening the attack with heavy discharges from their bow guns.[25] The boats swung into position opposite the batteries and fired broadsides with great rapidity. The storm of iron beat with great violence against the works, with but little effect. The position occupied by the First and Second regiments was torn up by the shot and shell, but our works gave us such protection that the loss on our part was very slight.

Our batteries, consisting of siege and field guns, in all about twenty pieces, replied with great vigor. The field pieces soon ceased firing, as they were not sufficiently protected. The lower or water batteries replied, and kept up the fire gallantly. The bombardment continued until about noon, when Commodore Porter withdrew his fleet, and proceeded up the river.

The infantry fire was kept up strongly, and directed at the port-holes of the boats. Volley after volley was poured into them. Two of the gunboats appeared to be disabled, as they withdrew from the battle. The gunboats were well handled and kept up a furious fire until noon, as stated before, when they hauled off, having suffered heavy loss and been fairly beaten, as shown by their own official reports.[26]

In this action Capt. William Wade of St. Louis was killed. He was a gallant soldier and in command of the lower battery. His loss was severely felt, as he was very popular.[27] He was buried next day and his funeral sermon preached by Rev. Father Bannon, also of St. Louis.[28] Among the other St. Louisans killed I remember the names of Ed. [P.] Woods and John Kearney of Wade's battery, Claib[orne] Ferguson and William Underwood of Guibor's battery. Capt. Guibor was severely wounded.

About 2 o'clock the gunboats, six in number, returned with the transports lashed to them. The gunboats were opposite to the batteries, with the transports covered as much as possible. As soon as they came in range our batteries opened on them, confining their fire to the transports. A heavy fire

FATHER JOHN B. BANNON, CA. 1861. BANNON
SERVED AS CHAPLAIN FOR THE MISSOURI STATE
GUARD AND FOR MISSOURI'S CONFEDERATES,
1861–1863. PHOTO BY A. T. URIE, ST. LOUIS.

was kept up on both sides for nearly half an hour, when the last of the boats passed. Only one of the transports was sunk in this action. She sank about three miles below, or just before reaching Bruinsburg.

Towards the close of the day the federal forces began crossing the river in transports that had passed.[29] Their decks were covered with men and could be seen plainly from our position. They landed just below the mouth of Bayou Pierre. This work was continued during the entire night, as we saw by the sparks from the chimneys and the lights passing to and fro.[30]

The next morning, Gen. Bowen moved his division toward the enemy, who had landed at Bayou Pierre, leaving the First and Second Missouri to guard the artillery at Grand Gulf.[31] Shortly after daylight the enemy attacked Bowen and the battle raged fiercely all day. We remained at our post, about five miles distant from the action. We could see the transports at work ferrying over troops and supplies. This inaction on our part was continued without molestation from the enemy until about 5 o'clock, when one of his gunboats steamed up and fired several rounds at the lower battery, which replied promptly. The gunboat returned at once to her station.

During the night the evacuation of Grand Gulf and Port Gibson was effected. All the valuable property was loaded upon the wagons and they were sent off towards Bovina Station, on the Vicksburg and Meridian railroad, about eight or ten miles from Vicksburg.[32]

After considerable skirmishing and very hard marching, closely followed by the enemy, we reached the above station several days after our wagons. Just before we got to this point the enemy abandoned the pursuit. We went into bivouac and all extra baggage and unnecessary material was sent off to Edwards' depot, in the neighborhood, to be shipped to Vicksburg. Very little in the clothing line was retained, and the command presented a very light marching appearance.[33]

In the meantime Grant had made a wonderful move, leaving us at our bivouac. He pushed to the right of our position and headed his troops for Jackson, the capital of the state, drove the small force that was between him and this point, and by quick marches appeared before the city. He captured the place without much resistance and his troops destroyed the most valuable park of the city and a large amount of the military supplies. The torch was

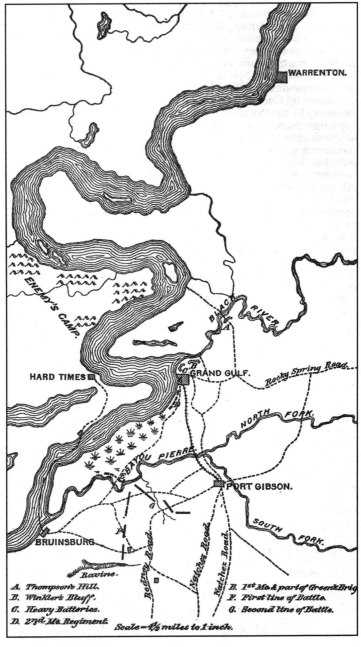

BATTLE OF PORT GIBSON, MISSISSIPPI. FROM THE *Official Records*,
SER. I, VOL. 24, PT. I.

applied freely and the flames lit up the surrounding country. So quickly was this move made that a great many knew only of his whereabouts by the fires raging in the city of Jackson and in the vicinity of it.[34]

After Sherman destroyed Jackson, Miss., Grant moved his forces at once towards our position, where we were bivouacked near Edward's Depot on the Vicksburg and Meridian railroad. At this point we were reinforced by the divisions of Gens. Loring and Stevenson, and during the afternoon of the 15th of May we marched on the Jackson road five or six miles to a point selected by Gen. Pemberton to give battle to Grant's forces now hurrying down this same road to attack us.[35] Our position was near Baker's creek. The hills on which nearly all the fighting was done were called Champion hills, so this battle, like several others, has two names.[36]

The position selected for us was an excellent one. We had the advantage of the ridge, while in our front the ground sloped gradually for nearly a mile, with little or no timber to obstruct our view. The batteries of Guibor, Landis and Wade, the latter commanded by Capt. Dick Walsh of St. Louis, were also in position on this line.[37] Looking along the front of the division, and taking into consideration the strength of our position it made us feel that the enemy would have to be in great force to defeat us.

May 16, 1863, about 9 o'clock a.m. our company, under command of Capt. Martin Burke, was ordered forward as skirmishers. We were joined by Capt. C[a]nniff's company of the Fifth Missouri, Col. McCo[wn].[38] This was the same that Capt. Joe Kelly of the St. Louis Washington Blues took away with him from Camp Jackson. It was made up of details of the several companies forming the First regiment captured there and was without doubt one of the best companies in the Confederate army.[39] It was drilled to perfection by that grand tactician, Col. Joe Kelly, and after his promotion transferred to Capt. Patrick Canniff, his protégé and worthy successor. This company was like regulars in every movement it made. They were veterans, for they had been in all the engagements from Boonville, Mo., to Corinth, Miss., under Gen. Price and Bowen after he assumed command of the division.

I have departed from my narrative to do this company justice, for really it was the pride of the Missouri division. I hope in the near future to hear a paper read before this society giving a history of "Kelly's men." It was the creation of the ablest tactician in Price's army, and he had no superior in either armies. His company reminded one of Ellsworth's Chicago zouaves; they were simply perfection.[40]

We were also joined by a company from the Second regiment, Col. F. M. Cockrell. The three companies formed a battalion and were placed under command of Lieut. Col. Hubb[ell] of the Third Missouri.[41] Our movements were executed by calls from a whistle instead of the bugle. We discarded the bugle some months previous through the influence of Capt. Burke, as the calls on this instrument were the same as those used by the federal forces. Hence, while we had the advantage of knowing his movements by the bugle calls, he could not anticipate our moves, as he was not familiar with our orders by the whistle. This change afforded us great advantage and amusement while we anticipated his every move.

Skirmishing continued for some time, when our batteries opened on the enemy in our front, firing over us and doing considerable damage to him. They were successful in blowing up several caissons and disabling a fine battery of Parrot[t] guns that replied vigorously to our artillery fire. Our side had the advantage of guns and the "Parrotts" were soon knocked out of time, to our great delight. We saw them limber up and we gave them all the encouragement we could by firing rapidly at them, hastening their departure. They left one gun badly broken, and quite a number of disabled horses and killed and wounded men.[42] This ended the engagement for the morning and we enjoyed a quiet rest for about two hours. The enemy, however, was not idle during this time. He moved quite a body of troops into the heavy timber on our left, we were moved in his front in the woods, and quietly awaited his movements. About 1 o'clock we were startled by a tremendous crash of musketry on our left where Stevenson's division lay. A moment later and all the batteries of Stevenson opened with an awful roar. The ball was opened, Grant and Pemberton were calling the figures, and we were to join in the dance of death.

The enemy had manoeuvered until he massed a large force in front of the weakest division we had in the command—Stevenson's.[43] This division was made up almost entirely of conscripts from Alabama and Georgia, and unfortunately had very little military training, one of its regiments,

MARTIN BURKE WAS THE FIRST CAPTAIN OF COMPANY
D, 1ˢᵗ MISSOURI INFANTRY, AND ADVANCED TO MAJOR
IN OCTOBER 1862. PHOTO BY CUMMINS, ST. LOUIS,
CA. 1861–1865.

the Forty-second Georgia, was known as the Forty-tooth Georgia.[44] This division occupied the extreme left of our line of battle, and when it was attacked with great vigor by the enemy it soon gave way, losing nearly all of its artillery.

It was at this time our brigade was hurried over at the run to restore our line. The command moved with a yell and fell upon the victorious federal troops with a fury they could not resist. Landis' battery opened a terrific fire on them at the same time and they were driven back in great confusion, followed by us until we had recaptured all of Stevenson's artillery and also a federal battery. The battle raged fearfully for several hours. This ground was fought over and over. It was the Missouri Confederates against Grant's army. Stevenson's division had left the field. We could hear nothing from Loring, and we were so hotly engaged that it was impossible to do anything but shoot, shoot. Point your gun in almost any direction and you could see a blue-coat to shoot at. At last the federal forces gave way before us, abandoning the batteries and leaving us almost in possession of their ammunition train. The drivers were whipping up their mules and making every effort to escape. We had burst Grant's centre and felt the day was ours.[45]

By this time the troops we had driven from our front began forming on our flanks. The situation at once changed, and we were about to be surrounded and captured by the overwhelming forces all about us. Had it not been for the quick movements of Guibor and Landis we were lost. They rushed their batteries into position on our right and left and opened a terrific fire on the mass of federal troops closing in upon us, throwing them into confusion, and by this means enabling Bowen to withdraw us. It was the artillery saving the infantry. They did us a good turn that day for the support we often gave them on other fields.

Our command fell back to Big Black river, about ten miles distant, where we found Stevenson's division. Loring left the field in another direction, and, after several days' march, escaped Grant's forces and arrived at Jackson. We reached Big Black bridge between nine and ten o'clock that night. This point was about twelve miles from Vicksburg.[46] A line of works had been constructed here which we moved into. They were about a mile and a half long, and conformed to a bend in the river at our rear with a pontoon bridge connecting us with the opposite bank. The railroad bridge had also been floored in case the infantry desired to use it. Unfortunately the works were placed on the wrong side of the river, and admitted of little or no defence. Some troops from Mississippi and Tennessee, a portion of the garrison of Vicksburg, were added to our force and placed on the left of the line of works. Stevenson's division was on the opposite bank as a reserve.[47]

At daylight the next morning we saw a very poor chance to defend such a position. The enemy attacked us soon after, and, after two hours' engagement, broke over the left of the works and soon were masters of the situation.[48] A wild rush for the pontoon and railroad bridges, and our army was fleeing for safety towards Vicksburg. It was a dreadful scene. Men shot down everywhere, others drowning in their attempt to swim the river. It was one of those appalling sights so usual to war. Such brave men to meet so dreadful a fate. To add to the awful picture, the boats and bridges were fired and many of the poor wounded fellows were burned to death.[49]

Those who escaped made their way to Vicksburg. On our way we passed Bovina Station where our clothing and other property had been stored, expecting to get a change of clothes at least, we found everything destroyed. The guard left with the property had become demoralized and set fire to everything to keep it from falling into the enemy's hands. By this great piece of military genius they kept it out of our hands, too. The usual army prayer was vigorously offered up for that guard.

That evening, May 17, 1863, we reached Vicksburg a little while before dark. We were sad at heart indeed. So many of our comrades killed in the two engagements, a great number captured, and all of our artillery in the hands of the enemy.[50]

IN DEFENSE OF VICKSBURG

ENDNOTES

1. Warner, *Generals in Gray*, 232–233. Archer Jones, *Confederate Strategy from Shiloh to Vicksburg*, 78–82. Van Dorn's performance at Corinth was a factor in his subordination to Pemberton.

2. *OR*, vol. 29, pt. 2, 729, 733, 736.

3. Hewitt, *OR Supplement*, vol. 38, 393–396.

4. Lieut. Gen. John C. Pemberton to Secretary of War George W. Randolph, October 31, 1862. *OR*, vol. 17, pt. 2, 739.

5. Lieut. Gen. John C. Pemberton to General S. Cooper, November 3, 1862. *OR*, vol. 17, pt. 2, 740.

6. Headquarters, Dept. of Miss. and East La., General Orders No. 17, December 7, 1862, *OR*, vol. 17, pt. 2, 787.

7. Ann York Franklin, transcriber, *The Civil War Journal of Lt. George R. Elliot, 2nd & 6th Missouri Infantry, Company F, 1862–1864* (Louisville, KY: privately printed, 1997), 13. Diary entry for December 9, 1862.

8. "Diary of Lieut. Col. Hubbell, of 3d Regiment Missouri Infantry, C.S.A.," *The Land We Love* 6 (1868): 104. Diary entry for March 10, 1863.

9. On October 20, 1862, the 1st Missouri joined five other Missouri infantry regiments in a brigade commanded by Brigadier General Martin E. Green. Bowen, the 1st Missouri's former brigade commander, was advanced to command a division containing Green's brigade and two others consisting primarily of Arkansas troops. Two days later, Bowen rationalized his command into two brigades, one exclusively of Missouri troops and another of Arkansas troops. *OR*, vol. 2, 729, 733, 736.

10. Archibald MacFarlane eventually recovered sufficiently from a gunshot wound to the head to return to active service commanding at Gainesville, Alabama, in November 1863. In 1878, MacFarlane was living in Jefferson City, Missouri. *CSR—Confederate, Missouri*. Robert S. Bevier, *History of the First and Second Missouri Confederate Brigades, 1861 – 1865* (St. Louis: Bryan, Brand & Company, 1879; reprint, n.p.: Walworth Publishing Company, 1985), Appendix: List of Survivors...with Present Residence and Occupation, 5. Bevier was an officer in the 5th Missouri Infantry.

11. Martin Burke was 32 years old when he left his position as a merchant in St. Louis, Missouri, to become captain of Company D, 1st Missouri Infantry, on June 30, 1861. Ephraim McD. Anderson, *Memoirs: Historical and Personal including the Campaigns of the First Missouri Brigade* (St. Louis: Times Printing Company, 1868), 536. Anderson was a veteran of the 2nd Missouri Infantry.

Attorney Hugh Garland, a native of Lynchburg, Virginia, was a member of the Missouri Volunteer Militia when it was captured at Camp Jackson in St. Louis in May 1861. He joined the 1st Missouri Infantry in July 1861 and became captain of Company F a month later. Garland became major to rank from May 26, 1862, and was formally promoted to lieutenant colonel while the regiment was at Grand Gulf, Mississippi, in May 1863. *CSR—Confederate, Missouri*.

12. Generals John Sappington Marmaduke and Joseph Orville Shelby, two of the Missourians' more popular leaders, led cavalry commands in Arkansas and Missouri. Warner, *Generals in Gray,* 211–212, 273–274.

13. Boyce covers nearly two months of campaigning with this sentence. Van Dorn's army withdrew south of the Tallahatchie River during the second week of November 1862. Price's troops, including Bowen's division, took position on the hills north of Abbeville, Mississippi. Flanked by Federal forces operating on the Mississippi River, the Confederates were soon hurried farther south. They completed crossing the Yalobusha River on December 7, Bowen's division forming the Confederate left. Edwin C. Bearss, *The Campaign for Vicksburg, Volume I: Vicksburg Is the Key* (Dayton, OH: Morningside House, 1985), 51, 110.

14. William H. Kavanaugh was a seventeen-year-old farmer living in Tipton, Missouri, when he enlisted in early 1862. As a soldier in the $2^{nd}/6^{th}$ Missouri, he participated in the grand review on Christmas Eve 1862 and recorded his impressions in his diary: "This was the first opportunity many of us had ever had of seeing an actual live president—and yet he looked very much like other men." William H. Kavanaugh Papers (SUNP1189), Western Historical Manuscript Collection–Columbia, University of Missouri.

15. In his campaign to capture Vicksburg, Grant's next move was to organize the Yazoo Expedition under General William T. Sherman. Sherman and four divisions moved along the Yazoo River but were stopped short of their goal at Chickasaw Bluffs on December 27–29, 1862.

16. On March 1, 1863, a review was held in honor of General Sterling Price. A soldier in the 5th Missouri Infantry recorded in his diary: "I never saw as many sad faces as I did when all the boys found Old Pap was surely going to leave us in Mississippi." William A. Ruyle Diary, typescript, Harrisburg Civil War Round Table Collection, U.S. Army Military History Institute.

17. In *Nicholson,* Boyce inserts the word "were" in this sentence.

18. A range of bluffs called Walnut Hills runs northeasterly from the Mississippi River just north of Vicksburg, converging on the Yazoo River at Snyder's Bluff. Haynes' Bluff is a short distance farther north along the Walnut Hills. Grabau, *Ninety-Eight Days,* Map 17: The Northeastern Approaches to Vicksburg.

On December 26, 1862, Sherman and four divisions supported by gunboats moved into the Yazoo River before debarking onto the low ground stretching from the river to Walnut Hills. After contending with terrain and a tenacious defense both more difficult than anticipated, Sherman's army began its withdrawal under cover of darkness on January 1, 1863. Bearss, *The Campaign for Vicksburg, Volume I,* 220–221.

19. Attorney Thomas Clement Fletcher campaigned actively for the election of Thomas Hart Benton for Missouri's governor in 1856, but with Benton's defeat, Fletcher joined Frank Blair and other former Democrats to organize

the Republican party in Missouri. With Blair's help, Fletcher recruited volunteers to form the 31st Missouri Infantry and led the regiment as its colonel in the Vicksburg campaign. He served as governor of Missouri from 1865 to 1869, supervising the state's adjustment to emancipation. William E. Parrish, "Fletcher, Thomas Clement" in *Dictionary of Missouri Biography,* ed. Lawrence O. Christensen et al. (Columbia: University of Missouri Press, 1999), 302–304.

William Theodore Van Doren enlisted in the 7th Missouri Cavalry, U.S.A., in St. Louis in March 1862 to serve as chaplain. He left the service in December after a few weeks in an Army hospital in Springfield, Missouri, which he left "permanently disabled" for his home in South Bend, Indiana. Edward T. Corwin, D.D., *A Manual of the Reformed Church in America (formerly Ref. Prot. Dutch Church), 1628–1902* (New York: Board of Publication of the Reformed Church in America, 1902), 819. CSR—*Confederate, Missouri.*

"Pine-top" is nineteenth-century slang for cheap, illicit whiskey.

20. The 1st/4th Missouri began the movement to Grand Gulf, Mississippi, on March 9, 1863, and arrived four days later. John T. Appler Diary, entries for March 9–12, 1863, typescript, Civil War Collection, MHM Archives. Appler belonged to Company H, 1st Missouri Infantry.

21. The position at Grand Gulf had been selected to interdict Union transports and to prevent Grant's forces from ascending the Big Black River from the Mississippi. Leonard Fullenkamp, Stephen Bowman, and Jay Luvaas, *Guide to the Vicksburg Campaign* (Lawrence: University of Kansas Press, 1998), 155.

22. A postwar "battle roll" published for the survivors of Guibor's battery shows that Sergeant William Corkery was wounded at Lexington, Missouri, in 1861. Promoted to lieutenant, he was wounded twice during the Vicksburg campaign. William's brother John served in the 1st Missouri Infantry. Guibor's Battery, Battle Roll, Civil War Papers, MHM Archives. Joseph Boyce to Isaac J. Fowler, May 10, 1913, Boyce Family Papers, MHM Archives.

23. Francis Marion Cockrell, a native Missourian, left his law practice in Warrensburg, Missouri, to enlist as a private in the Missouri State Guard in May 1861. His leadership potential quickly showed. He held the rank of colonel and command of the 2nd Missouri Infantry and would soon advance to command of the Missouri brigade. Ruth Warner Towne, "Cockrell, Francis Marion," in *Dictionary of Missouri Biography*, ed. Christensen, 197–198.

24. The Missouri troops crossed into Louisiana on April 4, 1863, to reinforce a small Louisiana cavalry unit in observing Grant's move south. A member of the 2nd Missouri described the unusual nature of this service: "During our stay here, our company was on picket duty most of the time, or reconnoitering the enemy's movements, the situation of their camp, and ascertaining if their advance was in force. This service was mostly discharged in small boats, of which a number had been provided, as the country was generally under water." Anderson, *Memoirs*, 283, 524.

25. John T. Appler, a member of the 1st/4th Missouri, was not unhappy when the Missourians boarded the steamer *Charm* on April 16 to recross the river. He had spent the previous day sparring with Federal pickets after marching "all night through mud and water knee deep." Appler Diary, Civil War Collection, MHM Archives.

Cockrell's command completed its return to Mississippi on April 17, 1863. Jno. S. Bowen to Lieutenant General Pemberton, April 17, 1863, *OR*, vol. 24, pt. 3, 755.

26. On April 29, 1863, Admiral David Dixon Porter directed seven Union gunboats in the bombardment of the Confederate positions at Grand Gulf, Mississippi. The purpose of the attack was to subdue the defenders preparatory to an assault by Grant's infantry. After more than five hours of work, Porter withdrew. Because of the strength of the defenses, Grant determined to move farther downstream in search of a crossing place. James R. Arnold, *Grant Wins the War: Decision at Vicksburg* (New York: John Wiley & Sons, 1997), 89–94.

27. William Wade, a native of Maryland, left his home in St. Louis to enter the Missouri State Guard at age forty-two in the summer of 1861. He left state service for Confederate service in December 1861 while in St. Clair County, Missouri, to become captain and senior officer of a company of the Missouri Light Artillery known as "Captain Wade's Company." In July 1862, he declined a request from General Price to become Price's chief of artillery, desiring to keep his commitment to the men of his battery who had elected him their captain. Wade was killed on April 29, struck in the head by a fragment of shot from a gunboat. At the time, he was serving as colonel and commander of the guns at Grand Gulf and of the light artillery of Bowen's infantry division. *CSR—Confederate, Missouri.* Winter, *The Civil War in St. Louis*, 122–123.

28. Father John B. Bannon served at St. John the Evangelist Church in St. Louis before the war, also serving as a chaplain in the Missouri Volunteer Militia and the pro-Confederate Missouri State Guard. The last known surviving letter from Father Bannon was written in March 1911 to Captain Joseph Boyce. Bannon described the physical limitations of his failing health and closed his letter with a blessing for the members of the Boyce family. William Barnaby Faherty, S.J., *The Fourth Career of John B. Bannon* (Portland, OR: C&D Publishing, 1994), 7–8, 80.

On March 8, 1914, Boyce read a memorial to his friend Father John Bannon to the United Confederate Veterans in St. Louis shortly after Bannon's death in Ireland. In it, he recalled: "He keenly felt Colonel Wade's death, as they were messmates, and the loss of a faithful friend. He preached his funeral service the day after the battle and saw his remains laid away at Port Gibson." Joseph Boyce, "Rev. John Bannon, Chaplain, Price's Missouri Confederate Division," Boyce Family Papers, MHM Archives.

IN DEFENSE OF VICKSBURG

29. The transports for Grant's army were assembled on the evening of April 29, but Grant's move across the Mississippi River did not begin until the morning of April 30. Arnold, *Grant Wins the War,* 97.

30. Grant's landing was made at Bruinsburg, Mississippi, south of the entry of Bayou Pierre into the Mississippi River. The course of Bayou Pierre runs roughly parallel to the course of the larger Big Black River to its north.

31. Bowen began moving troops toward Grant's landing force at 1:00 a.m. on April 30. The 1ˢᵗ/4ᵗʰ Missouri was stationed on the north bank of Bayou Pierre to prevent Grant's forces from gaining the most direct route to Grand Gulf. The 2ⁿᵈ Missouri remained in the fortifications at Grand Gulf. Arnold, *Grant Wins the War,* 101. Bevier, *History of the First and Second Missouri Confederate Brigades,* 178.

32. While the 1ˢᵗ Missouri guarded the approaches to Grand Gulf, the rest of Bowen's division, reinforced by Tracy's Alabama brigade and Baldwin's brigade of Mississippi and Louisiana troops, fought a vicious delaying action east of Port Gibson. Slowly the Federal advantage in numbers took its toll, and the Confederates retired to the north side of Bayou Pierre on the evening of May 1, 1863.

33. By May 5, 1863, Pemberton had repositioned his field forces behind the Big Black River in such a way that Bowen's division was now on the northern end of the Confederate line facing east at the Big Black River bridge. Grabau, *Ninety-Eight Days,* Map 35: Disposition of Forces in the Vicinity of Vicksburg, May 5, 1863.

In the midst of all this movement, John Appler reported that on May 7, the 1ˢᵗ/4ᵗʰ Missouri was armed with Enfield rifles. Appler Diary, Civil War Collection, MHM Archives.

34. Grant's army pushed aside a Confederate brigade at Raymond, Mississippi, fifteen miles southwest of Jackson on May 12, 1863. Two days later, Grant entered the state capital after a delaying action by two brigades of Joseph E. Johnston's army. Sherman and two divisions remained in Jackson on May 15 to destroy Confederate supplies as Grant turned west toward Vicksburg. Long, *The Civil War Day by Day,* 352–353.

35. William Wing Loring, the youngest line colonel in the U.S. Army when he resigned to join the Confederacy, was appointed brigadier general on May 20, 1861, and was promoted to major general nine months later. Carter Littlepage Stevenson resigned from the U.S. Army to command the 53ʳᵈ Virginia Infantry. In 1862, he led a brigade in the Kentucky campaign and was promoted to major general effective October 10, 1862. On December 15, 1862, Stevenson and his division of ten thousand troops were ordered away from the Army of Tennessee to the defense of Vicksburg. Warner, *Generals in Gray,* 193–194, 292–293.

36. Southern accounts of the battle at Champion Hill typically refer to it as the battle at Baker's Creek.

37. John C. Landis commanded a battery in the Missouri State Guard, transferring with his artillerymen to Confederate service in early 1862. Of "the indomitable Landis," an admiring infantryman claimed "the thunder of his guns was glorious music to us." Anderson, *Memoirs,* 314, 469.

 Richard C. Walsh, a native of Kilkenny, Ireland, was living in St. Louis before enlisting in the 1st Missouri Light Artillery, Captain Wade's company, in the Missouri State Guard in the summer of 1861. Walsh quickly became the battery's lieutenant, and he served as its captain following Wade's death at Grand Gulf. Wade's battery was renamed Walsh's battery. The unit served under his leadership for the remainder of the war. *CSR—Confederate, Missouri.*

38. Twenty-three-year-old Patrick Canniff, a native of Ireland and a saddler from St. Louis, joined the Missouri State Guard in 1861 as a private, soon becoming a lieutenant. On entering Confederate service in January 1862, he was elected captain of Company F, 5th Missouri Infantry. *CSR—Confederate, Missouri.*

 James C. McCown was born in Kanawha County, (West) Virginia. Then living in Warrensburg, Missouri, he raised a regiment for the Missouri State Guard and eventually led the 5th Missouri Infantry. The United Daughters of the Confederacy, Missouri Division, comp., Record of Missouri Confederate Veterans, Joint Collection, University of Missouri, Western Historical Manuscript Collection–Columbia and State Historical Society of Missouri Manuscripts.

39. The "First Regiment" is the 1st Regiment, Missouri Volunteer Militia, not the 1st/4th Missouri Infantry.

40. Colonel Elmer E. Ellsworth and the United States Zouave Cadets of Chicago, Illinois, won national attention for their precision in drill in the summer of 1860. Boyce was likely a spectator when Ellsworth and his Zouaves performed in St. Louis in August 1860. The *St. Louis Daily Evening News* estimated that ten thousand people watched the event on August 11. William C. Winter, "The Zouaves Take St. Louis," *Gateway Heritage* (Spring 1999): 20–29.

41. Finley L. Hubbell was born in Kentucky but was making his living as a merchant in Richmond, Ray County, Missouri, when war broke out. He served in the Missouri State Guard as major and retained that rank when his unit was organized as 3rd Missouri Infantry in Confederate service in January 1862. The following November, he was promoted to lieutenant colonel. Wounded in the left arm on May 16, 1863, at Champion Hill, he died twelve days later from complications. *CSR—Confederate, Missouri.*

 The three companies forming the skirmisher battalion under Lieutenant Colonel Hubbell were Company G, 2nd Missouri, under Captain James B. Wilson; Company F, 5th Missouri, under Captain Patrick Caniff; and Company D of the 1st/4th Missouri under Captain Martin Burke. Anderson, *Memoirs,* 310.

42. The guns were likely the six 10-pounder Parrott rifles of the 17th Battery, Ohio Light Artillery, brought forward to support the advance of Brigadier General Stephen Burbridge's brigade. Arnold, *Grant Wins the War*, 152.

43. Stevenson's division of four brigades was the largest in Pemberton's army. During the initial stages of the battle at Champion Hill, the Confederate left was held by the Alabama brigade that fought well at Port Gibson, where their commander, Edward D. Tracy, had been killed. Brigadier General Stephen D. Lee had only recently been given command of the brigade. As the Union forces began to shift around the Confederate left, Stevenson saw the danger and moved Brigadier General Seth Barton's veteran Georgia brigade from his right, leapfrogging Lee's brigade to extend the Confederate left. Herman Hattaway, *General Stephen D. Lee* (Jackson: University Press of Mississippi, 1976), 85–88. Edwin Cole Bearss, *The Campaign for Vicksburg, Volume II: Grant Strikes a Fatal Blow* (Dayton: Morningside House, 1986), 591, 597–598.

44. The 42nd Georgia was detached from Stevenson's division to hold the bridge across Baker's Creek on the army's line of communications to Vicksburg. They formed part of the army's rear guard after the defeat at Champion Hill. Joseph Bogle, *Historical Sketches of Barton's (later Stovall's) Georgia Brigade, Army of Tennessee, C.S.A.* (Atlanta: n.p., 1900; reprint, William Stanley Hoole, ed., Dayton, OH: Morningside House, 1984), 39.

45. Pemberton ordered Bowen to pull his two brigades and his batteries from their position in the Confederate center to reinforce the left, now beginning to disintegrate in the face of superior numbers. Cockrell's brigade led Green's brigade north, counterattacking and viciously contesting the Federal advance. Report of Lieut. Gen. John C. Pemberton, August 25, 1863, *OR*, vol. 24, pt. 2, 263–264.

46. The date was May 16, 1863.

47. The troops from Mississippi and Tennessee were under the command of Brigadier General John C. Vaughn: the 60th, 61st, and 62nd Tennessee Infantry and the 4th Mississippi Infantry and Company A, 1st Mississippi Light Artillery. In the line of works, Bowen's two brigades had been separated, Cockrell's brigade to the right and Green's brigade to the left. Vaughn's command was placed in the center. Stevenson's division was on the west bank of the Big Black River, out of reasonable supporting distance of Bowen's command. Bearss, *The Campaign for Vicksburg, Volume II*, 664, 689.

48. The Federal attack broke the Confederate line between the 61st Tennessee, the left of Vaughn's brigade, and the 62nd Tennessee to its right, driving a wedge into the Confederate line. Bearss, *The Campaign for Vicksburg, Volume II*, 668.

49. The railroad bridge over the Big Black River and the steamer *Dot*, turned across the river as a bridge, were the principal avenues of escape for Bowen's men. Colonel Samuel H. Lockett, Pemberton's chief engineer, waited "until all Confederates in sight were across the river" before he set fire to *Dot*.

The railroad bridge, piled with fence rails and loose cotton saturated with turpentine, soon followed. S. H. Lockett, "The Defense of Vicksburg," in *Battles and Leaders of the Civil War*, ed. Johnson and Buel, vol. 3, 488.

50. In a major tactical mistake, the teams for the Missouri artillery batteries and the 1st Mississippi Light Artillery had been moved to the opposite bank of the Big Black River. As a result, eighteen guns were abandoned to the Union army because there was no means to withdraw them. Bearss, *The Campaign for Vicksburg, Volume II*, 657.

CHAPTER 8
THE VICKSBURG SIEGE
MAY–JULY 1863

In the battle for Champion Hill (Baker's Creek), 172 officers and men of the 1ˢᵗ/4ᵀᴴ Missouri were killed or wounded.[1] More were lost in the defense of Big Black River Bridge. Now, the battle-weary Missourians made their way into the fortifications at Vicksburg. A Baptist minister in the city, chaplain of the 35ᵀᴴ Alabama, began a lengthy letter to his wife with a description of what he had seen in the last few days:

> We see the ditches all along filled with men, having taken their positions and now for the first time we learn of our sad defeat at Bakers Creek. We converse with men who were in the fight & they confess that they were badly beaten. With deep curses some denounced Gen. Pemberton as a traitor & as having sold the place. A strong and muscular Missourian swore with flashing eyes & compressed lips & a frowning brow, that if Pemberton surrendered V[icksburg] his life would pay the forfeit.[2]

Grant's Army of the Tennessee moved forward to Vicksburg on May 18, 1863. Sherman's XV Corps moved to the northeast corner of the Vicksburg lines, the corps' right flank stretching away to the Mississippi River. The Federal XVII Corps under McPherson watched the center, with McClernand and XIII Corps to its left (south). As other Federal divisions arrived, Grant used them to extend his army's left flank opposite the southern reaches of the city's defenses.

THE VICKSBURG SIEGE

WITHIN THE VICKSBURG FORTIFICATIONS, PEMBERTON ASSIGNED MARTIN LUTHER SMITH'S DIVISION TO THE NORTHERN SECTOR, JOHN FORNEY'S DIVISION TO THE CENTER, AND CARTER STEVENSON'S DIVISION TO THE SOUTH. BOWEN'S TWO BRIGADES—THE FIRST TO DEFEND AGAINST GRANT'S MISSISSIPPI CROSSING, THE COUNTERATTACKING FORCE AT CHAMPION HILL, AND THE REAR GUARD AT BIG BLACK RIVER—BECAME PEMBERTON'S RESERVE WITHIN THE VICKSBURG LINES. THEIR MISSION WAS TO MOVE TO REINFORCE THE DEFENDERS WHEREVER GRANT'S ARMY SURGED AGAINST THE CONFEDERATE DEFENSES. MARTIN GREEN'S ARKANSAS BRIGADE OF BOWEN'S DIVISION WAS SOON ASSIGNED A POSITION IN THE FORTIFICATIONS, LEAVING BOWEN'S MISSOURI TROOPS TO BE RUSHED TO WHEREVER GRAVE DANGER APPEARED.

We had no time to spare. The enemy would soon be upon us. We set to work at once to strengthen the defenses of Vicksburg. The artillerists of Guibor, Landis and Walsh took charge of the pieces in the works on our part of the line varying in calibre from the six to the twenty-four-pounder.[3] The earthworks surrounded the city, commencing at the fort on the bluff that commanded the river above the city and ending a mile below the lower part of Vicksburg, where they ended in a swamp that was impassable. The hills and forts on the line of works were in charge of the batteries, making the place quite formidable for a defence. Rifle-pits were beyond the works for the skirmishers. The place had been bombarded about a year before by Farragut and many evidences of the bombardment were still plainly to be seen—houses and churches in ruins, large holes in the streets where his shells had fallen, and bursting, tore up the ground in a fearful manner.[4]

Many of the citizens who remained during the first siege had adopted "cave life" as they termed it. The hills were used for this purpose. The people dug into the face of them, and in many cases families lived there in the rooms they dug out, carpeting them and moving their bedding there.[5]

Gen. Pemberton issued an order upon his arrival with the troops from Big Black river for all the women and children to leave the city while the chance still remained, by the Canton road. Very few left.

120

On the afternoon of the 18th the enemy appeared in our front on the Jackson road in considerable force, when he attacked the troops in his front with infantry and artillery. Our brigade was sent out to reinforce the command engaged. This attack continued until dark, when all the troops defending this point were withdrawn inside the works.

The next day we were assailed by a heavy fire from the enemy. He appeared to be getting his infantry and artillery into line. In the afternoon he made an assault on Gen. Shoup's line.[6] We were ordered over to the support of this brigade, and arrived just in time, as their ammunition was expended. We had to rush in just as this brave Louisiana brigade fixed bayonets for the last resort.[7] About dusk the enemy fell back, when the fighting ceased for the night. A detail from the Second Missouri went out during the night and set fire to a building in our front that afforded the enemy shelter during the attack. They removed the dead and wounded, and at the same time captured several prisoners.[8]

For several days the enemy kept up a brisk fire on the works everywhere. We were not idle. The works had to be strengthened and the gaps, where the roads led out of the city, closed. This work was promptly done.

Early in the afternoon of the 22[d] of May, 1863, the enemy was seen massing in front of our position.[9] About three o'clock the grand charge was made. They came out of the timber with a cheer and full of confidence. His front looked like a large blue wave surging towards us. We were waiting for them, every man in his place, and he got the warmest reception we could offer. Our batteries opened a tremendous fire of canister and their first line seemed to melt away under our fearful fire of artillery and musketry. Their second line advanced gallantly and some reached the ditch of our works and planted their flag. They were Gen. Blair's troops, mostly from Missouri.[10] I cannot recall the number of the regiment that planted the flag on our works, and if I could at this late date name it, I have too much respect for the memory of those brave Western men who fell in our front and for those now living who planted their standard in that bloody assault to remind them of their loss. The color sergeant and guard were shot down, while some of the men of the regiment tried to save the colors.[11]

Robert Bush, a young German boy from St. Louis, a member of the writer's company, sprang out of the works, seized the flag, and waving it defiantly at them, cried out: "Come and get your flag! The Camp Jackson boys are here. Don't you want to take us to the arsenal again? It's our time now." The brave fellow had to be dragged into the works by his comrades, carrying the flag with him. He escaped without a scratch. The flag was taken to General Pemberton's headquarters, and the captor was complimented and offered promotion, which he modestly declined. Poor fellow! he was afterwards killed at New Hope, Ga.[12] This young boy had been captured with our regiment at Camp Jackson in St. Louis [on] May 10, 1861, by Generals Lyon and Blair, whose troops were composed almost entirely of St. Louis Germans.

The assault was repulsed with dreadful slaughter, and not without heavy loss on our side. It was an attack in force by all of Grant's troops on the entire line. This defeat of the enemy gave our army great satisfaction, restored us to our usual good spirits, and strengthened our determination to hold the place. The failure of the enemy to carry the works by this charge, lasting nearly four hours, fully demonstrated the courage of the defenders and the strength of the defences of Vicksburg. No more assaults were made. The enemy settled down to a regular siege. He increased his force of skirmishers, enlarged his rifle pits, erected new batteries and opened a steady fire along the entire line of works. He made no attempt to bury the brave fellows that gave up their lives in the charge, and after two days the bodies of his dead became so offensive that at last he was compelled to grant a truce of a few hours to perform this act of humanity. This work done, the firing was resumed and kept up by the enemy day and night for about six weeks. His force was so great and his advantages by land and water so many that he was able by reliefs and reinforcements to keep up a continuous fire on Vicksburg from all points.[13]

At night the bombardment from the mortar fleet was fearful. Large shells were thrown high into the air where their lighted fuses looked like large sky-rockets. Then they would burst like a clap of thunder, and the fragments would be hurled down into the place, frequently killing and wounding the men. Others would plunge down into the streets and explode after entering the ground, tearing up the earth and leaving immense holes. Shells would tear through houses, causing dreadful destruction.[14] Hospitals were struck time and again, and many of the sick and wounded killed.

Father Bannon was daily at the breastworks and could not be kept away. He with doctors John A. Leavy of St. Louis and J. H. Britts of Clinton, Missouri, occupied a room in the hospital. One night a shell from the Federal fleet entered and burst in their room. Dr. Leavy was stunned by the explosion, and it was thought he was killed. Dr. Britts was struck by one of

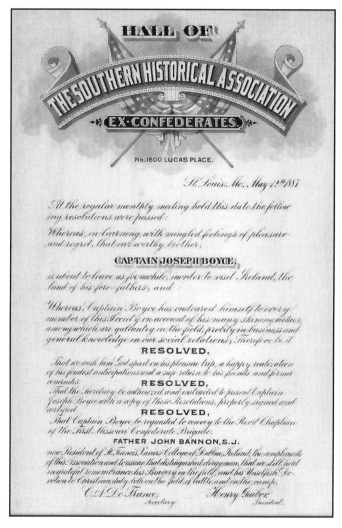

FATHER BANNON RETURNED TO IRELAND IN 1864 AND ENTERED
THE JESUIT ORDER. BOYCE CARRIED THIS GREETING TO BANNON
FROM THE CONFEDERATE VETERANS IN ST. LOUIS.

the fragments and his foot torn off. Father Bannon was unhurt, and by his quick action he rendered Dr. Britts, saving the doctor's life by stopping the flow of blood until help came.[15]

Dr. Sylvester Nidelet and the Rev. Father Bannon had many narrow escapes.[16] I think Dr. Jno. A Leavy was also wounded at the hospital.[17]

The bombardment by land and water was kept up. Notwithstanding the dreadful situation, the defenders were determined. During the first week our rations were issued in the usual quantities. After that they were cut down to fourteen ounces of food daily. This at last was changed when our beef and bacon gave out and mule meat substituted. For several days it was hard to get the troops to touch it, but hunger requires no sauce. Sickness prevailed to an alarming extent. Famine and want were ever present. We hoped against hope for Joe Johnston's command to relieve us. We heard so much by the "grapevine route," about the mighty army under Johnston that had been organized at Jackson, how Lee and Bragg had sent on their veterans to rescue us. It kept up our hearts and hopes, and every day we expected to hear their guns.

The enemy, in the meantime, had drawn his line closer and closer, until only a few yards separated us. He invented about this time a devil's mortar, made of wood, and bound with iron. It held just enough powder to throw a shell over our works, when it would burst right in our midst, killing and wounding our men dreadfully. We responded with hand grenades, and learned, after the siege with the same deadly effect upon the enemy. Nevertheless this wooden mortar was a terror to us.[18]

Then we mined and could hear the enemy in their tunnels at the same work. This continued until the first day of July at noon, when an immense mine was exploded in front of the Sixth Missouri, Col. Sent[e]ny. It seemed as if hell itself had joined the efforts of the enemy to dislodge us.[19]

The ground about us fairly trembled, clouds of earth were thrown high into the air with an appalling roar. The dreadful loss of life it entailed, and the deafening roar of fifty pieces of the enemy's artillery concentrated on this spot, it was thought would make our troops abandon this point. On the contrary, they stood firmer than ever. We moved into that awful breach, supporting the gallant Second Missouri, Col. Cockrell, who rushed to the front of his regiment crying out: "All of us must die here before this point is carried. Men of Missouri, stand firm; the fate of Vicksburg depends on you." We answered him with a cheer: "Stand to your ground, colonel, the First Missouri will die with you, too." Our colonel, Riley, was at his side in a moment to assure him of our help.[20] For two hours those two regiments lay in that breach, with bursting shells and hissing bullets all around us. The wounded from the explosion and those buried in the ruins were dug out under this dreadful fire. It was horrible to look upon the blackened and mutilated bodies taken out of this place.[21] The wounded were cared for as tenderly as possible. All this time we were expecting a charge, but it was not made.

At dark this part of the line was repaired and the following morning the line presented a very good defence. During the day we understood Johnston had arrived at Big Black River and was fighting his way towards us. Great excitement prevailed, and the troops desired to be led over the works and cut our way to Johnston's command.[22]

The next morning, July 3, about 9 o'clock, a flag of truce was sent out by Gen. Pemberton. The firing ceased, and shortly after Gen. Bowen and Col. Montgomery, Gen. Pemberton's chief of staff, passed out of the works. The interview that was held was not satisfactory for they returned about an hour later and the firing was resumed. About the middle of the afternoon another truce took place. Gens. Pemberton and Bowen and Col. Montgomery went out and held another interview with Gens. Grant, McPherson and others in plain view of the regiment. It was then settled and Vicksburg was surrendered. The formal surrender was to take place the following day. The storm had passed and quiet reigned that night, the first in almost fifty, that we passed amidst the horrors of war.

The silence was at first so unusual that it became in a manner painful, and produced a feeling of restlessness. This in time passed away and we slept that night without danger.[23]

About noon the next day, July 4, the troops marched out and stacked arms in front of the works. We returned to our former positions and the federal forces marched in a division and took formal possession of the city.[24]

About a week after the surrender we were ready for the march. Paroles had been furnished to all, and we bid adieu to our captors, who treated us royally indeed. There was nothing too good for the defenders of Vicksburg. We fraternized as readily as if the trouble had ever existed between us.[25]

Our brigade led the way out on the Jackson road and started for Enterprise, Miss., a point on the Mobile and Ohio railroad.[26] Gen. Bowen accompanied us. He was very ill and despite the endeavors of Gens. McPherson and Carr of the federal army, his classmates at West Point, he could not be prevailed upon to stay and go under medical treatment.[27] It was unfortunate that Gen. Bowen would not listen to their appeals. He was with us as far as Raymond, when his disease took a very serious turn and he stopped at this place for treatment. It was too late. He died a few days afterwards. He received while in Vicksburg his commission as major-general, a well-earned honor conferred upon him by the authorities at Richmond for his services at Grand Gulf and Port Gibson. His loss was deeply felt by the entire army, but more particularly by the members of his old regiment.[28]

The unerring judgment of the private soldiers proclaimed Gen. Bowen the ideal officer and gentleman. His zeal for the cause amounted to a passion, and caused sharp reproof to the sluggard and unmilitary, who in turn sometimes called him a "martinet." But after following that accomplished officer through one battle, the malcontents lauded him more enthusiastically than they had censured him. Happily blending the strict discipline of the old army with the kindly instincts of a natural nobility of character, he was almost universally pronounced the born leader in battle, and the gentleman and friend everywhere. So stunning a blow to the Missourians was his death that days passed in silent wonder before they could realize it. It appeared like a reversal of the decree of Providence. To them he was the one general in that army who could not be replaced.

The regiment suffered severely during the campaign just closed. Our killed was 83, and as for the wounded, very few escaped without some injury. Among the killed, I recall the names of Capt. W. C. P. Carrington, Lieut. Sam Howarth, Sergts. Jno. Shea, James Boyd, Tom Dwyer, Ben West, Privates Ed Fagan, Patrick Dolan, Peter L. Fitzwilliam and Lewis B. Beakey.

The wounded were Capts. Martin Burke, Sam Kennerly and James McFarland. Privates: Joseph R. Matthews, William Hopkins, John Plunkett, John Niblack, Charles Simpson, and many others whose names I cannot recall.[29]

After several days' march we arrived at Enterprise, but our stay here was very short. We were removed to Demopolis, Ala., and placed in the parole camp. Furloughs were granted to all who applied for them, by order of the secretary of war, as an evidence of the esteem the troops were held in that made such a heroic defence of Vicksburg.

THE VICKSBURG SIEGE

ENDNOTES

1. Bock, "Confederate Col. A. C. Riley, His Reports and Letters, Part II," 280.

2. Kenneth Trist Urquhart, ed., *Vicksburg: Southern City Under Siege, William Lovelace Foster's Letter Describing the Defense and Surrender of the Confederate Fortress on the Mississippi* (New Orleans: The Historic New Orleans Collection, 1980), 3.

3. The genealogy of the Missouri Confederate artillery units is often difficult to trace because of the practice of identifying the batteries by the names of their commanders. Guibor's battery was now commanded by Lieutenant W. Corkery. Lieutenant Richard C. Walsh commanded the unit formerly known as Wade's Battery. Edwin Cole Bearss, *The Campaign for Vicksburg, Volume III: Unvexed to the Sea* (Dayton, OH: Morningside House, 1986), 871.

4. David Farragut, a veteran of service in the U.S. Navy since 1810, was promoted to rear admiral in July 1862 for his success in opening the Mississippi River below Vicksburg to Federal navigation. Boatner, *The Civil War Dictionary*, 275–276.

5. One who did and later wrote about it was Boyce's fellow St. Louisan, Mrs. Mary Ann Webster Loughborough. Basing her book on a journal kept during the siege, Mrs. Loughborough published *My Cave Life in Vicksburg* in New York in 1864. Mary Ann Webster Loughborough, *My Cave Life in Vicksburg, with Letters of Trial and Travel* (D. Appleton and Company, 1864; reprint, Wilmington, NC: Broadfoot Publishing Company, 1989). Her husband, James, served during the siege as the assistant adjutant general for General J. C. Moore's brigade. *CSR—Confederate, Missouri.*

6. Francis Asbury Shoup, a graduate of the U.S. Military Academy in 1855, left the army in 1860 to practice law. He now commanded a brigade of Louisiana troops. Warner, *Generals in Gray*, 275–276.

7. Shoup reported that the 1st Missouri "moved promptly to support the point attacked and arrived in time to render valuable assistance." Report of Brig. Gen. F. A. Shoup, July 8, 1863, *OR*, vol. 24, pt. 2, 406.

8. Lieutenant Henry Gillespie led the detail recovering "two officers and seventeen killed or wounded" as well as eleven prisoners. He and his men then burned the house. Anderson, *Memoirs*, 329.

9. In "What Flag Was This?" *Confederate Veteran* XXVII, 235, Boyce revised the timing of the attack to "early in the afternoon."

10. Francis Preston Blair Jr. was the second son of a politically powerful family, a factor in Republican politics before the war. Although a congressman from St. Louis, Blair held a commission as a colonel of volunteers and commanded a regiment when he aided Nathaniel Lyon in the capture of the Missouri Volunteer Militia, precipitating the Camp Jackson massacre. Now he commanded a division in Grant's army. Montgomery Blair, his brother, served in Lincoln's cabinet as postmaster general. William E. Parrish, "Blair, Francis Preston, Jr.," in *Dictionary of Missouri Biography*, ed. Christensen, 79–81.

11. Private Howell G. Trogden, 8th Missouri Infantry, U.S.A., and a member of the volunteer storming party, planted the Union flag on the Confederate works. General Blair shared Boyce's admiration for the bravery of these men, recommending that all of the non-commissioned officers and enlisted men of the storming party be recognized with the Medal of Honor. Trogden was awarded his Medal of Honor on August 3, 1894. Report of Maj. Gen. Francis P. Blair, Jr., May 24, 1863, *OR,* vol. 24, pt. 2, 257–260. www.history.army.mil/html/moh.

12. The regiment's colonel, A. C. Riley, acknowledged Robert William Bush and three others in his official report because they "displayed great coolness and bravery during the siege and did valuable service sharpshooting with the enemy." Bock, "Confederate Col. A. C. Riley, His Reports and Letters, Part II," 282–283.

13. From May 24 until June 1, the 1st/4th Missouri served every other day in the trenches, alternating with the 3rd Missouri. With each turn, the 1st/4th Missouri lost from one to eight men killed or wounded. Bock, "Confederate Col. A. C. Riley, Part II," 282.

14. Pemberton's chief engineer observed the results of a mortar attack on June 27, 1863: "I measured one of the holes made by the mortar shells in hard, compact clay, and found it seventeen feet deep." S. H. Lockett, "The Defense of Vicksburg," in *Battles and Leaders of the Civil War,* ed. Johnson and Buel, vol. 3, 483.

15. John Henry Britts studied medicine first in Indiana and then in Missouri, beginning his own practice in Austin, Missouri, in 1859. When war broke out, he organized a company for the Missouri State Guard and was elected captain. He moved from his leadership position in the infantry to become a regimental surgeon in April 1862. On June 9, 1863, a shell exploded in his hospital tent, delivering wounds to Britts in the lungs and left knee and causing him to lose his right leg. He survived the war to return to his home in Clinton, Missouri, and practice medicine. At the time of his death in 1909 Dr. Britts was "one of Clinton's best-known citizens," having served the town as mayor and as state senator. Joanne Chiles Eakin and Donald R. Hale, comps., *Branded as Rebels: A List of Bushwhackers, Guerillas, Partisan Rangers, Confederates and Southern Sympathizers from Missouri During the War Years* (Independence, MO: Wee Print, 1993), 44–45. "Britts, John Henry," www.rootsweb.ancestry.com/~mohenry/obituary/b08obit.html.

16. Born in Philadelphia in 1821, Sylvester L. Nidelet graduated in medicine from Saint Louis University in 1852 and joined the U.S. Army as a surgeon. In 1861, he entered Confederate service as surgeon for the 2nd Texas Infantry. After the battle at Corinth in October 1862, Nidelet remained with the Confederate wounded and was detained three months in this work by Union authorities. Nidelet returned to his regiment at Vicksburg, where he was placed in charge of the Marine hospital and badly wounded by a

shell fragment while on duty. After the war, he returned to service with the U.S. Army but subsequently opened a private practice in St. Louis. Moore, *Confederate Military History: Missouri*, 379. "Death of Dr. Sylvester L. Nidelet," *St. Louis Medical Review*, LIV, no. 22 (July–December 1906): 517.

17. John A. Leavy, M.D., graduated from the Washington University Medical School in St. Louis in 1856. He joined the Confederate service in July 1861 at Memphis. He was appointed a surgeon by the War Department, passing his board of examination in Bowling Green in February 1862. At Vicksburg, he was the staff surgeon for Green's brigade in Bowen's division. Leavy was promoted to senior surgeon on May 31, 1864. Moore, *Confederate Military History*, 338. *CSR—Confederate, Missouri*.

18. Of hand grenades, Pemberton's chief engineer S. H. Lockett remembered: "As the Federals had the hand-grenades and we had none, we obtained our supply by using such of theirs as failed to explode, or by catching them as they came over the parapet." Small shells about the size of a goose egg filled with little bullets, the hand grenades exploded only if they struck something hard. They did not have fuses. As the Union siege lines closed in, the Confederates would roll lighted shells or barrels of powder toward their opponents. S. H. Lockett, "The Defense of Vicksburg," in *Battles and Leaders of the Civil War*, ed. Johnson and Buel, vol. 3, 491–492. Bevier, *History of the First and Second Missouri Confederate Brigades*, 211.

19. Lieutenant Colonel Pembroke S. Senteny commanded the 2nd Missouri Infantry, in reserve behind the 6th Missouri Infantry. Senteny was born in Ohio, moved to Kentucky as a child, and came to Missouri as a young man, making his living as a schoolteacher in Louisiana, Missouri. Taken prisoner with the Missouri Volunteer Militia at Camp Jackson in St. Louis in May 1861, he joined the Missouri State Guard to fight for the South. Senteny had commanded his regiment since May, when Cockrell was advanced to command the brigade. The day following these events, a soldier of the 2nd Missouri recorded in his diary: "A short time after dark our Lt. Col. P. Senteny was pierced through the head with a ball and expired without a groan. In him we lose a friend and an efficient and gallant officer. He was beloved by all his men and many are the hearts that have been made sad by his death." Moore, *Confederate Military History: Missouri*, 398–399. Theodore D. Fisher, "A Confederate Veteran's Diary as Written During the Siege of Vicksburg 1863," entry for July 2, 1863, typescript, Civil War Collection (B186), MHM Archives.

20. On July 1, before the mine exploded, the 1st Missouri had been moved to join the 2nd Missouri as a reserve force behind the 3rd Louisiana Redan, the target of the mine. Bock, "Confederate Col. A. C. Riley," 282.

21. A soldier of Company D, 2nd Missouri remembered: "The poor 6th Mo. Infantry, that grand old Regiment was almost annihilated." William H. Kavanaugh Papers (SUNP1189), Western Historical Manuscript Collection–Columbia, University of Missouri.

22. By late June, Johnston had collected a potential relief force north and east of Vicksburg, but he did not begin moving toward the city until July 1. Anticipating Johnston's threat, Grant had already turned Sherman's corps away from Vicksburg and prepared it to defend against any move by Johnston. Arnold, *Grant Wins the War*, 288, 291.

23. Not long after midnight on July 3, Confederate skirmishers detected what they believed to be an advance by the besieging Union troops. The thirty men of Company C, 1ˢᵗ /4ᵗʰ Missouri Infantry, under Lieutenant Robert F. Renick, were ordered to advance, scout, and resist if necessary. Crawling on their hands and knees in the darkness, Renick's men discovered Federal sappers, miners, and their escorts trying to advance the Federal lines. Renick's men fired, dispersing the threat and later claiming for the 1ˢᵗ/4ᵗʰ Missouri the honor of firing the last shots in the defense of Vicksburg. Captain W. T. DeWitt, "The Last Shots at Vicksburg," *Missouri Republican*, undated clip ca. 1885, Boyce Scrapbook, MHM Archives.

24. Grant appointed Major General John A. Logan as the military governor, and Logan's division and a brigade of Major General Francis A. Herron's division were designated to occupy the city. Bearss, *The Campaign for Vicksburg, Volume III*, 1293.

25. At the time of their parole, Boyce and the other members of the brigade numbered only 123 officers and 1,415 men. Consolidated statement of prisoners of war captured and paroled, July 1863, *OR,* vol. 24, pt. 2, 325.

Of the paroles, Grant wrote: "The paroles were in duplicate, by organization (one copy for each, National and Confederate), signed by the commanding officer of the companies or regiments. Duplicates were also made for each soldier, and signed by each individually, one to be retained by the soldier signing, and one to be retained by us." Ulysses S. Grant, "The Vicksburg Campaign" in *Battles and Leaders of the Civil War,* ed. Johnson and Buel, vol. 3, 536.

26. A Missourian in Lowe's battery wrote not long after: "We traveled hard after our famine. Our men were like skeletons, and many came out but to die. It was really lamentable to see men in last stages of chronic diarrhea eating green corn and green melons." James E. Moss, ed., "A Missouri Confederate in the Civil War: The Journal of Henry Martyn Cheavens, 1862–1863," *Missouri Historical Review* 57 (October 1962): 45.

27. Bowen, Eugene Asa Carr, and James Birdseye McPherson were cadets at the United States Military Academy at the same time, but they were not members of the same class. Carr graduated with the class of 1850; Bowen and McPherson graduated in 1853. Cullum, *Biographical Register*, vol. 2, 264–265, 333–334, 342–343.

28. Bowen was promoted to major general to rank from May 25, 1863. He died near Raymond, Mississippi, on July 13, 1863. Warner, *Generals in Gray,* 29–30.

THE VICKSBURG SIEGE

29. In his official report, Colonel A. C. Riley stated that the 1st/4th Missouri lost 98 officers and men killed or wounded between May 17 and the surrender on July 4, 1863. These casualties were in addition to the 172 officers and men killed or wounded at Champion Hill on May 16. Bock, "Confederate Col. A. C. Riley," 280, 282.

CHAPTER 9
WITH JOHNSTON'S ARMY OF RELIEF

MAY–JULY 1863

AFTER THE SURRENDER AT VICKSBURG, THE MISSOURIANS MARCHED TO A CAMP FOR PAROLEES SET UP AT DEMOPOLIS, ALABAMA, SOME 170 MILES EAST OF VICKSBURG. DEMOPOLIS, THEN "A SMALL TOWN NOT DENSELY OR REGULARLY BUILT," SITS ON THE EAST BANK OF THE TOMBIGBEE RIVER.[1] ONE VETERAN REMEMBERED THAT THE PEOPLE OF DEMOPOLIS WERE "ALMOST UNIVERSALLY HOSPITABLE" TO THE MISSOURIANS, GIVING THEM "A FREE AND HEARTY WELCOME."[2] ANOTHER MISSOURIAN, A ST. LOUISAN HOPING TO JOIN GUIBOR'S BATTERY, FOUND THE CAMP AND DESCRIBED IT AS "DOLEFUL ENOUGH, IN A LOW SWAMPY THICKET, JUST OUTSIDE TOWN—MEAN WATER, POOR FOOD (AND LITTLE OF THAT) AND NO DISCIPLINE."[3] THE MISSOURIANS BEGAN ARRIVING AT DEMOPOLIS ON JULY 26, 1863.

WHEN THE PAROLED VICKSBURG VETERANS ARRIVED, THEY MAY HAVE BEEN SURPRISED TO SEE THEIR COMPATRIOT, JOE BOYCE. IN A LETTER WRITTEN FROM DEMOPOLIS TO HIS BROTHER ON SEPTEMBER 14, 1863, BOYCE EXPLAINED THE CIRCUMSTANCES OF HIS SEPARATION FROM HIS REGIMENT DURING THE VICKSBURG CAMPAIGN.[4] THIS EPISODE WAS NOT INCLUDED IN BOYCE'S PUBLISHED MATERIALS, PERHAPS BECAUSE BOYCE CONSIDERED IT TOO PERSONAL TO INCLUDE IN WHAT HE INTENDED AS AN OFFICIAL HISTORY, NOT A PERSONAL REMINISCENCE, OF THE 1ST MISSOURI INFANTRY.

IN NOVEMBER OF THE PREVIOUS YEAR, PRESIDENT DAVIS ASSIGNED GENERAL JOSEPH E. JOHNSTON TO THE POST OF COMMANDER OF THE DEPARTMENT OF THE WEST. HIS RESPONSIBILITY INCLUDED THE WESTERN CONFEDERACY'S TWO

WITH JOHNSTON'S ARMY OF RELIEF

PRINCIPAL ARMIES, THE ARMY OF TENNESSEE UNDER BRAXTON BRAGG AND THE ARMY OF MISSISSIPPI UNDER JOHN PEMBERTON. DAVIS'S GOAL WAS TO USE THIS SENIOR GENERAL TO ACHIEVE UNITY OF COMMAND ACROSS THE FORCES DEFENDING THE CONFEDERACY'S VULNERABLE HEARTLAND. SINCE HIS ARRIVAL FROM RICHMOND IN DECEMBER 1862, JOHNSTON SPENT MOST OF HIS TIME IN THE REGION IN TENNESSEE NEAR BRAGG'S ARMY. ON MAY 9, WITH GRANT NOW ACROSS THE MISSISSIPPI RIVER, SECRETARY OF WAR JAMES SEDDON ORDERED JOHNSTON TO MISSISSIPPI "TO TAKE CHIEF COMMAND OF THE FORCES."[5] THOUGH SUFFERING FROM THE LINGERING EFFECTS OF ILLNESS, JOHNSTON MOVED TO JACKSON, MISSISSIPPI, ARRIVING THERE ON MAY 13. AS HE ARRIVED, THE CONFEDERATES WHO HAD FOUGHT GRANT THE DAY BEFORE AT RAYMOND MOVED INTO THE CITY, THE FIRST ELEMENTS OF WHAT WOULD OPTIMISTICALLY BE NAMED JOHNSTON'S ARMY OF RELIEF.

MAJOR GENERAL WILLIAM T. SHERMAN AND THE UNION XV CORPS, ACCOMPANIED BY GRANT, ARRIVED AT JACKSON ON MAY 14 WITH MAJOR GENERAL JAMES B. MCPHERSON'S XVII CORPS TO HIS LEFT. AFTER BRIEF RESISTANCE, JOHNSTON RETREATED NORTHWARD TOWARD CANTON, MISSISSIPPI. SHERMAN'S CORPS REMAINED A DAY IN JACKSON TO DESTROY THE ARSENAL, A FOUNDRY, FACTORIES, AND THE RAILROAD. GRANT TURNED THE REST OF HIS ARMY WEST TOWARD CHAMPION HILL AND VICKSBURG.

FOR THE NEXT SEVEN WEEKS, JOHNSTON AND PEMBERTON COMMUNICATED FUTILELY ON WHEN, WHERE, AND HOW TO COMBINE THEIR FORCES TO DEFEAT GRANT. IMMEDIATELY FOLLOWING THE VICKSBURG SURRENDER, GRANT SENT SHERMAN TO LEAD THE PURSUIT OF JOHNSTON'S HOVERING ARMY OF RELIEF. THE FEDERAL ARTILLERY BEGAN SHELLING JACKSON ON JULY 11, AND AFTER "USING OUR ARTILLERY PRETTY FREELY," SHERMAN ENTERED THE CITY ON JULY 16.[6] JOHNSTON, RECOGNIZING THAT HIS FORCE COULD NOT WITHSTAND A SIEGE, HAD AGAIN WITHDRAWN FROM THE STATE CAPITAL. GRANT DID NOT PURSUE.

BOYCE'S LETTERS DURING THE WAR RARELY LAMENT HIS CIRCUMSTANCES, BUT THE WEEKS AFTER THE LOSS OF VICKSBURG WERE CLEARLY A LOW POINT FOR

134

HIM. VICKSBURG HAD SURRENDERED, AND NEWS ARRIVED THAT HIS WIDOWED MOTHER HAD PASSED AWAY IN ST. LOUIS.[7] "OH GOD! THAT MY MOTHER SHOULD DIE WHILE I AWAY FROM HOME," HE WROTE TO HIS BROTHER, "TO THINK ON MY RETURN THAT THE HOME I LEFT SO HAPPY & I WAS TO RETURN IN SIX WEEKS OR TWO MONTHS AT THE FARTHEST HOW LITTLE MY INEXPERIENCED MIND KNEW OF WAR—YES, BLACK BLOODY WAR—THAT IS NOW DESOLATING OUR HOMES & FIRESIDES, MY COMPANY OF BRAVE BOYS KILLED OR MAIMED FOR LIFE."[8]

Now about myself and why I was not in Vicksburg during the siege. At the opening of the campaign, when Grant and his forces were moving down the west bank of the Mississippi river, my regiment being a part of Bowen's division, was in camp at Bovina Station on the Big Black river, about 20 miles from Vicksburg when the division was ordered by Genl. Pemberton to go at once to Grand Gulf and Port Gibson about 30 miles south of where [we] were stationed, and orders issued for the sick and those not fit for service to be sent to Clinton, Miss., and placed in hospital.[9] I was among the former, being down with weakness from my wounds received at Shiloh and at the same time suffering with chills and fever, a most common disease in this land of the "Sunny South," and I did not get over them and [become] fit for duty till the city was surrounded by Grant's forces after driving Bowen and his men from Grand Gulf and Port Gibson and then overwhelming them at Baker's Creek and forcing them and all the others who had resisted unavailingly into Vicksburg. Then Genl. Jos. E. Johnston was sent out by Pres. Davis to take charge of the department and relieve Vicksburg and rescue the besieged. Then an order [was issued] calling those who were fit for duty to report at Genl. Johnston's headquarters in Jackson for assignment. Major Wallace Butler of St. Louis was paymaster of the post at Jackson (and with whom I stayed whenever I was in town from Col. Wm. Hinton's plantation near Clinton). The day I made my usual visit I found him engaged with Col. ———, chief ordnance officer on Johnston's staff.[10] The colonel asked him if he knew an officer who could get the teams and overcome the confusion existing about two blocks south of the State

House on the Main street. He must know how to handle men and ship out the ammunition in boxes, cases, etc. Just then I entered. "Well, major, here is your man…my young friend Capt. Boyce from St. Louis, and it's his regular line of business." That was enough. I was told to come with him to headquarters and my written orders were handed to me by Col. Johnston's chief of staff and—by the way—his brother is librarian of the Mercantile Library at St. Louis.[11]

I was about a week emptying a big warehouse filled with all kinds of explosives. When I took charge the men were carrying out some of the ammunition from the first floor. This I stopped at once because the heighth of the building was four stories and I feared when the Yankees would commence shelling the city their shells would probably strike this building. Genl. Johnston accompanied by two of [his] staff came to the building during the afternoon and asked for the officer in charge. I was called downstairs and the general remarked "Why are you not emptying this building? There is hardly anything off this floor." "I am unloading the top, general, and have it pretty well cleaned now. The wagons will be back in a few minutes and I hope to have all the top floors cleaned." "Why do you want to do that?" "Because the fourth floor is too good a mark for the Yankee artillerymen and if a shell or round shot struck that floor there would be no longer anything in this house or neighborhood to be moved."

The general looked seriously at me and then turned to his officers and went out and looked up at the building, came back and looked at me, and then said "I'll see you again, sir."[12]

I thought I had offended him but I was too busy to think about it, so the work went on. By the end of the week all the floors and the entire building were cleared of their contents. I was then put in charge of the ordnance train and sent to Brandon where I was kept sending ammunition to Jackson as was required.[13] This work lasted about two weeks when I was ordered to Enterprise and told to turn over my train and ammunition to the commandant of the post and to report to headquarters, which I did.[14]

The chief of ordnance thanked me and said I was the best man he ever had to do the work and Genl. Johnston intends to keep me permanently on his staff, but I told him I could not take the promotion, that the boys in my company were all my friends in St. Louis and I was sure Colonel Riley would not willingly let me go. In fact I did not want to leave the regiment and I told the same thing to Genl. Johnston. He laughed and said to the colonel "Well, our young friend is right and I approve of his determination to stay with his home comrades." I thanked both Genl. Johnston and the colonel and here I am in command of the regiment because I was the ranking officer not paroled and now I have been getting the regiment reorganized and ready for duty as it is about to be exchanged and put back into service. I have it fully equipped and am awaiting the exchange roll to turn it over to Colonel Riley who with most of the officers have returned from furlough. I never had a furlough and in fact never cared for one as I have nowhere to go except home and God only knows when that shall be—if ever. I hope for the best and ask you to pray for the safe return of your affectionate brother.

———◆◆◆———

Our camp at Demopolis was on the bluffs overlooking the Tombigbee river, and just below the mouth of the Black Warrior river. It was a delightful place and worthy of the state, Alabama, which means "Here we rest."

The citizens of the town and neighboring country came to visit us, and nearly every visitor carried away several soldiers to take care of and distribute among those who could not get to Demopolis. The kindness we received at the hands of those people, and the unbounded hospitality they offered can never be forgotten. Our reception at Demopolis was so hearty, and the pleasure it gave us so lasting that it is only necessary to say Demopolis or Alabama among the survivors of the command to start every tongue in praise of that time and place. The attractions were so great and the ladies so pretty that many of the boys fell victims to Cupid's dart, and married there. The command left several of its bravest and best there at the end of the war, many of whom are now filling important positions in Alabama. At Demopolis, as the men daily bathed in the Tombigbee, the citizens noted with wonder that nearly all were scarred by gunshot wounds.

WITH JOHNSTON'S ARMY OF RELIEF

ENDNOTES

1. Anderson, *Memoirs*, 373, 557.

2. *Ibid.*, 373.

3. Nathaniel Cheairs Hughes, Jr., *The Civil War Memoir of Philip Daingerfield Stephenson, D.D.* (Baton Rouge: Louisiana State University Press, 1998), 125.

4. Joseph Boyce, "Now about myself and why I was not in Vicksburg during the siege." Boyce Family Papers, MHM Archives. The narrative is written in pencil, apparently somewhat hurriedly, and shows few marks of editing. It appears to have been intended as part of a letter written to Anthony Boyce on September 14, 1863.

5. Craig L. Symonds, *Joseph E. Johnston: A Civil War Biography* (New York: W. W. Norton & Company, 1992), 202. Jones, *Confederate Strategy from Shiloh to Vicksburg*, 193.

6. William T. Sherman, *The Memoirs of William T. Sherman* (1885, second edition; reprint, New York: The Library of America, 1990), 357.

7. The death of Mrs. Sarah Boyce to pulmonary consumption was reported to authorities on May 13, 1862. She was forty-seven years old. Missouri State Archives, Missouri Birth and Death Records Database accessed at www.sos. mo.gov/archives/resources/birthdeath.

8. Joseph Boyce to "My Dear Brother" (Anthony Boyce), September 14, 1863, from Demopolis, Alabama, Boyce Family Papers, MHM Archives.

9. Bowen's division began its movement to Grand Gulf on March 10, 1863.

10. Boyce could not recall the name of the staff officer.

11. Boyce's reference to "his brother" is to Edward William Johnston, the general's older brother. Edward Johnston was first employed by the Mercantile Library in St. Louis in 1858. Refusing to take the "test oath" to support the Union, he was forced to resign in 1862. Recognizing his valuable services as a librarian, friends kept him on the payroll as "Edward Johnson" to avoid further scrutiny by Federal officials. Winter, *The Civil War in St. Louis*, 29.

12. Boyce may have had reason to feel intimidated. British observer Lieutenant Colonel James Fremantle was in Jackson at the time and described Johnston as of "rather below middle height, spare, soldierlike, and well set up; his features are good, and he has lately taken to wear a grayish beard." James Fremantle, *The Fremantle Diary*, quoted in Bearss, *The Campaign for Vicksburg, Volume III*, 973.

13. Brandon is east of Jackson and south of the line of the Southern Railroad of Mississippi. Bearss, *The Campaign for Vicksburg, Volume III*, 974 (map).

14. In his manuscript, Boyce adds a postscript: "I forgot to say a few days after we removed the ammunition the Yankees sent a shell through the roof of the building at Jackson. We were lucky to have emptied it out."

CHAPTER 10
REST AND REORGANIZATION

◆◆◆◆◆

SEPTEMBER 1863–APRIL 1864

WITH THE BENEFIT OF TIME AND PERSPECTIVE, THE CONFEDERATE SURRENDER AT VICKSBURG BECAME UNDERSTOOD AS A PIVOTAL EVENT IN THE WAR'S PROGRESS. AT THE TIME, HOWEVER, THE MISSOURIANS' VIEW WAS MUCH DIFFERENT. WRITING ONLY THREE MONTHS AFTER THE SIEGE, THE COLONEL OF THE $1^{ST}/4^{TH}$ MISSOURI INFANTRY TOLD HIS MOTHER:

> YOU MUST NOT JUDGE FROM MY LETTERS THAT I AM AT ALL DISPONDENT. NEVER MORE HOPEFULL IN MY LIFE. MY LETTERS MAY BE GLOOMIER THAN I INTEND FROM MY NATURAL DESIRE TO SEE THE LOVED ONES AT HOME. I NEVER WANT TO SEE YOU ALL UNTIL THE LAST FOUL BREATH OF THE INVADER HAS BEEN OBLITERATED FROM OUR SOIL....[1]

WHILE IN THE HOSPITAL AT LAUDERDALE SPRINGS, MISSISSIPPI, IN NOVEMBER, CAPTAIN BOYCE HAD THE OPPORTUNITY TO RESPOND TO A FRIEND WHO HAD FORMERLY LIVED IN ST. LOUIS. THE FRIEND, MR. EDWARD WARREN, HAD WRITTEN TO OFFER HIS SYMPATHY AFTER THE DEATH OF BOYCE'S MOTHER. AFTER RECOUNTING THE NEWS OF ACQUAINTANCES, BOYCE DESCRIBED ST. LOUIS, THE HOME HE HAD LEFT BEHIND:

> YOU REMARK THAT THE CITY HAS CHANGED SINCE YOU LEFT. MR. WARREN, YOU HAVE NO IDEA HOW ST. LOUIS HAS CHANGED SINCE YOU LAST SAW IT. 4TH ST. YOU WOULD NOT KNOW FROM ST. CHARLES TO FRANKLIN AVE. THE MOST MAGNIFICENT STORES HAVE BEEN ERRECTED ON THE OLD SITE OF COLLIERS MANSION AND

REST AND REORGANIZATION

THE METHODIST CHURCH. ABOVE MORGAN [STREET] THERE IS A
SPLENDID MARBLE FRONT HOTEL & IN FACT THROUGHOUT THE
WHOLE CITY—TOO NUMEROUS TO ENUMERATE. JUST PREVIOUS TO
THE WAR THERE WAS NOT MECHANICS ENOUGH IN THE CITY TO
SUPPLY THE DEMAND FOR LABOR.

THE MISSOURIANS WERE NOW PART OF THE DEPARTMENT OF THE SOUTHWEST
(MISSISSIPPI AND EAST LOUISIANA), RENAMED THE DEPARTMENT OF ALABAMA,
MISSISSIPPI, AND EAST LOUISIANA IN THE SPRING OF 1864. GENERAL LEONIDAS
POLK, UNDER WHOM THE REGIMENT HAD SERVED BRIEFLY TWO YEARS PRIOR,
WAS NOW THE DEPARTMENT COMMANDER. OF THE MOBILE MILITARY FORCES
WITHIN POLK'S COMMAND, MAJOR GENERAL LORING LED ONE INFANTRY
DIVISION, AND MAJOR GENERAL FRENCH LED THE OTHER. POLK'S CAVALRY
WAS COMMANDED BY STEPHEN D. LEE AND NATHAN BEDFORD FORREST.[2] POLK
ESTABLISHED HIS HEADQUARTERS AT MERIDIAN, MISSISSIPPI.

AFTER THEIR EXPERIENCE WITH NORTHERN-BORN PEMBERTON, THE
MISSOURIANS MAY HAVE BEEN SOMEWHAT RELUCTANT ABOUT NEW JERSEY
NATIVE SAMUEL GIBBS FRENCH. A WEST POINT GRADUATE IN 1843 AND A
VETERAN OF THE MEXICAN WAR, FRENCH MARRIED A MISSISSIPPI BELLE IN 1856
AND REMAINED TRUE TO HIS ADOPTED HOME WHEN WAR CAME. FRENCH WAS A
COMPETENT LEADER, AND MUTUAL ADMIRATION SEEMS TO HAVE GROWN QUICKLY
BETWEEN THE MISSOURIANS AND THEIR NEW DIVISION COMMANDER.[3]

COLONEL COCKRELL WAS PROMOTED TO BRIGADIER GENERAL AND
CONTINUED IN IMMEDIATE COMMAND OF THE MISSOURI BRIGADE. THE
VICKSBURG CAMPAIGN HAD SERIOUSLY DEPLETED THE BRIGADE'S RANKS, HOWEVER,
AND MORE CONSOLIDATIONS BECAME NECESSARY. THE 2ND AND 6TH MISSOURI
INFANTRY WERE COMBINED, AND PETER C. FLOURNOY BECAME COLONEL. THE
3RD AND 5TH MISSOURI INFANTRY WERE UNITED UNDER THE LEADERSHIP OF
COLONEL JAMES MCCOWN. THE 1ST MISSOURI CAVALRY REGIMENT AND 3RD
MISSOURI CAVALRY BATTALION WERE ALSO CONSOLIDATED. THE MEN HAD
SERVED AS INFANTRY AFTER LEAVING THEIR HORSES IN ARKANSAS AND CROSSING

SEPTEMBER 1863–APRIL 1864

EAST OF THE MISSISSIPPI RIVER IN 1862. PART OF GREEN'S BRIGADE DURING THE VICKSBURG CAMPAIGN, THE CONSOLIDATED UNITS WERE NOW ADDED TO COCKRELL'S BRIGADE. THE REDOUBTABLE ELIJAH GATES LED THE DISMOUNTED TROOPERS. ENOUGH ARTILLERYMEN REMAINED ONLY TO STAFF A FOUR-GUN BATTERY OF 12-POUNDER NAPOLEONS. CAPTAIN HENRY GUIBOR COMMANDED THESE CANNONEERS.[4]

BEFORE LEAVING THE CAMP OF PAROLE AT DEMOPOLIS FOR MERIDIAN, MISSISSIPPI, THE MISSOURIANS WERE REVIEWED BY GENERAL JOHNSTON. BOYCE WROTE TO A FRIEND THAT FOLLOWING THE REVIEW "GENL. JOE" ORDERED THE MISSOURI BRIGADE "TO CHARGE IN REGULAR MISSOURI STYLE WITH THE YELL. WE FORMED OUR LINE OF BATTLE IN FRONT OF HIM & STARTED FORWARD AT THE DOUBLE QUICK, CHARGED BAYONETS & RAISED THE YELL. IT WAS A GRAND SIGHT." AFTER THE EVENT, "GENERAL JOHNSTON TOLD OUR FIELD OFFICERS THAT HE HAD BUT ONE OBJECTION TO THE MISSOURIANS & THAT WAS THAT HE DID NOT HAVE FORTY THOUSAND OF THEM."[5]

PRESIDENT DAVIS ARRIVED THE NEXT DAY, AND THE MISSOURIANS WERE AGAIN REVIEWED. THE PRESIDENT "RODE DOWN OUR LINES AND STOPPED IMMEDIATELY IN FRONT OF MY REGT. (THE 1ST INFTY)," BOYCE RECORDED. "WE WERE ON THE EXTREME LEFT. HE SAID 'MISSOURIANS, YOUR RANKS ARE DECIMATED BUT A GRATEFUL COUNTRY & MYSELF KNOW THE CAUSE. FROM AFAR I HAVE THANKED YOU BUT NEVER UNTIL NOW HAVE I HAD THE PLEASURE TO THANK YOU WITH YOU ALL BEFORE ME. NOBLEST! AND BRAVEST OF MEN. LET THE TROOPS OF THE CONFEDERACY EMULATE THE EXAMPLE YOU HAVE SET THEM.'"

"IS IT NOT ENOUGH TO MAKE ONE FEEL PROUD OF BELONGING TO THAT BRIGADE?" BOYCE MUSED.[6]

———◆◆✕◆◆———

Early in the following September the command was exchanged, and in a short time it was fully equipped and ready for service.[7] The regiments comprising the division were consolidated and formed into a brigade, under Gen. F. M. Cockrell. It was wonderful to see how well the Missourians

141

REST AND REORGANIZATION

FRANCIS M. COCKRELL. STEEL ENGRAVING,
MID– TO LATE NINETEENTH CENTURY.

looked in their new uniforms of gray, faced with blue, and the new Enfield rifles, which had been imported from England and successfully carried through the blockade at Charleston, S.C., were grasped with pride.[8] The men felt that they were themselves again.

The familiar sounds of guard mounting and drill call again resounded through the camp, and in a short time everything had resumed its usual course of military duty. When the regiment was reported for duty our field officers and staff were as follows:

A. C. Riley, colonel; Hugh A. Garland, lieutenant-colonel, Martin Burke, major; Thomas T. Tunstall, adjutant; Capt. James Pritchard, commissary; Capt. Frank Stewart, quartermaster; John Blades, commissary sergeant; Albert O. Allen, ordnance sergeant; John K. Newman, sergeant-major. We were assigned to Cockrell's brigade. This was very satisfactory to us as we held Gen. Cockrell in high esteem, as a brave and gallant soldier, who had earned his commission as brigadier-general for his services at Grand Gulf, Baker's Creek and Vicksburg.[9]

Just before leaving Demopolis we were reviewed by President Davis. He was on a tour of inspection. We were drawn up in line on one of the main streets of Demopolis and occupied the left of the brigade. He rode along the line of the command accompanied by Gen. Johnston and staff. When he reached the colors the regiment saluted. Reining in his horse, he raised his hat and with uncovered head returned the salute. He looked at the regiment a moment and then addressed us as follows:

> Men of the First Missouri, my heart goes out to you. In every fibre of it I hold you in the deepest affection. When I look upon your thinned ranks and remember how far you are from your homes, how nobly you have borne yourselves in every engagement you were in, your soldierly bearing, which stamps you as veterans of the first class, of undoubted courage and discipline, I sincerely hope the day is not far distant when you can go back to that state which has done so much for the cause of the South. Again I thank you in the name of the Confederacy.

AMONG BOYCE'S PAPERS IS AN UNDATED TYPESCRIPT FROM ONE OF BOYCE'S CORRESPONDENTS, IDENTIFIED ONLY AS "E. P. R." WHETHER THIS VERSION OF EVENTS WAS SENT TO BOYCE BEFORE OR AFTER PUBLICATION OF HIS ACCOUNT IS NOT KNOWN. THE TEXT OF E. P. R.'S ACCOUNT IS INCLUDED HERE.

At 3 o'clock the President, accompanied by a splendid cortege, reviewed the brigades of Generals Cockrell, Pe[ttus] and Moore.[10] The line was formed on the Main Street of the town and was nearly a mile long. The troops made a creditable appearance and elicited the highest encomiums from the Chief Magistrate.

Each regiment as the President reached its colors "presented arms," dropped its ensign and greeted with rapturous cheers the President. When the President came opposite the flag of the 1st Missouri (Bowen's Regiment) he halted and made a few stirring remarks as follows:

"Gallant Missourians! I look with sadness on your reduced ranks and feel it a high honor to be in the presence of such chivalrous soldiers. I have heard of your heroism on the bloody fields of the west and must express to you the high regard which I cherish for your privations and positive suffering in the cause of liberty. I thank you from the deepest recesses of my heart, from its very fibre, for your dauntless courage and untiring devotion to our common cause. Be assured that I express but the sentiment of our entire countrymen when I address you in the most fervid terms of gratitude and impress upon you that you have but to be true to the past, and the memory of your proudest desires for our country. May you live to see the flag of our infant Republic the ensign of a great nation—floating proudly among the national colors of the world. When this vision of joy is ours it will be due to your own brave heads and stout arms. Again, I thank you."[11]

His words burned deeply into our hearts, and as he turned to ride away we gave him the regimental cheer and tiger, counting rapidly from one to nine, with the right hand keeping time, and dwelling upon the nine until it swelled into a roar, with caps in hand and waving above our heads. This cheer was introduced by Gen. Bowen when the regiment was organized, and was retained as such until its dissolution. We felt that to be complimented as Missouri soldiers by President Davis was the highest honor he could confer upon our state through us.

The newspapers of the day were filled with complimentary articles upon the First Missouri, and the remarks of Mr. Davis published. All our sufferings and hardships vanished. The fame of the regiment was acknowledged, and we tendered our honors to Missouri and our people at home. We were Missourians, and our state could well be proud of her First regiment of infantry.

Early in October we were ordered to Meridian, Miss., and became a part of French's division. Gen. Joseph E. Johnston was in command of the army and his headquarters were at this place.[12]

While at Meridian the command received many kind attentions from Gen. Johnston and his excellent wife.[13] Accompanied by her lady friends they visited the encampment almost daily, and attended our dress parades with a great deal of pleasure. The grounds were kept remarkably clean and in perfect order.

At Meridian Gen. Cockrell brought the command to perfection in brigade drill. The First Missouri had long before earned the reputation of the "crack regiment" of every command with which it had served. From this time to the end this reputation was, in a measure, merged into that of the brigade, the wonderful efficiency of which can be judged by the following. The brigade drills usually lasted one hour, every movement being executed invariably in double-quick time. An expert tactician was in the habit of watching these drills to see if he could detect one man out of step during the hour, and was almost always unsuccessful. The spectacle of nearly eighteen hundred men performing most of the complicated evolutions of the line in double time without a single man losing step, looks like exaggeration now, but is simply the truth, and in our ranks excited no special comment. But the reputation spread far and wide, and brought the old tacticians out as spectators wherever we went.

The command remained at this point until after Christmas, when it was hurriedly ordered to Mobile. While at Mobile Gen. Dabney Maury put up a stand of colors to be awarded to the best drilled regiment of infantry in the department of the Gulf.[14] Many entries were made by states, Alabama, Arkansas, Louisiana, etc., had representative regiments. The eyes of the Missouri brigade turned towards the old First. The others discovered soon that Missouri would be represented.

This prize drill took place just west of our camp on a broad, level field well adapted for the necessary movements. The day was all that could be hoped for. The sun shone out bright and clear, the air was warm and pleasant; overcoats were thrown aside, the men appearing in nice-fitting jackets of grey, and all equipped in first-class style.

The first regiment to move out was from Arkansas. It did very well, indeed. This was followed by commands from Alabama, Tennessee, Louisiana, etc. These battalions moved very handsomely and attracted a great deal of attention and applause from the large attendance of citizens, soldiers and ladies. The navy was also well represented by Admiral Buchanan and his fleet officers stationed in Mobile harbor.[15]

This was the first challenge to drill which the regiment received since its entry at Bowling Green, Ky. It is well to state here that all entries were limited to five companies. The companies selected were under the command of Capts. Lewis H. Kennerly, Chas. Edmondson, Keith Goah Stewart and Joseph Boyce, Col. Riley in command of the battalion.[16]

The command moved out at quick time. The immense crowd received us with cheers, the ladies in carriages waving their handkerchiefs and speaking kind words of encouragement. It was not known to many outside of our brigade that we were to drill by the bugle. Coming promptly into line by platoons we saluted Gen. Maury and Col. Olin F. Rice of his staff, who had charge of the drill. Col. Rice, by the way, was one of the original captains of the regiment. He ordered Col. Riley to proceed with the drill.[17]

The bugle sounded "Deploy." Away went the men at the "double-quick," deploying from the colors; then "commence firing," which was continued standing, kneeling and lying down, then rallying by fours, platoons, by companies, then again thrown out as skirmishers, the entire battalion on the run, wheeling, the men four paces apart, until it completed a circle, never out of line, moving like a solid front, then rallying upon the colors the next movement in line of battle at a charge bayonets, all this done at the "double quick." It was a revelation to the crowd. Such cheering for old Missouri and her regiment. It was a proud day for Missouri. The colors were won and awarded to the regiment. The command left the drill grounds company front at the "double quick," amidst the plaudits of all. The brigade seemed to take more pride in our success than we did. It was late that night, or rather early the next morning, before the men of the brigade left our camp. The canteen was passed freely, and we were overpowered by good wishes and peach brandy. Healths were drunk and songs were sung until the command was too full to reply to any more compliments.[18]

A few days after the drill the regiment was ordered with the rest of the brigade into Mobile, to be reviewed by Gen. Patrick Cleburne. This officer had seen the regiment often while we were a part of the army while at Bowling Green, Ky.[19] He complimented Col. Riley after we had passed before him and spoke very feelingly to him about our reduced ranks, then about 300 men. When he last saw the regiment we mustered at least a thousand strong; this was a short time before the battle of Shiloh.

About this time a movement was made by the federal forces under Gen. Sherman from Vicksburg, their objective point being Meridian. Our forces were moved by rail via Meridian to Morton, Miss.[20] We arrived in good time and formed with our brigade in line of battle, just south of the town, about 4 p.m. Some skirmishing was going on in our front, but night soon put a stop to it. During the early part of the night we were drawn off and had a night march, with torches made of pine, through a swamp just in rear of our line. Such a march through the mud. The night was very dark. It was enlivened, however, by the men of the regiment, as the torches gave it the appearance of a political procession, by cries of "Three cheers for Missouri Dick." This was the name given to Hon. J. Richard Barrett, M. C. from our district at home. These cheers were given with a will. To keep up the excitement and good nature a voice would cry out, "Three cheers for Frank P. Blair."[21] This would be received by tremendous cheering. Then some one would exclaim with a rich Irish accent, "I am Shanghai Connors (a then noted pugilist), the terror of the Ninth ward and the best Dimmycrat in St. Louis. Who'll deny it? I have a new baby at home, and I calls him Stephen A. Douglas Connors."[22] This was continued until midnight at which time we reached solid ground and rested until daylight. About 7 o'clock that morning we resumed our march and continued it without interruption until we reached Meridian. After two days stay there we proceeded to Demopolis. It was the intention to go back to Mobile when we reached the Tombigbee river, just south of Gain[e]sville, Ala., as the boats were there to transport us.

A very short stay at Demopolis, and the last forever for the command, as we were ordered to Lauderdale Springs, Miss., where we remained several weeks.

REST AND REORGANIZATION

Endnotes

1. Bock, "Confederate Col. A. C. Riley," 282–283.

2. Joseph H. Parks, *General Leonidas Polk, C.S.A., The Fighting Bishop* (Baton Rouge: Louisiana State University Press, 1962), 355–356.

3. Warner, *Generals in Gray,* 93–94.

4. Anderson, *Memoirs,* 371. Bevier, *History of the First and Second Missouri Confederate Brigades,* 225–226.

5. Captain Jos. Boyce to Edward Warren, November 2, 1863, from Officer's Hospital, Lauderdale Springs, Mississippi, Boyce Family Papers, MHM Archives.

6. *Ibid.*

7. The command was officially exchanged on September 12, 1863. *OR,* ser. II, vol. 6, 113, 279–280.

8. The Enfield rifle musket was the standard weapon of the British army. The .577 caliber weapon was fifty-five inches long and weighed more than nine pounds. The British Enfield was second in popularity only to the Springfield rifle musket of the U.S. Army. Time-Life Books, *Echoes of Glory: Arms and Equipment of the Confederacy* (Alexandria, VA: Author, 1998), 36–37.

9. Cockrell was appointed brigadier general to rank from July 18, 1863. Warner, *Generals in Gray,* 57.

10. The typescript E. P. R. account identifies the general as "Pelters" but "Pettus" is likely correct. Edmund Winston Pettus, brother of the Mississippi governor, commanded the brigade of Isham Garrott after Garrott was killed in the Vicksburg lines. He was promoted to brigadier general on September 18, 1863.

John Creed Moore graduated from the U.S. Military Academy in 1849 but resigned from the army in 1858. In 1861, he organized the 2nd Texas Infantry and was elected its colonel. He was promoted to brigadier general in May 1862 and served in the Corinth and Vicksburg campaigns. After he was exchanged, he served with Bragg at Chattanooga and Maury at Mobile before resigning from the service in 1864. Warner, *Generals in Gray,* 219, 238–239.

11. "The President's Address to the Missourians," a typescript by E. P. R. (unidentified except as a self-styled "Conservator of the Facts") in Boyce Family Papers, MHM Archives. This document dates the review as occurring on September 14, 1863.

12. Joseph E. Johnston remained in command in Mississippi until he was ordered to the Army of Tennessee, then defending northern Georgia, on December 27, 1863. Thomas Lawrence Connelly, *Autumn of Glory: The Army of Tennessee, 1862–1865* (Baton Rouge: Louisiana State University Press, 1971), 281.

13. General Johnston's "excellent wife" was Lydia Mulligan Sims McLane Johnston. They had married on July 10, 1845; she was fifteen years his junior. Symonds, *Joseph E. Johnston,* 51.

14. Dabney Herndon Maury graduated from the U.S. Military Academy in 1846 and served continuously until resigning to join the Confederacy. Maury was familiar with the Missourians because of his service on Van Dorn's staff and as a division commander at Corinth. Warner, *Generals in Gray*, 215–216.

15. Admiral Franklin Buchanan is best known as captain of the CSS *Virginia (Merrimack)* during its attack on the Federal ships at Hampton Roads, Virginia, on March 8, 1862. Wounded in the attack, Buchanan was not at the helm when CSS *Merrimack* dueled USS *Monitor* the next day. Buchanan was now commander of the naval forces at Mobile, Alabama. Patricia Faust, ed., *Historical Times Illustrated Encyclopedia of the Civil War* (New York: Harper & Row, 1986), 86.

16. Lewis H. Kennerly was twenty-five when he enlisted at Memphis in June 1861, giving his occupation as "Indian trader." Badly wounded in the leg and thigh at Shiloh, Kennerly returned to duty and was elected captain of Company F in July 1862. In May 1864, Kennerly was deemed unfit for field service because of the lingering effects of his wounds, and he was assigned to the staff of Lieutenant General Stephen Lee to assist with court-martial records. He was surrendered and paroled on May 10, 1865. *CSR—Confederate, Missouri.*

17. Olin Rice was a native of Georgia but entered the U.S. Military Academy from Kentucky. Graduating with the class of 1861, he was assigned to the 9th U.S. Infantry but resigned to join the 1st Missouri Infantry. He served with distinction at Shiloh but left the regiment in late 1862 to join the staff of General Buckner. He served for the remainder of the war in Mobile in both line and staff responsibilities. Sergent, *They Lie Forgotten,* 174.

18. Lest Boyce be accused of "old soldiering" in his praise for his fellow Missourians, Lieutenant Colonel Walter A. Rohr, 20th Mississippi Infantry, observed a review in March 1864 and described it to his cousin: "Next came the fair fancied Missouri brigade, they are the brag men of this or any other army, they fight better, drill better and look better than any other men in the army, clean clothes, clean faces and all in Uniform and every man in the step." Walter A. Rohr to My Dear Cousin Susan, March 22, 1864, Kennesaw Mountain National Battlefield Park.

19. Major General Patrick Ronayne Cleburne commanded a division in the Army of Tennessee. He had a reputation as a superb combat officer, and the Missourians would have been highly complimented by his praise. Warner, *Generals in Gray*, 53–54.

20. The 1st Missouri moved from Meridian, Mississippi, to Mobile, Alabama, and from Mobile to Morton, Mississippi, by the railroad. From Morton, they marched to Demopolis, Alabama, a distance of approximately 150 miles. *OR Supplement,* vol. 38, 406.

21. In 1858, Democrat "Missouri Dick" Barrett opposed Republican Francis P. Blair Jr., for the seat in the U.S. House of Representatives representing

REST AND REORGANIZATION

Missouri's first district, St. Louis. Blair contested Barrett's narrow victory through the Congressional Committee on Elections, and Congress unseated Barrett in June 1860. Frederick A. Culmer, *A New History of Missouri* (Mexico, MO: McIntyre Publishing Company, 1938), 332–333, 347.

22. In the presidential contest in 1860, Democrat Stephen A. Douglas carried only one state: Missouri. Culmer, *A New History of Missouri*, 332–333, 347.

CHAPTER 11
DEFENDING ATLANTA UNDER JOHNSTON
———◆◆◆◆◆———
MAY–JUNE 1864

On May 2, 1864, General Polk ordered the Missouri Brigade from Demopolis into north Alabama for the purpose of clearing "tories, deserters, and conscripts evading the obligations of service."[1] On the next evening, Boyce and the 1ˢᵗ/4ᵀᴴ Missouri Infantry established camp at New Lexington in Tuscaloosa County, Alabama, and on the following day, the regiment captured more than a dozen of the miscreants.[2] Not long after the regiments of Cockrell's brigade dispersed on this duty, the scattered regiments were abruptly recalled. General William T. Sherman was on the move, and General Joseph E. Johnston, now in command of the Army of Tennessee in northern Georgia, wanted Polk and all of his available force to unite with his army as quickly as possible.[3]

Polk's ten thousand infantry and four thousand cavalry began arriving at Resaca late on May 11 to form the left of Johnston's army. On May 25, Polk's corps—including the 1ˢᵗ/4ᵀᴴ Missouri—formed the Confederate center between Hood's corps at New Hope Church on the right and Hardee's corps at Dallas on the left. On May 26, Polk moved from the center to the far right to counter a flanking move by Sherman. On May 27, Johnston again shifted to his right to counter Sherman. Late in the day on May 28, Johnston launched a counterattack against the Federal right near Dallas

JOHNSTON'S BATTLES	
May 7	Rocky Face Ridge
May 8	Dug Gap
May 13–15	Resaca
May 16	Rome Crossroads
May 25	New Hope Church
May 27	Pickett's Mill
May 28	Dallas
June 22	Kolb's Farm
June 27	Kennesaw Mountain

THAT WAS REPULSED. THE MOST SIGNIFICANT OUTCOME OF THESE FOUR DAYS OF FIGHTING WAS TO CONVINCE THE SOLDIERS OF THE BENEFITS OF BREASTWORKS. ENTRENCHING BECAME A SPONTANEOUS ACT, AND IT SIGNIFICANTLY INCREASED THE POWER OF THE DEFENSE. THE FIGHTING ALSO ESTABLISHED THAT IF SHERMAN THREATENED A FLANK, JOHNSTON WOULD EVENTUALLY RETIRE. THE CONFEDERATE WITHDRAWALS COUNTERED SHERMAN'S TURNING MOVEMENTS, OFTEN SUCCESSFULLY DEFLECTING THE UNION SUPERIORITY IN NUMBERS, BUT WITH EACH MOVE, THE CONFEDERATES MOVED SOUTHWARD TOWARD ATLANTA.

ON JUNE 14, 1864, LIEUTENANT GENERAL POLK, COMMANDER OF THE ARMY OF MISSISSIPPI OF WHICH THE 1ST/4TH MISSOURI WAS A PART, WAS KILLED BY ARTILLERY FIRE. WILLIAM LORING COMMANDED THE CORPS UNTIL ALEXANDER PETER STEWART TOOK COMMAND ON JULY 7.[4] JOHNSTON NEEDED TO MOVE QUICKLY TO FIND A PERMANENT REPLACEMENT FOR POLK. IN RECOMMENDING STEWART TO PRESIDENT DAVIS, JOHNSTON REASONED THAT STEWART, A WEST POINT GRADUATE IN 1842, WAS THE "BEST QUALIFIED" OF THE MAJOR GENERALS THEN SERVING WITH HIS ARMY.[5]

FOR THE MISSOURIANS, MORALE REMAINED HIGH. JOHNSTON'S SUPPLY LINES SHORTENED AND SHERMAN'S GREW LONGER AS THE ARMIES MOVED CLOSER TO ATLANTA. AFTER THE WAR, AN OFFICER OF THE 5TH MISSOURI INFANTRY

REMEMBERED JOHNSTON'S RETREAT AS "A MARVEL OF STRATEGIC SKILL AND MILITARY ABILITY." "TO THIS POINT," HE WROTE, "THE INCIDENTS OF THE CAMPAIGN HAD ALL BEEN IN FAVOR OF THE CONFEDERATES. THE ENGAGEMENTS AT RESACA, NEW HOPE CHURCH, AND KENNESAW MOUNTAIN HAD ALL BEEN CONFEDERATE VICTORIES."[6]

THE 1ST/4TH MISSOURI AND THE OTHER REGIMENTS OF THE BRIGADE PLAYED A KEY ROLE IN REPULSING SHERMAN'S ASSAULT ON KENNESAW MOUNTAIN, WHERE THE MISSOURIANS OCCUPIED "THE STRONGEST AND MOST EASILY DEFENDED WORKS TO WHICH THE BRIGADE HAD EVER BEEN ASSIGNED."[7] A MEMBER OF GUIBOR'S BATTERY EXPLAINED THAT THE FEDERAL ASSAULT WAS DIRECTED MOST HEAVILY AGAINST THE MISSOURI REGIMENTS, THE FEDERALS "COMING ON IN EARNEST, CHARGING IN THREE LINES, AND REPEATING THE CHARGE WHEN REPULSED. LARGE NUMBERS OF THEIR DEAD LAY WITHIN THIRTY YARDS OF OUR INFANTRY LINE...." BECAUSE OF A CURVE IN THE LINE AND THE ROCKY TERRAIN, GUIBOR COULD BRING ONLY ONE GUN TO BEAR. THE GUN HAD BEEN LOWERED BY ROPES INTO "A NATURAL EXCAVATION" AND ITS FIELD OF FIRE NOW ENFILADED THE FEDERAL ADVANCE. THE GUN WAS FIRED SO OFTEN THAT THE BARREL COULD NOT BE TOUCHED WITH BARE HANDS. WET BLANKETS WERE THROWN OVER IT TO COOL IT. IN OTHER CIRCUMSTANCES, ANOTHER GUN MIGHT HAVE REPLACED IT, BUT "THE SHOOTING WAS TOO GOOD TO LOSE THE TIME OF CHANGING FOR ANOTHER PIECE."[8]

TACTICAL VICTORIES THESE ENGAGEMENTS MAY HAVE BEEN, BUT EACH RESULTED IN A WITHDRAWAL CLOSER TO ATLANTA.

At this time Gen. Jos. E. Johnston was in command of the Army of Tennessee, having succeeded Gen. Bragg. Gen. Sherman now commenced his move against Johnston's forces. The latter's line of couriers between Tuscumbia and Florence, Ala., was very much disturbed, and the couriers frequently murdered by a gang of deserters from both armies who infested this locality. We were ordered by Gen. Polk to proceed at once to Tuscaloosa and break up this gang. After several days march the command arrived at its destination and the work immediately commenced.

Gen. Cockrell ordered the brigade to deploy as skirmishers and we were marched in this way, the men about twenty and in some places 100 paces apart, so that our line covered a front of several miles, practically rounding up a whole county at one sweep. A detail of one or two companies followed to take charge of the prisoners. Our orders were to march directly to the front, regardless of obstacles or the heighth of hills or bluffs. We must scramble up or down, when we reached water wade, or swim if necessary. The number of animals we started in our front was amazing: wolves, foxes, deer, rabbits, etc., went scampering away for dear life. Not a shot to be fired. Move to the front as quietly but as rapidly as possible. The bushwhackers and deserters sought refuge in their caves. They were soon unearthed by building fires in the front of them of leaves and twigs, and by this means smoking them out, when they were turned over to the guard and sent back to Tuscaloosa, where they were placed in jail. This work was accomplished in a few days and the entire colony of rascals broken up.[9]

Just as this work was completed, and upon our return to Tuscaloosa, we received orders from Gen. Johnston to come at once by forced marches to Rome, Ga., about 200 miles distant.[10]

This march will never be forgotten by any who made it. Night and day, little or no rest, "push on, men, push on," was the only command we heard. At last nature was about to give way. We were, on the fourth day, within a few miles of Rome, about 4 o'clock in the afternoon, when suddenly the boom of a cannon was heard; again and again it came to our ears in rapid succession. It was electrical. It infused new life into the men. With a wild cheer the ranks were closed up, a steady tramp, almost at the "double quick," and we came in sight of Rome. The attack was made upon the place by some federal cavalry, but they were driven back by Ector's Texan brigade of our division, which had preceded us a day, and only reached Rome about two hours before us.[11]

The next morning we were placed on flatcars and hurried off to Kingston, on the Georgia Central railroad, where we arrived about 10 o'clock that morning, and became a part of Johnston's army, participating in engagements from that point to Atlanta.[12] From the middle of May until the last of August hardly a day passed that we were not under fire. When I look back after twenty years have passed, it seems like yesterday—not that time flies so quickly, but the impression of that dreadful campaign is so fresh that I am sure time can never remove those scenes from the memory of those who passed through them.

Fighting every day in trenches on the skirmish line, at night called up to resist an expected attack. How we lived, and observed order and discipline is wonderful. Yet, we were always ready and cheerful. New Hope church— how that name recalls the terrors of death. Here it was we lost so many of our brave comrades by the enemy's sharpshooters. They climbed into trees, covered themselves with leaves fastened to their coats, attached them to their hats, and with branches of trees carried in front of them, approached our line so quietly that they were unobserved by us. The enemy were terribly aggressive and enterprising at this place. Our men in the rifle-pits in our front could not be relieved until dark, and any poor fellow so unfortunate as to be wounded had to remain until night to be removed. It was sure death to attempt to visit our advanced line of skirmishers during the day.

This continued for nearly a week, when a sudden fit of desperation seized the brigade; simultaneously the men sprang over the works and dashed upon the enemy's line with a yell and drove them back. The men in the trees came down in a hurry, but they were badly used up. Many sharpshooters were captured. The attack was so sudden and without orders that our skirmishers were run over by the men charging. The line was advanced, and during the rest of our stay here, we had at least some comfort and safety.[13]

It was here we lost our colonel, A. C. Riley, who was killed by a sharpshooter while he was talking to the writer. Other accounts of Col. Riley's death state [he] was killed by a fragment of a shell. Such was not the case. It was a severe blow to the regiment. He was an excellent officer, a thorough soldier and as gentle as a child; brave, watchful and always with his men.[14]

We had quite an exciting time one dark night at this point. About 10 o'clock the brigade on our left (Sears') opened a tremendous fire of musketry and artillery.[15] Some of their officers ran down our line and cried out: "Missourians, why are you idle and silent? Why don't you fire?" Of course we were astonished, but as our skirmishers had not been driven in, we could not open fire, for if we did we might kill our men at the front. This uproar continued for some time, when at last it subsided. Gen. French and staff in the meantime came plunging through the woods, and wanted to know "What in the —— is up? What's the matter?" etc. It was soon explained. Sears' men mistook the lightning-bugs, which were quite numerous through the woods and flashing their lights vigorously, made it appear that the enemy were making a night attack. The next morning the report was circulated that a bottle of ink was to be issued to every man in Sears' brigade so that he could assist in painting the fiery end of the lightning-bugs, and hereafter avoid such a scare.

It was here that for the first time in two years we had genuine coffee issued to us, as the boys called it, the genuine "Lincoln green." Thirteen grains, or kernels, to each man. It was carefully parched, the companies making the coffee in large camp-kettles and everybody placing his ration of coffee in the kettle. It was indeed a treat. The morning we got it was wet and cold, but the coffee was nectar, without sugar, etc. It was a drink that is still remembered for the sweetness and comforting effect. This was the last coffee issued to us during the war.

Notwithstanding the hardships we endured and the dangers which surrounded us, we were never confused or driven out of any point or works in which we were placed to defend, one instance alone excepted. Early in June the skirmish line in front of the brigade, under the command of Col. McDowell of the Sixth Missouri and the writer, was overpowered at a place called Lat[ima]r house.[16] Our left rested in an angle, exposing our flank to a fire which could not be avoided.[17] The enemy, it appears, knew this weak spot, and commenced moving up in small squads to a point in our front, where he was pretty well protected by an old line of abandoned works. This was continued for some time, until he had in our front at least two regiments. In the meantime word had been sent back to Gen. Cockrell stating the position of affairs, and what the enemy were doing.

Col. McDowell returned saying that our original orders were repeated to him, "Hold the position at all hazards." Col. McDowell and the writer had a quiet laugh over this matter. It was raining torrents and had been all day. This was about 4 o'clock in the afternoon. Our ammunition was wet, the men were standing in the rifle-pits in water up to their waists, under a steady fire from men armed with Henry rifles and metallic cartridges which were waterproof, themselves covered with rubber blankets.[18] Our guns and ourselves were soaking and only occasionally were we able to fire a shot. I recollect saying: "Mac, go back to the general and tell him that I say the first Yank who jumps up and yells at us, I am going to order my part of the line to make for the brigade as quick as it can. We can't shoot any more and I don't intend to go to Johnson's island just yet."[19] He had hardly left of his mission when the Yank jumped up, sure enough, and yelled, with two regiments at his heels, "Hold the position at all hazards!" Why, a log-chain wouldn't have held us then. We got back in double-quick time, every man, save himself. The way we went over the old line of abandoned rifle-pits, fortifications and trenches made the federal force which charged us think they had gained a great victory. We got off with small loss, but we were under a terrible fire of infantry and artillery until nightfall, when we fell back to Kennesaw mountain. This is the only time I can recollect when we gave up a position.[20]

We had quite a laugh at Joe Donovan, who came limping into the line of works where our regiment was stationed saying, "Boys, I am shot; take off my shoe; be careful now." His shoe was removed and his foot examined; no wound was found. The shoe was looked at next, and it was discovered the heel was shot away. Well, Donovan was wild, and said "—— a Yank who couldn't shoot an inch or two higher and give a poor fellow a sixty-day furlough at least after such a run as that."[21]

On the 27th of June a general assault was made upon our position, and from the prisoners captured it was learned the command which moved up in our immediate front was Blair's division. This battle was simply a slaughter. Our position was on Little Kennesaw mountain, while in our front was a small valley formed by Big Kennesaw mountain on our right. The federal troops moved up steadily and into this valley of death, where they were met by a terrible fire of musketry from our brigade. The artillery fire from Guibor's battery on our right was frightful. His Napoleon guns seemed to roar louder than usual, while the cannister tore through their ranks fearfully. It was really sickening to see those brave fellows struggling up that valley. Our infantry did not return their rammers as usual, after loading, but stuck them in the ground and snatched them up when wanted, just to save time. No troops could stand such a concentrated fire long. They were driven back in confusion, and with dreadful loss in killed, wounded, and prisoners. The latter told us they were under the impression that Gen. Johnston had entrusted this naturally strong position to the Georgia state troops, composed of old men over the age for regular military service. They were very much surprised to find that they had charged the same troops which repelled them a year before at Vicksburg.

On the night of the 3d of July we left Kennesaw mountain and fell back to Marietta, where we made a stand and had a lively skirmish with the enemy on the glorious Fourth. Our loss was slight, being only a few wounded—among them our major, Feagan of Palmyra, Mo.[22] We continued to fall back, with our usual daily skirmishing, until we reached Atlanta.

MAY–JUNE 1864

ENDNOTES

1. *OR*, vol. 38, pt. 4, 658.

2. Report of Brig. Gen. F. M. Cockrell, May 5, 1864, *OR*, vol. 38, pt. 4, 666–667.

3. Adjutant and Inspector General S. Cooper to Lieut. Gen. L. Polk, May 4, 1864, *OR*, vol. 38, pt. 4, 661.

4. Report of General Joseph E. Johnston, October 20, 1964, *OR*, vol. 38, pt. 3, 617.

5. Sam Davis Elliott, *Soldier of Tennessee: General Alexander P. Stewart and the Civil War in the West* (Baton Rouge: Louisiana State University Press, 1999), 191–192.

6. Bevier, *History of the First and Second Missouri Confederate Brigades*, 238.

7. *Ibid.*, 235.

8. "Guibor's Missouri Battery in Georgia," *The Kennesaw Gazette*, May 15, 1889. Files, Kennesaw Mountain National Battlefield Park. Much of the account is extracted from a diary maintained by Ward Childs of Guibor's battery.

9. Boyce was likely unaware that the orders to a staff officer accompanying the brigade explained that members of a "secret society" were suspected of armed resistance in the area. If found "in arms and offering resistance," they were to be "put to death on the spot." *OR*, vol. 38, pt. 4, 657–658.

10. The Missourians left Tuscaloosa on May 1, 1864, and arrived in time to evacuate Rome, Georgia, on May 16. *Official Records Supplement*, Record of Accomplishments, vol. 38, 380.

11. Brigadier General Matthew Duncan Ector, a Texas legislator when war broke out, gained his military reputation leading the 14th Texas Cavalry (Dismounted). Warner, *Generals in Gray*, 80.

12. The Missouri Brigade arrived in Kingston, Georgia, on May 18, 1864. *OR*, vol. 39, pt. 1, 899.

13. Sherman and Johnston struggled in a series of actions in the vicinity of New Hope Church northwest of Atlanta. On May 25, Polk's corps—including the 1st/4th Missouri—formed the Confederate center between Hood's corps at New Hope Church on the right and Hardee's corps at Dallas on the left. On May 26, Polk moved from the center to the far right to counter a flanking move by Sherman. On May 27, Johnston again shifted to his right to counter Sherman. Late in the day on May 28, Johnston launched a counterattack against the Federal right near Dallas that was repulsed. The most significant outcome of these four days of fighting was to convince the soldiers of the benefits of breastworks. Entrenching became a spontaneous act, and it significantly increased the power of the defense. Horn, *The Army of Tennessee*, 329–331.

14. Brigadier General Francis M. Cockrell reported Riley's death to division commander French not long after the event, writing: "I am grieved to inform

you that about 10 minutes before 2 o'clock p.m. today, Col. A. C. Riley, comdg 1ˢᵗ/4ᵗʰ Mo. Infty, one of the most gallant, skillful & meritorious officers of our army was pierced almost through the heart by a minnie ball and died in a few moments. My loss is almost irreparable." *CSR—Confederate, Missouri.*

In his report on the battle at New Hope Church, French claimed that Riley's death "will be irreparable to his regiment and to the brigade, and the country will mourn the loss of one of her most valuable soldiers." *OR*, vol. 38, pt. 3, 900.

After the war, Riley's father "with his trusty Servt during all the war" traveled to A. C. Riley's grave in Atlanta and removed the body for burial in the family burying ground near New Madrid, Missouri. In relating these details to his cousin, C. N. Riley added "but as I know but little about the Battles he fought I will refer you to Capt. Joe Boyce of St. Louis who has gained considerable notoriety by writing Articles about the War." C. N. Riley to A. R. Taylor, June 27, 1886, Boyce Family Papers, MHM Archives.

15. Claudius Wistar Sears graduated from the U.S. Military Academy in 1841 but left the army to become a teacher. Brigadier General Sears now led a brigade in French's division. Warner, *Generals in Gray*, 271–272.

16. Born in Ohio in 1838, James Kelsey McDowell moved to Ray County, Missouri, twenty years later and became a teacher. He served as a captain in the Missouri State Guard in 1861, later becoming an officer in the 3ʳᵈ Missouri Infantry. Advanced to lieutenant colonel effective May 16, 1863, McDowell would die in August 1864 while leading a skirmish line. Of McDowell, division commander Samuel French recorded in his diary: "What an excellent man and gallant officer gave his life for the Confederacy! Peace to him and his friends!" James Bradley, *The Confederate Mail Carrier* (Mexico, MO: James Bradley, 1894; reprint, Bowie, MD: Heritage Books, 1990), 268. Samuel Gibbs French, *Two Wars: An Autobiography of Gen. Samuel G. French* (Nashville: Confederate Veteran, 1901; reprint, Huntington, WV: Blue Acorn Press, 1999), 221.

17. The Latimar House and farm were located near the intersection of Stilesborough (now Stilesboro) Road and New Salem Road near Kennesaw, Georgia, on land now largely occupied by the Marietta Country Club and Marietta Country Club Estates. W. R. Johnson, Kennesaw Mountain National Battlefield Park, to author, February 3, 2004, email.

18. The Henry rifle was a coveted weapon. Its magazine containing fifteen .44 caliber cartridges could be emptied in fewer than eleven seconds. The rifle's metallic cartridges gave it an additional advantage in wet weather. Jack Coggins, *Arms and Equipment of the Civil War* (1962; reprint, Wilmington, NC: Broadfoot Publishing Company, 1990), 36.

19. Johnson's Island lies less than three miles north of Sandusky, Ohio, in Lake Erie. In 1862, the three-hundred-acre island became a prisoner of war camp for officers, enlisted men, and civilian political prisoners. In June

1862, Johnson's Island became the concentration point for all Confederate officer-prisoners. The prison appeared especially formidable in winter when surrounded by ice, but conditions within the overcrowded, hastily built prison were good compared to conditions in other Federal prisons. As many as twelve thousand Confederate officers were confined at Johnson's Island during its forty months of operation. Edward T. Downer, "Johnson's Island," in *Civil War Prisons,* ed. William B. Hesseltine (Kent, OH: Kent State University Press, 1962), 98–113.

20. Johnston's line was now two miles north of Kennesaw Mountain. The Latimar House and farm, just north of Mud Creek, was near the center of the Confederate line. Held by French's division, the position was a bend in Johnston's line. The Union army soon discovered that the salient could be subjected to enfilade from the north and west. Soldiers from Major General Oliver O. Howard's command made a quick thrust against the position on the evening of June 17, 1864, and the enfilade fire of the Federal artillery caused a rapid evacuation by French's command. Johnston withdrew to Kennesaw Mountain. Jim Miles, *Fields of Glory: A History and Tour Guide of the Atlanta Campaign* (Nashville: Rutledge Hill Press, 1995), 96.

21. St. Louisan John T. Donovan was twenty years old when he enlisted in Company D, 1st Missouri Infantry, in August 1861. Severely wounded in the left leg at Shiloh in 1862 and in the hip at Franklin in 1864, Donovan's luck held. He survived the war to return to St. Louis and engage in the real estate business. Moore, *Confederate Military History: Missouri,* 279–280. *CSR—Confederate, Missouri.*

22. Jeptha D. Feagan served in the Missouri State Guard before joining the Confederate service as a captain in the 4th Missouri Infantry and now served as major in the consolidated 1st/4th Missouri Infantry. Wounded at Champion Hill in May 1863, Feagan was wounded again on July 3, 1864, near Vining Station, Georgia. The wound to his right leg led to partial paralysis in the knee, and in March 1865 he was found unfit for duty. Feagan survived the war to die at his home in Palmyra, Missouri. *CSR—Confederate, Missouri.* Bevier, *History of the First and Second Missouri Confederate Brigades,* Appendix, 3.

CHAPTER 12

DEFENDING ATLANTA UNDER HOOD

◆✦◆

JULY–SEPTEMBER 1864

ON JULY 17, 1864, JOSEPH JOHNSTON WAS RELIEVED OF COMMAND AND FRESHLY PROMOTED LIEUTENANT GENERAL JOHN BELL HOOD WAS GIVEN THE RESPONSIBILITY OF ARRESTING SHERMAN'S ADVANCE. EIGHT DAYS EARLIER, IN PART BASED ON HOOD'S ADVICE, JOHNSTON WITHDREW HIS ARMY SOUTH OF THE CHATTAHOOCHEE RIVER IN ANTICIPATION OF ANOTHER OF SHERMAN'S ATTEMPTS TO TURN THE ARMY'S FLANK. PRESIDENTIAL PATIENCE FINALLY RAN OUT. A VETERAN OF THE 2ND/6TH MISSOURI INFANTRY RECORDED THAT "THE ARMY WAS OPPOSED" TO THEIR SEPARATION FROM JOHNSTON, "IN WHOM ITS FAITH AND CONFIDENCE WERE STRONG AND ABIDING."[1] SAMUEL BALDWIN DUNLAP, A CANNONEER IN THE MISSOURI ARTILLERY, REMEMBERED THAT JOHNSTON'S DEPARTURE "CAUSED GREAT SURPRISE & DISSATISFACTION." WRITING AFTER THE WAR AND PERHAPS INFLUENCED BY SUBSEQUENT EVENTS, DUNLAP NOTED THAT JOHNSTON WAS ADMIRED BECAUSE OF "HIS CEASELESS EFFORTS IN TRYING TO PROTECT THE LIVES OF HIS MEN."[2] JOHNSTON HAD BEEN A CAREFUL STEWARD OF THE RESOURCES UNDER HIS COMMAND, BUT HE HAD USED THEM TO NO SIGNIFICANT PURPOSE. EACH OF JOHNSTON'S TACTICAL CHECKS OF SHERMAN'S ADVANCE WAS FOLLOWED BY A STRATEGIC WITHDRAWAL.

HOOD, HOWEVER, VIEWED HIS TASK SOMEWHAT DIFFERENTLY. ON JULY 20, BOYCE AND HIS MISSOURIANS WERE IN RESERVE AS HOOD'S ARMY STRUCK AT THE FEDERALS WHO HAD ADVANCED SOUTH OF PEACH TREE CREEK ON ATLANTA'S NORTHERN SIDE. THE NEXT DAY, HOOD MET A FEDERAL ADVANCE AGAINST HIS RIGHT AT BALD HILL, 1.5 MILES FROM THE EASTERN OUTSKIRTS OF

DEFENDING ATLANTA UNDER HOOD

HOOD'S BATTLES	
July 20	Peach Tree Creek
July 21	Bald Hill
July 22	Atlanta
July 28	Ezra Church
August 6	Utoy Creek
August 31	Jonesboro
September 1	Jonesboro
September 2–3	Lovejoy's Station

ATLANTA.[3] ON JULY 22, HOOD TURNED THE DEFENSIVE ACTION INTO A FULL-SCALE ATTACK, RESULTING IN WHAT IS KNOWN AS THE BATTLE OF ATLANTA. RECOGNIZING THAT SHERMAN RESPONDED BY SHIFTING HIS FORCES TO THE WEST OF THE CITY, HOOD ATTACKED AGAIN AT EZRA CHURCH ON JULY 28. WHILE THESE ATTACKS MAY HAVE BEEN TEMPORARY DETERRENTS TO SHERMAN'S ADVANCE, NONE HAD ANY LASTING EFFECT ON THE FEDERAL ARMY. THE IMPACT ON HOOD'S FORCE, HOWEVER, WAS SIGNIFICANT. IN THE FEW WEEKS SINCE ASSUMING COMMAND, HOOD HEAVILY DEPLETED THE VALUABLE RESOURCE THAT JOHNSTON HAD HUSBANDED FOR THE LAST SEVERAL MONTHS: THE SOLDIERS OF THE ARMY OF TENNESSEE.

CASUALTIES IN THE $1^{ST}/4^{TH}$ MISSOURI INFANTRY			
May 18–September 5, 1864	Killed	Wounded	Missing
New Hope Church	2	–	–
Latimar House	–	16	11
Kennesaw	1	25	–
Smyrna	–	3	–
Chattahoochee	–	6	–
Peach Tree Creek	–	–	–
Atlanta	4	10	–
Lovejoy's Station	5	3	–
Total	**12**	**63**	**11**
Source: *OR* I, vol. 38, pt. 3, 908.			

JULY–SEPTEMBER 1864

August passed in constant skirmishing and continued artillery fire until the last week of the month, when most of Sherman's army seemed to vanish from the Confederates' front. To cut the last railroad link into Atlanta, Sherman swung to the city's west and south before turning east to strike at the Macon & Western Railroad. On August 31, Hood sent two-thirds of his army, the corps of Hardee and Stephen D. Lee, to stop the Federal Army of the Tennessee from seizing the road and rail junction at Jonesboro south of Atlanta.[4] Their attack changed nothing other than adding to the casualty lists. That night, Hood recalled Lee's corps to Atlanta, only to discover that Sherman's Army of the Ohio under General John Schofield had seized the railroad between Jonesboro and Atlanta. The Federals counterattacked at Jonesboro the next day, badly damaging the isolated and imperiled force under Hardee.

On September 1, while Hardee was under heavy attack at Jonesboro, Hood ordered preparations to begin for the evacuation of Atlanta. That evening, the Confederates blew up the immense supply of arms and ammunition parked in Atlanta's railyard. Late that night, their route "lighted by the glare of fires, flashes of powder, and bursting shells," the 1ST/4TH Missouri and the other regiments of the division marched slowly out of the city.[5] As they had been at Nashville, Shiloh, Davis Bridge after Corinth, and Big Black River at Vicksburg, once again the 1ST/4TH Missouri Infantry was part of the rear guard of the army. The division arrived at Lovejoy's Station south of Jonesboro late on September 3.

Just before 'we reached Atlanta Gen. Joe Johnston was relieved from command of the army and Gen. Hood appointed in his place.[6] This change of commanders was the source of universal regret and created a great deal of talk among the men as to our future actions. Gen. Johnston had the entire confidence of the army. This faith was the natural result of the general's masterly and deliberate campaign of seventy-two days, in presence of an enemy outnumbering him over two to one, and composed of the best fighting material assembled under the Union flag during the war. Constantly offering battle, a general engagement was never accepted by his opponent, while all partial attacks were speedily repulsed. When Sherman, after intrenching an equal number in front, would swing on our flank with another force equal to ours, "Old Joe," after holding on until the last minute, and until matters began to look desperate, would quietly move back a few miles in the dark, and by daylight everyone would be in his place on a new line, wagons would drive up with the day's supply of cooked rations, and we were again ready to "entertain company."

Gen. Hood was looked upon as a brave, energetic officer, and his address, which was read to the army, was very well received.[7] Notwithstanding the regret at Johnston's removal, and that Gen. Hardee would have been much more acceptable as his successor, the army received Gen. Hood as its commander with every show of good faith and earnestness. His orders were obeyed cheerfully, and in a few days after he assumed command it was very evident in battle that no change had taken place in courage or discipline. This was not strange, as the Army of Tennessee was composed in the main of veterans, men who had seen service for three years, and who were trained under Johnston, Beauregard, Bragg, Hardee, Price, etc.

While at Atlanta our left rested near the McDonough road, where a large fort was erected. This fort was very formidable in appearance, but owing to some defect was not suitable for the heavy guns, which were placed at the rear of our regiment. Whenever the time came to fire those huge pieces we "hunted our holes," because the shells were too small for the bore, and it addition to this the fuses were defective; the shells were just as liable to burst upon leaving the guns as on reaching the enemy's line. So that during this artillery practice we were between two fires. The enemy always responded vigorously. Our shells, when leaving the guns, turned over very rapidly and sounded like a train of cars rushing along. The boys would yell out: "All aboard the Ohio and Mississippi railroad!! This way, gentlemen, all aboard for St. Louis." At night the artillery fire from Sherman's line was very heavy, at times, the shells passing over us and bursting in the city a mile in the rear.

The weather had changed from rainy and disagreeable and the sun shone bright and hot during the day, but the nights were brightly moonlit and delightful. The men in both armies seemed to grow tired of fighting about night fall and singing took the place of firing. One night our company was visited by the members of Capt. Owney Barrett's Tenth Missouri battery, who were on the right of our position and entertained by some delightful singing.[8] This command had an excellent quartette composed of Gus. Ward, Gus. Beakey, Frank Turnbull and John Murtaugh, all St. Louis boys. They attracted quite a crowd from our line, and among the visitors were many from our brigade. Lieut. John A. Ladd of the Sixth Missouri added his voice to the entertainment and sang "When off the Blue Canaries I Smoked my last Cigar."[9] This song gave rise to a great deal of debate, and John was requested to tell us what a cigar was, it was so long since we had seen or smoked one. Dick Sa[lsbu]ry of the writer's company said he could tell because the last one he smoked was a stump, and it was off the Planters' house steps.[10] "Yes," said someone, "and you picked it up there, too." For this he was compelled to tell a story or sing a song.[11]

"Well, boys," said he. "I'll tell you how I came to save my leg, and my life. One day I was digging a cellar in St. Louis, along side a large three-story house; there were quite a number of hands with me, when all of a sudden the big house fell, and every divil escaped but me. The house was down on the top of me, and when I came to the boys were hard at work digging me out. At last they came to where I was pinned down with a big rock on my legs, another over my head, and so on. Well, I was badly hurt. My head was awfully cut and bleeding. My right leg was all bruised, and you would not give a fig for my life. They carried me off to the hospital and doctors gathered about me and gave me chloroform—I was wishing it was whiskey—and had me stupid. I heard them say they didn't know whether it would be best to cut off my head or my leg. I brightened up at once and told them to put me under the house again, as I felt safer there than in their hands. I said they should never cut off my leg, because without my leg I had no chance at all in this world. If they were going to cut, then cut off my head, as I would have a show for heaven. Well, boys, I raised such a laugh that the doctors took pity on me and said I was such a queer divil they could not trust me in heaven, and in a few weeks after I left the hospital all right. But upon me soul I was afraid of my life for several days for fear the young doctors would experiment on me."

"Very good, Dick; now for the song." So he complied and rendered the following:

The Song

Then fare ye well ould Erin, dear,
  To part my heart does ache well;
From Carrickfergus to Cape Clear
  I'll never see your equal.[12]
Although to foreign parts we're bound,
  Where cannibals may eat us,
We'll ne'er forget the holy ground
  Of poteen and potatoes.[13]
When good St. Patrick banished frogs,
  and shook them from his garment,
He never thought we'd go abroad
  To live upon such varmint.
Nor quit the land where whiskey grew,
  To wear King George's button,
Take vinegar for mountain dew
  And toads for mountain mutton.

This was received with great applause by all, and Dick was freely forgiven. We had many such evenings during the siege.

While we stayed here our loss was considerable in officers and men. We lost Maj. Bradford Keith, one of the original officers of the regiment. He was mortally wounded on the skirmish line and died about an hour after.[14]

During the afternoon of the 22[d] of July we found ourselves actively engaged on the left of Hardee's corps. It was a bloody engagement, lasting until dark. The heaviest fighting was done by Hardee's command. We were well protected by works in our front, which we gladly occupied. The fire from the small arms was annoying but not very destructive. The enemy's artillery fire was heavy, and their guns well handled. They got our range in short order, but the shells burst just as they passed over our position, and as the fragments were blown forward, injured no one.[15]

We were ordered to prepare to charge these two batteries, and just as we were rising to move over the works it was discovered the guns were on the far side of Peach Tree creek. It was fortunate that Gen. Cockrell made this discovery, as it would have been impossible for us to reach them, and our loss would have been necessarily great. After dark we were ordered to our former position in the works.

That night we heard the result of the battle and the death of Gen. McPherson of the federal army. This news was received with sympathetic expressions from all, as we looked upon him as a gentleman, and one of the best officers opposed to us. He was Gen. Bowen's friend, and we remembered his kindness and the interest taken in Bowen at Vicksburg.[16]

Fighting became the order of the day under Hood, and hardly an hour passed without some kind of a brush with the enemy. Battles were too common to receive formal names; simply the date was enough to distinguish them.[17] This continued right along until the last days of August, when it was discovered one morning that no enemy was in our front. Heavy clouds of dust were seen away to the rear of his position, and our skirmishers coming in reported no enemy in sight for at least a mile to the right or left. Upon this information Gen. Cockrell had all the batteries along his front open fire with shell at the roads from which the clouds of dust were rising. Guibor's and Barrett's guns were worked with a will, but no response came from the enemy.

Then the brigade, with the exception of the First Missouri, left behind to guard the position, was ordered over to find the enemy or to determine if he had really withdrawn. Shortly after the brigade had disappeared over the enemy's works heavy firing was heard, but died away as suddenly as it began. Some of the wounded came in and reported that a heavy federal skirmish line had been discovered, which was immediately driven off and quite a number of prisoners captured belonging to an Ohio command. These prisoners reported that Sherman had moved his forces during the night and had left them to hold the line until the afternoon, when they were to withdraw. If the attack had been delayed for a few hours it is probable no enemy would have been found. At once the idea took possession of us that Sherman was falling back, and the pleasure it gave cannot be described. It was almost too good to be true, but the men believed it and were wild with hope and joy.[18]

Permission was given to visit the enemy's position. Judging from appearances they got into the ground pretty well. All kinds of secure places were discovered. How they dug and tunnelled from one line to another to escape our fire! The trees about were cut all to pieces; many had fallen and some were ready to fall from the almost incessant fire which had been kept up from our lines for the past six weeks. We found our fire had been deadly from the newly made graves so near their line. The head logs were filled with our bullets, and there was no living brush about; everything except the largest trees was dead and they were dying. Fire only could make a cleaner sweep. The enemy must have passed a dreadful time in our front.[19]

The next morning orders were issued to cook three days' rations and be prepared to move at a moment's notice. It was known by this time that Hardee's corps had left its position on our right, and that Stephen D. Lee's corps was moving out then and passing a little to the left of our position.[20]

Everybody seemed to be in good humor, but despite this, there was a dread in our hearts that everything was not all right, and it wasn't either. Sherman, instead of being in retreat towards Kennesaw mountains, had started his forces in the direction of Jonesboro, a station about twenty miles south of Atlanta, and began tearing up the railroad, which supplied us with provisions, etc. He had placed himself between us and one of our most important sources of supplies, Columbus. It was now September 1, and we were saddened by the announcement that Atlanta must be given up.[21]

That night about 10 o'clock we left our works and marched through Atlanta. Such destruction was going on that it really appalled us, veterans as we were. Buildings on fire everywhere, cars of ammunition blowing up, shells bursting, and destruction of every kind going on. It was the dark side of war, drunken men going about with buckets of whiskey asking everybody to take a drink, and in their maudlin way singing how they would "Hang Abe Lincoln to a Sour Apple Tree," and others were "Not Going Home Till Morning."[22]

As our command was kept well in hand by the officers no straggling was allowed and we were pushed rapidly through those scenes to help Hardee, who, we learned, had been attacked that day by Sherman and almost overwhelmed. The instant this news was given to the men the cry passed along the line. "Push on to Hardee." "We must reach him by daylight." Every man strode on as if he alone could rescue "Old Reliable" and his matchless corps. Fortunately Lee's corps had marched ten or twelve hours before us, and daylight found them alongside that superb soldier.[23]

It was a close call. Any general in that army could be better spared than Hardee. For we thought he was the only one who could come near filling Johnston's place. The march was continued with very little rest during the night. At dawn we rested about an hour, and then we were pushed like on the march from Tuscaloosa to Rome. We could hear the firing distinctly, and every effort was made to lessen the distance between us and the enemy. We arrived about 10 o'clock, just as the firing was dying away and the enemy withdrawing from the front of Hardee and Lee. We took our position on the left of Hardee, just west of a deep railroad cut, and threw up temporary works. The enemy had withdrawn from our immediate front, but we could see his line some distance from our left, which kept up a musketry fire on our position. About 3 o'clock in the afternoon two shots were fired from an unseen battery which enfiladed our position. These two shots were the most destructive we received during the entire war. Capt. Sam Kennerly of Co. A was literally torn to pieces and twelve men of the regiment instantly killed.[24] If this fire had been continued for ten minutes longer our loss would have been appalling. To this day it makes me shudder.[25] This battery moved out at a trot and joined their infantry, who had quit firing and were moving off briskly towards Atlanta. Orders were given to pursue. Canniff's company of the Fifth Missouri and the writer's were thrown out as skirmishers, and kept up the chase until dark. We captured a company composed almost entirely of half-breed Indians, belonging to a Minnesota regiment, and a lot of stragglers who were too footsore to keep up.[26] The next morning we returned to our position, and during the day were moved to Palmetto station, and the Atlanta and Western railroad, about twenty miles distant, where we remained about two weeks.[27]

In the meantime, Gen. Sherman, who was now occupying Atlanta, determined to send out the women and children and the few citizens left there.[28] Quite a correspondence took place between him and Gen. Hood, but the order prevailed and the stream of vehicles which carried those poor creatures seemed to be without end. We were living on very small rations at this time, but the Missouri troops voted to do without rations for one day and give them to the "refugees." It was an act of self-denial which the "refugees" gratefully acknowledged. All these trials and hardships are usual in war.[29]

Our loss during the campaign just ended was very large. I can't recall many names. I remember only the following officers: Col. A. C. Riley, Maj. Bradford Keith, Capt. Sam Kennerly, Lieuts. Bumpis, William Shumate; Privates John Scott, John Crowley, Robert Bush, Joseph Weaver. Wounded: Maj. Feagan, Capt. Chas. L. Edmondson, Lieuts. John Redmond, L. A. Haynes, [George Riley] Cannon; Privates Patrick Crawls, Wm. Smith, Chas. Fannin, Robert Bonner, John O'Malley, John Dempsy and Chas. Barrell.[30]

President Davis visited the army here and addressed the men several times. He was listened to with great attention and his remarks well received. Several changes were made. Hardee left to take command of the district of South Carolina and Gen. Frank Cheatham took command of the corps.[31] Gen. Stephen D. Lee retained the command of Hood's corps, and Gen. A. P. Stewart was kept in command of ours (Polk's old corps). Gen. Hood had by this time perfected his plans for a march through Georgia, over the ground where we had fallen back before Sherman.

JULY–SEPTEMBER 1864

Endnotes

1. Anderson, *Memoirs*, 390.
2. Suzanne Staker Lehr, *Fishing on Deep River: Civil War Memoir of Pvt. Samuel Baldwin Dunlap, C.S.A.* (St. Joseph, MO: Platte Purchase Publishers, 2006), 301. Samuel's brother and fellow artilleryman, Robert Dunlap Caldwell, lost an arm while serving his gun during Johnston's defense of Kennesaw Mountain.
3. Russell S. Bonds, *War Like the Thunderbolt: The Battle and Burning of Atlanta* (Yardley, PA: Westholme Publishing, 2009), 211, 243. July 20 also marks the beginning of the Federal shelling of the city itself, a bombardment that continued for another five weeks.
4. Lee assumed command of Hood's former corps on July 27, 1864. Report of Lieut. Gen. Stephen D. Lee, January 30, 1865, *OR*, vol. 38, pt. 3, 762.
5. French, *Two Wars*, 222.
6. Johnston received the order relieving him from command around 10:00 p.m. on July 17, 1864. Connelly, *Autumn of Glory*, 421.
7. Hood issued an address to the army on July 19. It concluded: "I look with confidence on your patriotism to stand by me, and rely upon your prowess to wrest your country from the grasp of the invader, entitling yourselves to the proud distinction of being called the deliverers of an oppressed people." Quoted in Richard M. McMurry, *John Bell Hood and the War for Southern Independence* (Lexington: University Press of Kentucky, 1982), 124.
8. Overton "Owney" W. Barrett's Light Battery was organized in 1862. Though serving east of the Mississippi, Barrett's cannoneers had been separated from the main body of Missouri troops to serve in Kentucky before they were reunited in Georgia. Crute, *Units of the Confederate States Army*, 225.
9. John A. Ladd, a native of St. Louis, served initially with Turner Ashby's cavalry in Virginia and was wounded at the battle at Romney. Transferring west, he was elected to the rank of first lieutenant in Company D, 6th Missouri Infantry, in August 1862. He was again wounded during the Vicksburg campaign. In September 1864, he was captured near Cummins, Georgia, and sent north to the prisoner of war camp at Johnson's Island, Ohio. He was released from prison on December 31 of that year, consenting to an amnesty oath, and returned to St. Louis after the war. *CSR—Confederate, Missouri.* Bevier, *History of the First and Second Missouri Confederate Brigades*, Appendix, 5.

    "When off the Blue Canaries" is the last line of "The Last Cigar" by Joseph Warren Fabens (1821–1875). In 1887, his wife, Love Fry Stickney Fabens, published a collection of the poems of her late husband, including this one, with an introduction written by Julia Ward Howe (J. Warren Fabens, *"The Last Cigar" and Other Poems*, New York: M. L. Holbrook & Co., 1887). The preface remarks that Fabens wrote the poems "in his youth," likely while a student at Harvard College or the Theological Seminary at Andover.

10. The Planter's House Hotel opened in St. Louis in 1841. A hotel and civic meeting place, the Planter's House soon became known as "a center of lavish entertaining and extravagant spending." Winter, *The Civil War in St. Louis*, 67.

11. Richard Salsbury enlisted in Company D, 1st Missouri, on August 29, 1861, at New Madrid, Missouri. Boyce identified him as "Saulsberry." In the Confederate personnel records, he is identified as Saulisbery, Salisbury, Salsberry, Salsbury, and Salesbury. *CSR—Confederate, Missouri*.

12. Carrickfergus is at the northern end of Ireland, and Cape Clear is its southernmost reach.

13. "Poteen" is Irish moonshine.

14. After living as a farmer near Point Pleasant in New Madrid County, Missouri, Bradford Keith was twenty-four years old when he enlisted. He began his service with the 1st Missouri as a lieutenant in Company H and was quickly promoted to captain. After the consolidation of the 1st and 4th Missouri Infantry regiments, he was sent to Missouri on recruiting duty but was captured. He was held at the Gratiot Street Prison in St. Louis and at Fort Delaware, Delaware City, Delaware, before he was exchanged and returned to the regiment in October 1863. Brigadier General F. M. Cockrell recommended his promotion to major on August 16, 1864, to rank from May 30, 1864. Keith was killed on August 25, 1864. *CSR—Confederate, Missouri*. *OR*, vol. 38, pt. 3, 918.

15. On July 21, elements of McPherson's Army of the Tennessee under Major General Francis Preston Blair attacked the Confederate positions at Bald Hill near Decatur, Georgia. That evening, Hood sent Hardee's corps on a flanking movement to the northeast, hoping to strike McPherson, whom they believed to be out of supporting distance from Sherman's army. The battle fought on July 22 became known as the Battle of Atlanta. Unable to make their complicated maneuver work as planned, Hood and Hardee were soundly repulsed. McPherson was killed in the battle. Connelly, *Autumn of Glory*, 445–451.

16. Bowen and McPherson both graduated from the U.S. Military Academy at West Point in the Class of 1853. Cullum, *Biographical Register*, vol. 2, 333–334, 342–343.

17. Boyce uses only two sentences to describe a month of static warfare. The Confederate army remained in its entrenchments on the east, north, and west sides of Atlanta after the Battle of Ezra Church on July 28. Sherman turned temporarily to siege tactics, and for the next month both sides endured daily losses to combat and disease. McMurry, *John Bell Hood*, 135.

18. This reconnaissance occurred on August 6, 1864. *OR*, vol. 38, pt. 3, 917.

19. The 1st/4th Missouri and the other regiments of the Missouri brigade remained in defensive positions shielding Atlanta during the battle at Ezra Church on July 28. This time, Hood chose to strike the Federal right, expecting it to be unprepared. It was not. The poorly coordinated

Confederate assaults against the entrenched Federals nearly bled Hood's army to death. Bevier, *History of the First and Second Missouri Confederate Brigades,* 240. Sam Davis Elliott, *Soldier of Tennessee* (Baton Rouge: Louisiana State University Press, 1999), 209–214.

20. On the evening of August 30, 1864, Hood met with Hardee and Lee to explain his orders to attack the Federals west of Jonesboro on the next day. Bonds, *War Like the Thunderbolt,* 253–254.

21. On August 31, division commander Samuel French recorded in his diary: "Featherston and Walthall have been withdrawn from the city. My division and some State troops under the charge of Gen. G. W. Smith alone are in the city today." The 1st/4th Missouri was among the last Confederate troops to leave Atlanta. French, *Two Wars,* 222.

22. "The greatest explosion of the American Civil War" resulted from Hood's orders to destroy the reserve ordnance train parked on the Georgia Railroad just east of the city. The surprise of the explosion and its scope "would cause the common misconception that it was the Confederates, and not Sherman" who burned Atlanta. In 1939, the misconception was reinforced when the explosion became a climactic element in the film *Gone with the Wind.* Bonds, *War Like the Thunderbolt,* xvii–xviii, 270–272.

23. Sherman's army shifted west of Atlanta and then struck southeast in an attempt to sever the city's supply lines to the south. Hardee moved quickly to contest the Federal advance on August 31 at Jonesboro, south of Atlanta on the railroad line, but the Union army beat him to the objective. After costly assaults against prepared positions, Hardee withdrew. Sherman organized a counterattack the next day, nearly decimating Hardee's corps before it retired farther south to Lovejoy Station. Miles, *Fields of Glory,* 153–155.

24. Samuel Augustin Kennerly was the brother of Mary Kennerly Bowen, widow of the 1st Missouri's first commander. He was twenty-one when he enlisted in 1861. At the battle at Champion Hill, Mississippi, on May 16, 1863, Sam Kennerly was wounded and left for dead. He subsequently returned to duty as captain of Company C, 1st/4th Missouri, only to be killed at Lovejoy's Station, Georgia, on September 5, 1864. Drumm, "The Kennerlys of Virginia," 109. *CSR—Confederate, Missouri.* Drumm erroneously reports that he was killed at Second Manassas in 1862.

25. Brigade commander Cockrell reported that the two shots killed seven and wounded six, some of whom may have died later from their wounds. Report of Brig. Gen. Francis M. Cockrell, September 20, 1864, *OR,* vol. 38, pt. 3, 919.

26. Only the 2nd and 4th Minnesota Infantry regiments were assigned to Sherman's army. Both regiments had originally been mustered at Fort Snelling, Minnesota. Dyer, *A Compendium of the War of the Rebellion,* 1296–1301.

27. The corps of Stewart and Lee joined Hardee's corps at Lovejoy's Station, seven miles south of Jonesboro, on September 4. Hood's army remained there until September 21, 1864, when it moved about twenty miles west to

Palmetto Station. Palmetto Station was on the line of the Atlanta & West Point Railroad, Atlanta's former connection to Selma and Montgomery, Alabama. William R. Scaife, *War in Georgia: A Study of Military Command and Strategy* (Atlanta: Author, 1994), 24. Bonds, *War Like the Thunderbolt*, 296.

28. Elements of the Federal XX Corps first entered Atlanta on the morning of September 2 to receive the city's surrender. Sherman himself came into the city on September 7 after arranging his troops around the city. Report of Maj. Gen. Henry W. Slocum, September 3, 1864, *OR*, vol. 38, pt. 2, 20. Report of Maj. Gen. W. T. Sherman, September 15, 1864, *OR*, vol. 38, pt. 1, 82–83.

29. On September 7, 1864, Sherman informed Hood that "all citizens now residing in Atlanta should remove, those who prefer it to go South and the rest North." W. T. Sherman, Major General Commanding, to General Hood, Commanding Confederate Army, September 7, 1864, *OR*, vol. 38, pt. 5, 822.

30. Between May 18 and September 5, 1864, the 1st/4th Missouri Infantry lost twelve killed, sixty-three wounded, and eleven missing, an aggregate loss of eighty-six soldiers. *OR*, vol. 38, pt. 3, 908.

31. After Atlanta's fall, Hood blamed Hardee for the outcome and repeatedly asked President Davis to relieve Hardee from command. Davis visited the army at Palmetto Station, and he heard from each a litany of the other's shortcomings. Hardee was reassigned, and Major General Benjamin Franklin Cheatham was advanced to command Hardee's former corps. Hood recommended Cheatham despite his "fervent devotion to Joe Johnston." Cheatham was the senior of Hardee's division commanders and had exercised interim command of the corps on several occasions. Christopher Losson, *Tennessee's Forgotten Warriors: Frank Cheatham and His Confederate Division* (Knoxville: University of Tennessee Press, 1989), 195–197.

CHAPTER 13
NORTH THROUGH GEORGIA

SEPTEMBER–OCTOBER 1864

HOOD COULD NOT RECOVER ATLANTA FOR THE CONFEDERACY. ON SEPTEMBER 21, 1864, HE REGROUPED HIS BATTERED ARMY AT PALMETTO STATION, ABOUT TWENTY-FIVE MILES SOUTHWEST OF ATLANTA ON THE ATLANTA & WEST POINT RAILROAD. HIS OFFICERS AND MEN WERE INCREASINGLY DISSATISFIED. PRESIDENT DAVIS, ACCOMPANIED BY GOVERNOR HOWELL COBB OF GEORGIA AND GOVERNOR ISHAM HARRIS OF TENNESSEE, VISITED THE ARMY ON SEPTEMBER 25 IN AN ATTEMPT TO BOOST MORALE. BOYCE REMEMBERS THAT DAVIS'S REMARKS WERE "WELL RECEIVED," BUT A VETERAN OF THE 2ND MISSOURI INFANTRY DISAGREED. WRITING IN 1868, HE REMEMBERED DAVIS'S REMARKS: "SOLDIERS, IN GIVING YOU A NEW COMMANDER I HAVE CHOSEN ONE WHO HAS STRUCK IN THE CAUSE OF THE CONFEDERACY AN HONEST IF NOT A SUCCESSFUL BLOW." THE WORDS WERE IMMEDIATELY CONSTRUED "TO IMPUGN THE HONOR, FIDELITY AND STANDING" OF GENERAL JOHNSTON, QUALITIES WHICH "WERE BEYOND SUSPICION OR THE SLIGHTEST TAINT."[1]

DAVIS AND HIS GENERALS AGREED THAT THE BEST AVAILABLE COURSE OF ACTION WAS FOR HOOD TO MOVE HIS ARMY NORTH OF THE CHATTAHOOCHEE RIVER IN AN ATTEMPT TO WORK AGAINST SHERMAN'S LINES OF COMMUNICATION. STEWART'S CORPS, INCLUDING FRENCH'S DIVISION AND THE 1ST/4TH MISSOURI INFANTRY, WAS ORDERED NORTHWARD FOLLOWING THE LINE OF THE WESTERN & ATLANTIC RAILROAD, SHERMAN'S SUPPLY LINE TO CHATTANOOGA. ON OCTOBER 4, STEWART'S CORPS SWEPT UP SMALL FEDERAL GARRISONS AT BIG SHANTY (NOW KENNESAW) AND ACWORTH. THAT AFTERNOON, FRENCH

NORTH THROUGH GEORGIA

RECEIVED ORDERS FOR HIS DIVISION TO CONTINUE TO THE NORTHWEST TO IMPEDE THE RAILROAD AT ALLATOONA AND CONTINUE ON TO DESTROY THE RAILROAD BRIDGE OVER THE ETOWAH RIVER BETWEEN ALLATOONA AND CARTERSVILLE. AS FRENCH PREPARED TO MOVE, HE LEARNED FROM LOCAL CIVILIANS THAT THE UNION ARMY HAD BUILT FORTIFICATIONS AT ALLATOONA PASS AND STILL OCCUPIED THEM.[2]

AN EAST-WEST RIDGE WAS THE PROMINENT FEATURE AT ALLATOONA. TO MAKE THE RIDGE PASSABLE FOR THE WESTERN & ATLANTIC RAILROAD, A NORTH-SOUTH CUT SIXTY-FIVE FEET DEEP HAD BEEN MADE IN THE RIDGE. ALLATOONA LAY AT THE SOUTHERN END OF THE RAILROAD CUT, THE ALLATOONA PASS. ON THE RIDGE EAST OF THE CUT, THE UNION ARMY BUILT THREE REDOUBTS. ON THE WESTERN SIDE OF THE CUT, A PENTAGON-SHAPED WORK OF RAILROAD TIES CALLED THE STAR FORT HAD BEEN BUILT, PROTECTED BY "OUTER WORKS AND APPROACHES."[3]

FEWER THAN 2,000 UNION SOLDIERS UNDER BRIGADIER GENERAL JOHN M. CORSE HELD THE POSITIONS AT ALLATOONA PASS. FRENCH'S THREE BRIGADES NUMBERED ABOUT 3,200 MEN. COCKRELL'S MISSOURI BRIGADE FORMED THE DIVISION'S RIGHT AND ATTACKED THE STAR FORT FROM THE WEST. ECTOR'S TEXAS BRIGADE, UNDER GENERAL WILLIAM H. YOUNG, WAS TO COCKRELL'S LEFT. SEARS' MISSISSIPPI BRIGADE ATTACKED THE FEDERAL POSITIONS FROM THE NORTH TO OCCUPY THE ATTENTION OF THE FEDERAL TROOPS ON THE EASTERN SIDE OF THE ALLATOONA RAILROAD CUT.

IN RECOUNTING THE STORY OF ALLATOONA, BOYCE MENTIONS THAT HE HAD JUST RECEIVED HIS COMMISSION AS THE CAPTAIN OF COMPANY D. IN THE BATTLE, BOYCE RECEIVED HIS SECOND WOUND OF THE WAR, A WOUND TO THE NECK, AND IN RECOUNTING THE CASUALTIES, BOYCE AGAIN IDENTIFIES HIMSELF AS A CAPTAIN. UNFORTUNATELY, NO EVIDENCE OF HIS PROMOTION IS FOUND IN HIS SERVICE RECORDS. AFTER AUGUST OF 1863, BOYCE ROUTINELY SIGNED THE MUSTER ROLLS FOR COMPANY D, 1ST/4TH MISSOURI INFANTRY, AS COMMANDER OF THE COMPANY WHILE INDICATING HIS RANK AS FIRST LIEUTENANT. GIVEN

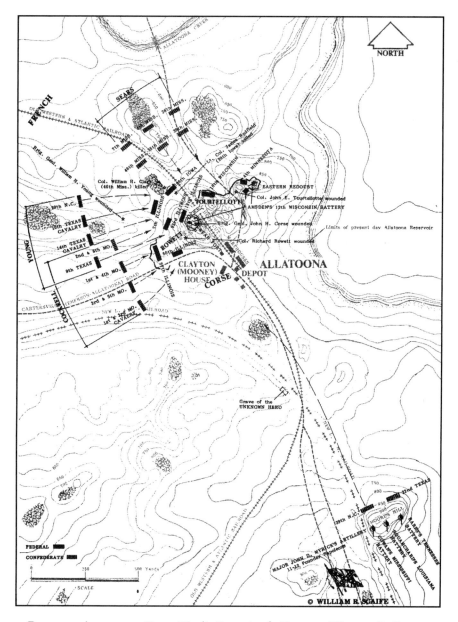

BATTLE OF ALLATOONA. FROM *Hood's Campaign for Tennessee,* WILLIAM R. SCAIFE, 1986, WITH PERMISSION FROM THE WILLIAM R. SCAIFE FAMILY.

NORTH THROUGH GEORGIA

THE REGIMENT'S CONSTANT MOVEMENT AND TERRIBLE CASUALTIES IN THE LAST FEW MONTHS OF THE WAR, IT IS LIKELY THAT ARMY ADMINISTRATION RECEIVED MINIMAL ATTENTION. BOYCE'S SIGNATURE ON HIS PAROLE AT MERIDIAN, MISSISSIPPI, ON MAY 19, 1865, IDENTIFIES HIM AS FIRST LIEUTENANT OF COMPANY D, 1ST/4TH MISSOURI INFANTRY, BUT HE WAS WITHOUT DOUBT "CAPTAIN JOE" TO THOSE WITH WHOM HE SERVED.

About the last of September the reorganization of the army was completed and we started north, striking the Georgia Central railroad near Marietta. This was the road which Sherman depended upon for his supplies. "To destroy is a soldier's joy." Here was property belonging to our friends, but this was no concern of ours. The orders were to tear up the tracks, and at once the work was begun. Huge fires of ties were built, rails laid across them, the centre heated to a red heat, when they were carried over to the trees and bent until the ends met. In some cases the rails were twisted around the trunks of the trees forming a ring, and in every way possible destroying their usefulness. We continued this work until we reached the vicinity of Allatoona, when on the morning of the 5th of October we formed line of battle and sent a demand to Gen. Corse, commanding the federal forces, to surrender.[4] To this he refused compliance so we were ordered by Gen. French to assault the works.

The fortifications of Allatoona, as near as can be remembered from hasty glances at them during the fight, consisted of first, a line of rifle-pits for skirmishers, next, a strong abatis and an infantry parapet with two six-pounder guns firing through embrasures, next in rear was a strong enclosed fort about twelve feet high surrounded by a ditch too deep for escalade.

Gen. Cockrell formed the brigade for attack with First and Third Missouri cavalry dismounted, Col. Gates, on the right; Third and Fifth Missouri infantry commanded by Maj. Waddell, right centre; First and Fourth Missouri, left centre, Col. Garland; Second and Sixth Missouri, Col. Flourn[o]y, on the left.[5] Ector's brigade of Texans, commanded by Gen. Young, were supporting us in a second line.[6] Our skirmishers were already out, among them Capt. Goah Stewart's company of the First Missouri, and

PETER C. FLOURNOY COMMANDED THE
2ND/6TH MISSOURI INFANTRY. COPY FROM
AN 1865 PHOTO.

they were now ordered forward.[7] The federal skirmishers were quickly driven in, and the Missouri brigade surged forward for another deadly struggle with the boys in blue, who received us with a hot fire as we charged up the hill, some 300 yards long. Our first trouble was in scrambling through and over the abatis, which was, I think, thickly laced with telegraph wire, where we lost many men.[8] This passed, the men instinctively reformed and the brigade preserving fair alignment, went on with a yell. As we gained the smoking, roaring parapet I observed the federal flag right in front and made for it; then the thought came up, "I have just gained my captain's commission, give others a chance," and I yelled at Sergt. John Ragland of our regiment, "John, go for those colors," and with a daring leap John tore them from their bearer's grasp, who received a clod of hard clay from the hand of the writer between the eyes at the same instant.[9] The flag belonged to an Illinois regiment. John Ragland was sent to Richmond with this flag, and won his lieutenant's commission.[10]

The federals stood right up to their work, and we, for a few seconds, had what the boys call "a —— of a time." Our Texas friends in the second line— Ector's brigade—caught up and went over with us. As our boys swarmed over the parapet the bayonet was freely used by both sides, officers firing their pistols, and many throwing sticks and stones. This melee was quickly ended by the surrender of most of the defenders, very few of whom reached their large fort in the rear. All this time our own batteries were silent. They had been ordered to a hill on our right, to enfilade the position and why they did not open fire was and still is a mystery.[11]

This was, for the time engaged, the bloodiest fight we were ever in, and our loss was heavy. Corse's men fought like devils.

We now received and replied to a hot fire from the big fort, and soon stopped their artillerists from looking through their embrasures, silencing their guns. At this point Gen. French ordered the line to fall back. This order was disregarded, but a second peremptory order soon came, and was reluctantly obeyed.[12]

We moved back to the point where we commenced the attack. The loss of the First Missouri was very heavy in killed and wounded. We lost several excellent officers, among the killed I recollect Capts. [A. C.] Patton and Andrew J. Byrne; Lieuts. William Dunnica, Thomas Shelby, Girard A. Foote; Sergts. Chandler Parsons and Gus O'Neil. Wounded, Capts. Stewart and Boyce, Lieut. William A. Byrd, color-bearer; Sergts. John J. Corkery, Ed. J. Stiles and John Spane. On leaving Allatoona we left our killed with the enemy and such of the wounded as were unable to keep up with us on the march.[13]

A detachment of the garrison at Allatoona, which occupied a blockhouse in the vicinity, was captured by a portion of our division while the assault on Allatoona was going on.[14] It consisted of several companies of infantry from Wisconsin, commanded by Capts. Carpenter and O'Brien. The latter was from Mineral Point. These officers, if alive, will recollect the writer, as he divided his scanty rations with them. Capt. O'Brien and I had quite a laugh at Capt. Carpenter, who had just received his commission, and with it a new uniform, which he had put on that morning. In talking to us O'Brien said: "It's a shame to send a man to prison who is as nicely dressed as Carpenter."

He replied: "O'Brien, it's all right for you, as your clothes are not much account anyhow, and you have been a captain for some time; but just think of my case; I am so well fixed up that really I hate to sit down anywhere. If I had my old clothes on I wouldn't feel so bad about it." Then he would say: "Boyce, that's mighty poor cooking you have got in your haversack. If you fellows had gone into this fight for grub, instead of blood and prisoners, you would have a d—d sight better spread to offer your unwilling guests."

Carpenter was a trump. I hope he and O'Brien escaped the hardships of prison life. If they are alive I sincerely trust they are happy and prosperous, and that hard times have never forced them to Confederate fare.[15]

We continued our march up the railroad for several days, destroying the rails and ties, and about the 12th of October our command reached Tilton, a station on the Western and Atlantic railroad, about fifty miles north of Allatoona. This place was a natural defence. A creek ran by the camp, and in the middle of it was a small island, on which the blockhouse was erected. A foot-bridge connected the island with the shore. The position was guarded by the Seventeenth Iowa regiment.[16]

The writer was ordered forward by Gen. Cockrell to demand the surrender of the place, and while doing so, took occasion to view the defences. The walk across the foot-bridge was only wide enough for one man, and the water surrounding the island too deep to ford, so that really to attempt to take the place by a rush would have been disastrous. The logs forming the walls were set in the ground on end, and small holes were cut for the infantry to fire through. The line of fire was on a level with the slope up to the house, and as the house was made of heavy pine logs and the door so arranged that only one man at a time could enter, it was just impossible to take it with infantry. This was a discovery rather startling. I took a good look at the camp and found it deserted, as everybody belonging to it had been ordered to the block-house. A large lot of supplies was in the army wagons near by, and coffee, bacon and shoes, etc., in great abundance. Going out to the enemy with a flag of truce and demanding a surrender is mighty ticklish work, and you will be in good luck if they don't shoot you down for your answer. You have got to look sharp and think quick. If you don't bring back the desired answer, you had better have plenty of news for the general. Well, I sized up the place while waiting at the end of the bridge. The door was swung open and the colonel came forward. He was a large, handsome man, from Keokuk, I believe.[17] I delivered my message, when he started to say he was there to defend and not to surrender, etc.

I smiled and said: "That's all right, colonel, but we have a mighty big force."

"Yes," he replied, "I know how you fellows talk. Why, you are only a lot of cavalry on a raid." I showed him the facings on my coats, which were blue, and called his attention to the fact that the facings of the cavalry were yellow, but he would not believe me. I kept up the conversation as long as I possibly could, as Gen. Cockrell said: "If you can't get the surrender out of the commanding officer, give him all the talk you can until I can get a battery up behind that hill over there to our left."

Well, at last the colonel laughed and said: "My young friend, you just go back to Gen. Cockrell with my compliments, and tell him, if he wants this place worse than I do, to come and take it."

I reported the interview to Gen. Cockrell, who ordered me to take charge of my company, which was on the skirmish line. In the meantime the battery was taking position, and, as the firing was renewed by our boys, we kept the defenders of the blockhouse pretty busy. Upon reaching the company I called up Joe Donovan, Robert Bonner and John Plunkett and told them where the supplies were. We arranged then and there that they would each take three men of our company, and when the Iowa boys surrendered they were to make a rush and carry off the bacon, sugar, shoes, clothing, coffee and rubber blankets. They were instructed under no circumstances to take off anything except that for which they were detailed.

We just "laid low" and waited with watering mouths for the good things the writer had seen. We could afford to wait, as our position secured us against the enemy's fire. Suddenly four pieces of artillery opened on the blockhouse. They were not over 100 yards distant from it. Only two or three rounds were necessary. The defenders came out like bees from a beehive overturned. The first thing thrown out was the flag, a nice silk one. Then came the men and the big colonel.

"Don't shoot, we surrender!" "We surrender!" throwing down muskets, waving handkerchiefs and holding up hands. This was just what we were waiting for. [18]

Then the grand rush took place. We made right for the wagons and for the supplies. The details carried out their instructions to the letter, and it was the wonder of our regiment how well we selected our plunder. It was a glorious victory for Co. D. We had "sure enough" coffee, condensed milk, hams, bacon, sauerkraut, sugar, corned beef, crackers, etc., etc. The entire brigade was well supplied with good things for many days after. That night we had a regular banquet, and we earned it, too, as rations were scarce and far between.

We were fortunate in securing late papers from St. Louis, the *Republican* and *Democrat*. We were greatly amused at the list of names published of those drafted, as many of them were old friends. Sergt. Denny Callahan said, "We are very lucky to be where we are, for if we were at home the divils in St. Louis would draft us into the service to fight against ourselves."[19]

I hunted up the big colonel and congratulated him upon his escape from injury.[20] He was very glad to see me. He lost only one man killed and one wounded. It was impossible to stay in the blockhouse under artillery fire. The affair at Tilton was really a picnic. There was no loss of life on our side, and I believe the only man hurt in the entire brigade was a sergeant in the Second Missouri regiment, who was trying to roll off a barrel of corned beef before the place surrendered. He was stung in the heel by a ball fired by a sharpshooter, but he got away with the beef before he complained of his hurt. His devotion to his mess was rewarded by a ride in the commissary wagon until he was able to walk.

The experience of some of the command was amusing. One of the brigade made for the sutler's tent, and dashing into the crowd which had preceded him, he saw a large open trunk which had been fully examined by his comrades. He cried out: "Well, boys, you have certainly left something." He made a dive at the trunk with both hands and secured a handful of fish-hooks, which kept him busy for several hours cutting out of his fingers. He took it in good part and laughed at his mishap after he got through swearing at the boys, who laughed heartily at his share of the plunder.

The next morning we started up the railroad with our prisoners and well supplied haversacks, continuing our march without any further trouble from the enemy. We soon reached Dalton, where we found a part of Cleburne's division in charge of a lot of negro soldiers who had been captured at this point. We were relieved of our prisoners here by some of our cavalry.[21]

NORTH THROUGH GEORGIA

ENDNOTES

1. Anderson, *Memoirs,* 390–391.

2. French, *Two Wars,* 225.

3. *Ibid.,* 232.

4. John Murray Corse began his military service as a major in the 6th Iowa Infantry in 1861. Promoted to brigadier general for his accomplishments at Vicksburg, he had been badly wounded at Chattanooga. At this point he commanded the garrison at Allatoona. Warner, *Generals in Gray,* 94–95.

5. Elijah Gates was a farmer in Buchanan County, Missouri, near St. Joseph when the war started, and he organized a company of militia and was elected its captain. When the 1st Missouri Cavalry was organized, Gates was elected its colonel. When the 1st and 3rd Cavalry were consolidated, he continued to command the combined units. Moore, *Confederate Military History: Missouri,* 296–297.

Owen Waddell began his service as a lieutenant in the Missouri State Guard. When the 5th Missouri Infantry was organized, he was elected its major. Waddell was leading his regiment in Colonel McCown's absence. He was mortally wounded, shot in the abdomen, on the parapet at Allatoona. Anderson, *Memoirs,* 564. Bevier, *History of the First and Second Missouri Confederate Brigades,* 246.

Peter C. Flournoy began his military experience as a private in the 1st Virginia Infantry during the Mexican War. In 1861, Flournoy was a physician living in Linneus, Missouri. He was elected captain of Company K, 2nd Missouri Infantry in January 1863. Flournoy's advancement to colonel of the regiment was "a rather unusual occurrence," as a member of his regiment recalled it. By seniority, Major Tom Carter should have advanced when the position became vacant, but Carter and the other captains senior to Flournoy waived rank in favor of Flournoy's advancement because "the Missourians were fighting for objects far dearer than self-advancement, and they wanted men to direct and lead them who were most capable of command." Anderson, *Memoirs,* 372, 559.

6. William Hugh Young was a native of Boonville, Missouri, but grew up in Texas. In September 1861 he returned to Texas from the University of Virginia to recruit a company for Confederate service. Wounded twice at Kennesaw Mountain, Young was promoted to brigadier general on August 15, 1864, after Ector lost a leg in the Atlanta campaign. Warner, *Generals in Gray,* 348– 349.

7. Goah W. Stewart of Pemiscot County, Missouri, tried to visit his home following his parole at Vicksburg but was captured in New Madrid County, Missouri, and imprisoned in the Gratiot Street Prison in St. Louis. He escaped on February 4, 1864, and succeeded in returning to his regiment. Goah W. Stewart Papers (R699), Western Historical Manuscript Collection, University of Missouri–Rolla.

8. Abatis typically consisted of trees felled with their tops facing in the direction of the anticipated attack. When time was available, the tips of the branches would be cleared and sharpened into spikes. Abatis were very effective in delaying the attacker's advance. Paddy Griffith, *Battle in the Civil War: Generalship and Tactics in America, 1861–1865* (Mansfield, England: Fieldbooks, 1986), 35.

9. Boyce inserted the phrase "of our regiment" with an annotation in *Nicholson.*

10. Sergeant John Ragland of the 1st/4th Missouri Infantry captured the flag of the 39th Iowa Infantry. An officer of the 5th Missouri described the event somewhat more dramatically than Boyce did: "Sergeant John Ragland of the First and Fourth Infantry, captured the flag of an Iowa regiment on the breastworks, waved it in defiance at the enemy and carried it safely away." The 39th Iowa had been driven from its position north of the Star Fort by the attack of Sears' brigade and into the path of Cockrell's attack. The 39th Iowa had apparently become intermingled with the Illinois troops to Boyce's front. Bevier, *History of the First and Second Missouri Confederate Brigades*, 245. Phil Gottschalk, *In Deadly Earnest: The History of the First Missouri Confederate Brigade, C.S.A.* (Columbia: Missouri River Press, 1991), 420.

11. French positioned the division's artillery, eleven 12-pounder Napoleon smoothbore guns, on Moore's Hill more than 1,500 yards to the southeast of the Star Fort. The guns opened fire at 7:00 a.m. while the infantry moved into their assault positions. Around 8:00 a.m., the guns ceased fire while French offered Corse the opportunity to surrender. William R. Scaife, *Hood's Campaign for Tennessee* (Atlanta: Author, 1986), 14. French, *Two Wars*, 226.

12. Around midday, French received a dispatch reporting that Union forces had reached Big Shanty (now Kennesaw) and were moving north to Allatoona. French, his ammunition running low and fearful of being separated from the other divisions of his corps, called off the assault and moved west to rejoin Hood's army. Horn, *The Army of Tennessee,* 376.

13. One of those left behind was Edmund J. "Ned" Stiles. He had been "shot through the center of the breast" at the peak of the attack and was subsequently reported dead. Discovered by Federals after the battle, he was saved by the skill of a Union surgeon. He was later exchanged, returning to the 1st/4th Missouri at Mobile late in the war. Hughes, *Philip Daingerfield Stevenson*, 253, 355–356.

14. In the early hours of October 5, 1864, General French detached the 4th Mississippi Infantry and one piece of artillery to burn the bridge and capture the blockhouse where the Western & Atlantic Railroad crossed Allatoona Creek south of Allatoona. About one hundred Federals garrisoned the blockhouse. French, *Two Wars,* 225.

15. Luman N. Carpenter of Plover, Wisconsin, was promoted to captain of Company E, 18th Wisconsin Infantry, on March 11, 1864. After his capture at

Allatoona, he was sent to a prison camp but escaped to return to duty. Captain O'Brien has not been identified. State of Wisconsin, Adjutant General's Office, *Roster of Wisconsin Volunteers, War of the Rebellion, 1861–1865,* 1886, 95, 134. http://www.wisconsinhistory.org/roster.

16. The action at Tilton, Georgia, occurred on October 13, 1864. *OR,* vol. 39, pt. 1, 758–760.

17. Samson M. Archer commanded Federal infantry at Tilton. Report of Lieutenant Colonel Samson M. Archer, 17th Iowa Infantry, October 16, 1864, *OR,* vol. 39, pt. 1, 758 – 760.

18. The artillerymen aimed at the narrow loopholes in the oak blockhouse and succeeded in getting shells through them, exploding inside. Dense smoke ensued, and 350 men soon surrendered. French, *Two Wars,* 286.

19. Denis Callahan was a resident of St. Louis before enlisting in the 1st Missouri in August of 1861. He was promoted to corporal in the summer of 1862 and to sergeant in Company D, 1st/4th Missouri, in November of the following year. He was wounded on August 17, 1864, during the Atlanta campaign. Callahan is also identified as "Dennis Callaghan." *CSR— Confederate, Missouri.*

The *Missouri Republican* and *Missouri Democrat,* both published in St. Louis, were among the most prominent newspapers in the region. Ironically, the *Missouri Republican* tended to support the positions of the Democrats, while the *Missouri Democrat* strongly supported the Republican party.

20. Archer, "not being well," was paroled rather than retained as a prisoner of war. French, *Two Wars,* 286.

21. The soldiers belonged to the 44th United States Colored Infantry. They had been captured with a company of the 7th Kentucky Cavalry (U.S.), together nearly eight hundred men, at Dalton on October 13. Report of Colonel Lewis Johnson, 44th U.S. Colored Infantry, October 17, 1864. *OR,* vol. 39, pt. 1, 717, 719.

CHAPTER 14
FRANKLIN, TENNESSEE
OCTOBER–DECEMBER 1864

Briefly, ever so briefly, Hood's strategy succeeded. Sherman was uncertain how to respond to Hood's move north. Sherman and his army arrived at Allatoona, Georgia, on October 9, four days after French's attack, and on October 12, he moved north and west to Rome. Hood's army left Dalton on October 14, 1864, and moved south and west to Gadsden, Alabama, arriving there on October 20. French's division camped at the home of Mrs. Sansom, whose daughter Emma had become a Southern heroine.

In late April 1863, Confederate cavalry under Nathan Bedford Forrest were in pursuit of a much larger column of Federal troopers under Colonel Abel D. Streight raiding across northern Alabama. The Union horsemen soon realized that they were the ones in danger, but their hope rallied when they checked Forrest's pursuit after crossing Black Creek near Gadsden. Ever resourceful, Forrest remembered a young girl who had watched his column from a nearby farmhouse, and as he suspected, she volunteered to guide him to a ford. Lifting Emma Sansom up behind him on his horse, Forrest rode off to his guide's instructions and, having seen the route that would allow him to flank his opponent, he quickly returned her to her home. The next day, May 3, Streight and nearly 1,500 Union soldiers surrendered to Forrest and his 600 troopers.[1] Now camped on the Sansom farm, French called on the band of the Missouri brigade

FRANKLIN, TENNESSEE

TO HONOR EMMA'S SERVICE BY PLAYING FOR THE YOUNG WOMAN AND HER MOTHER.[2]

HOOD'S MARCH CONTINUED WEST AND NORTH TO DECATUR, ALABAMA, ON THE TENNESSEE RIVER. ADVANCE ELEMENTS ARRIVED THERE LATE ON OCTOBER 26, BUT FINDING THE PLACE GARRISONED, THE ARMY LEFT THE AREA ON OCTOBER 29 AND FOLLOWED THE TENNESSEE RIVER WEST TO TUSCUMBIA.[3] SHERMAN HAD FOLLOWED BUT STOPPED AT GAYLESVILLE, ALABAMA, JUST A FEW MILES WEST OF THE STATE LINE. GAYLESVILLE WAS IMPORTANT FOR SHERMAN BECAUSE IT ALLOWED HIM TO COVER THE APPROACHES TO EITHER CHATTANOOGA OR ATLANTA, SHOULD HOOD DECIDE HIS ARMY HAD THE STRENGTH TO TRY TO TAKE THEM.

THE CONFEDERATES, HOWEVER, WERE IN NO BETTER POSITION THAN WHEN THEY BEGAN THEIR MOVEMENT A MONTH AGO. THE ARMY WAS STILL TOO BRITTLE TO TURN AND ATTACK SHERMAN. HOOD DECIDED THAT HIS BEST COURSE OF ACTION WAS TO CONTINUE TO MOVE WEST BEFORE MOVING NORTH INTO TENNESSEE. THERE, HOOD SAID, HE COULD "AGAIN DESTROY SHERMAN'S COMMUNICATIONS...[AND] MOVE UPON THOMAS AND SCHOFIELD AND ATTEMPT TO ROUT AND CAPTURE THEIR ARMY BEFORE IT COULD REACH NASHVILLE."[4] SHERMAN BROKE OFF PURSUIT AND RETURNED TO ATLANTA. THERE HIS ARMIES WOULD REMAIN UNTIL MID-NOVEMBER WHEN HE BURNED THE CITY AND SET OUT ON HIS MARCH THROUGH GEORGIA.[5]

IN SHERMAN'S ASSESSMENT, THE SOLDIERS OF MAJOR GENERALS GEORGE THOMAS AND JOHN SCHOFIELD WOULD BE SUFFICIENT TO DEAL WITH HOOD. THOMAS COMMANDED THE UNION FORCES IN MIDDLE AND SOUTHERN TENNESSEE FROM HIS HEADQUARTERS IN NASHVILLE. OPERATING SOUTH OF NASHVILLE, SCHOFIELD LED A FEDERAL COMMAND AS LARGE AS HOOD'S CONSISTING OF IV CORPS, XXIII CORPS, AND A SIZABLE CAVALRY FORCE UNDER BRIGADIER GENERAL JAMES WILSON. AS EVENTS WOULD SHOW, SHERMAN WAS RIGHT.

WHEN HOOD CROSSED THE TENNESSEE RIVER AT TUSCUMBIA IN MID-NOVEMBER, A COLD WIND BLEW AND SNOW FELL INTERMITTENTLY FOR A WEEK.

OCTOBER–DECEMBER 1864

THE ONLY BENEFIT OF THE BITTER WEATHER WAS THAT IT TURNED ROADS OF MUD MORE THAN FOUR INCHES DEEP INTO GROUND FROZEN SO HARD THAT IT WOULD BEAR THE WAGONS. POORLY PROVIDED WITH THE MATÉRIEL NECESSARY FOR A WINTER CAMPAIGN, HOOD'S TROOPS SLEPT ON THE GROUND IN THE SNOW.[6]

MEANWHILE, AS SHERMAN HAD FORESEEN, SCHOFIELD AND HIS TROOPS WERE WAITING BEHIND THE LINE OF THE DUCK RIVER NEAR COLUMBIA, TENNESSEE. THOMAS WAS RAPIDLY CONCENTRATING HIS DISPERSED FORCES INTO THE FORTIFICATIONS AT NASHVILLE.

We left Dalton to our right, and continued our march to Tuscumbia, Ala., distant about 200 miles west, where we arrived after a fatiguing march of several weeks. During October the nights were cold and the frosts very heavy. It was a dismal journey. Our clothing was not suitable for the severe weather; we were without overcoats, and shoes were scarce. We were obliged to leave behind at Tuscumbia and Florence many men who were so badly shod and clothed that they could not make the march toward Nashville.

The following day we were moved to a point on the river bank (the Tennessee), where we bivouacked for several days. We were bivouacked at Tuscumbia from November 1 until the 20th awaiting the arrival of pontoon boats and supplies so that we could cross the Tennessee River, which was out of banks owing to the heavy and almost incessant rains. Despite the dreary march through cold and rainy weather, exhausting and depressing on troops not prepared for such trials and not enthused by past victories in Georgia, they were anxious to push on to the end and accomplish the defeat of the enemy at all hazards.[7]

In the meantime our pontoon corps had effected a landing on the opposite bank, and in a short time the bridge was laid and we crossed over to Florence. I can't allow this opportunity to pass without paying a deserved compliment to the pontooniers of our army. This bridge was securely constructed and rapidly laid. The river at this point was very wide and the water very high and swift, owing to the winter rains at this time (November). The first section was connected with an island, nearly in midstream, while the second section was laid at the opposite side of the island, connecting with the main shore. I would judge the width to be greater than the Mississippi opposite St. Louis. The entire army crossed on this bridge without any loss of life or baggage. It was really a grand affair, and most of it constructed under fire of the enemy.

On the 20th of November we crossed the river on pontoons and marched through Florence on a cold, rainy day.[8] The mud was thinned by the rain and snow to the consistency of gruel. The road-bed was macadam and our footing sure, but we waded through this awful mess for several miles before reaching the point where we were to bivouac. It took the best part of the night to clean up and make ourselves comfortable.

We were much cheered at this place by meeting Forrest and his cavalry. They had just returned from Johnsonville and other points on the Tennessee River after a grand and victorious campaign. Among his troopers we saw our old friends of the famous Second Missouri Cavalry, Col. Bob McC[ulloch], and King's 2nd Missouri Battery.[9] This was a superb company of flying artillery, well equipped and drilled to perfection, commanded by Captain Farris and J. Russell Dougherty.[10] Most of its members were from St. Charles, Mo.[11] These two commands represented Missouri with Forrest's cavalry during most of the war, and they always bore Missouri's banner in the front of the conflict with the enemy.

After a few days at Florence we started north with the army for Middle Tennessee. The morning we moved out on the road was gloomy and cloudy. Presently a snowstorm set in, the first heavy snow of the season. The men set up a shout and hurrahed for Missouri. "This is the kind of weather we want, regular old Missouri weather. This is none of your Southern rains; this is something decent. Hurrah for old Missouri! We are on our way home." After several hours the sun came out. We had by this time reached the pike road, and from that time on we had delightful weather and most excellent roads. Very little rain, the nights cool and slightly frosty, the days warm and pleasant.

This march was kept up for several days. We were received everywhere with great kindness by the people along our route. We passed through the finest farming country we ever saw, and, to the enemy's credit, there were not signs of destruction to private property, such as we saw in Georgia and Alabama.

We had several brushes with the enemy during our advance, but they were only skirmishes and did not give us any concern until the morning of the 30th of November, when a heavy skirmish line was thrown out from our brigade on the left of us. We marched in parallel lines and we (the main body) mostly on the road or pike passing through Spring Hill. I believe we were the advance infantry of Hood's army that day.[12]

Forrest was in our front with his cavalry, and he crowded the enemy fiercely at every point. This was very evident to us as he abandoned wagons of commissary stores. The enemy was too hotly pressed to have time to unhitch the mules. We found the poor creatures dead in their harness, having been shot through the head by the drivers or rear guard. Their bodies were still warm and smoking from the great exertion made to escape our advance.

Forrest was certainly the "Wizard of the Saddle," and he must have traveled like the wind, for on the road near Franklin we saw two locomotives which he captured, steam up and blowing off seemingly with indignation at their bad luck.

The citizens, nearly all old people or boys too young for military service, and any number of enthusiastic young ladies lined the fences, cheering us and crying out, "Push on, boys; you will capture all of the Yanks soon. They have just passed here on the dead run." We received this news with joyous cheers, and kept our double-quick step along the road for several hours. About noon we reached a point near Franklin, a range of hills, and after passing over them came out in full view of the federal position.[13]

The ground appeared to us as level as a floor. The main army came on the field, and the divisions of Loring and Walthall of our corps (Stewart's) took position for the battle. In the rear of Cheatham's and Cleburne's divisions our division (French's) was the reserve. It consisted of Cockrell's and Sears' brigade. Our other brigade, Ector's Texans, was not with us that day, having been left behind at Florence on guard duty of some kind.[14] After considerable delay the Army of Tennessee was in position. It was a beautiful sight. As far as the eye could see it beheld troops moving into position for

FRANKLIN, TENNESSEE

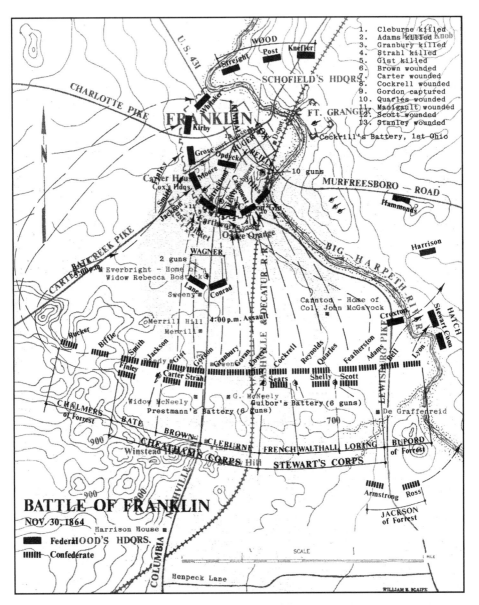

BATTLE OF FRANKLIN. FROM *Hood's Campaign for Tennessee*, WILLIAM R. SCAIFE, 1986,
WITH PERMISSION FROM THE WILLIAM R. SCAIFE FAMILY.

the attack. It looked like a magnificent review. The troops were placed in echelon, and while moving to their places, were it not for the shells which rushed over us, one would think we were getting ready for inspection.

While we were in line of battle some one in the company, impressed with the scene, quoted Nelson's famous order at Trafalgar, "England expects every man to do his duty."[15] Sergt. Denny Callahan took it up at once and said, "It's d——d little duty England would get out of this Irish crowd." (Nearly all the company, and regiment too, were composed of Irishmen or their descendants.) "If I thought we were helping England in any way I would quit right here. This is not a free fight by any means. The Yanks are bad enough, but the Lord deliver us from England. May the curse of the crows rest on her."[16] The laugh Denny raised at this was long and hearty. They were noble fellows, indeed, laughing and joking in the face of death. Four years of war hardens men, and yet there was hardly one in the command over 22 years of age.

About 4 o'clock the corps of Lee and Cheatham were ready for the grand assault.[17] The sun was going down behind a bank of dark clouds, as if to hide from his sight the impending slaughter. His slanting rays threw a crimson light over the field and intrenchments in front, prophetic of our fate. Our brigade was in the rear, formed in the same order as at Allatoona's bloody field, recollections of which were so many thrilling reminders that it was no boy's play to charge this veteran Western infantry when well intrenched.[18] Gen. Cockrell gave orders to march straight for the position in quick time and not to fire a shot until we gained the top of the works; then, when the decisive moment arrived, in clear, ringing tones, gave the final commands. "Shoulder arms! Right shoulder shift arms! Brigade forward! Guide centre! Music! Quick time! March!" and this array of hardened veterans, every eye straight to the front, in actual perfection of drill and discipline, moved forward to our last and bloodiest charge.

Our brass band, one of the finest in the army, went up with us, starting off with "The Bonnie Blue Flag," changing to "Dixie" as we reached the deadly point.[19] As it was an unusual thing for the 'tooters' to go up in a charge with the 'shooters,' I give the names of the veterans composing the band. Every one had carried his musket in the ranks for two years and through many battles, and I believe all of them would have instantly exchanged their instruments for muskets if ordered to remain in the rear. They were: Prof. John O'Neil (leader), John and Chris O'Neil, James and Thad Doyle, Charles Ketchum, Samuel Lyon, James Young, Shelby Jones, James Roboinet, and Simeon Phillips.

The enemy instantly opened heavily with musketry and artillery in front and an enfilading fire from a battery on our right, on the other side of Harpeth river, which was deliberate and deadly, as we fired not a shot in return. Men commenced dropping fast from the start. The distance we marched from our position where we first formed line of battle to the enemy's works was about 900 yards. In that space our flag fell three times. J[ohn] T. Donovan, ensign, of St. Louis was the first to fall, struck down and badly hurt by a fragment of shell. Two other members of the regiment, John S. Harris and Robert Bentl[e]y, were killed in a few moments after while carrying it.[20] Sergt. Denny Callahan was the last bearer, and this brave Irish boy carried it successfully to the works where he planted it, and was wounded and captured, the flag falling into the hands of the Federals, when we were forced from the position.[21]

Advancing in echelon (stair-step) order, our long swinging step soon brought us abreast of Cleburne's division, just to the right of the Franklin pike, and with that superb command we crossed the enemy's advance line of rifle pits, raised the glorious old yell, and rushed upon the main works, a frantic, maddened body of devils, every sense lost in the delirium of the charge save one overpowering impulse to reach the enemy and kill, murder, destroy. On and on we went, right up to the murderous parapet, delivered one smashing volley as Gen. Cockrell had directed, and the line rolled over the works with empty guns, the bayonet now their only trust. I should have said what was left of the line, for the ground in the rear was all too thickly covered with the bodies of our comrades.[22] Our colonel, Garland, of St. Louis was killed soon after we started, and as senior captain the command of the regiment devolved upon me.[23]

As we crossed the rifle-pits our line was delayed a second or two, and unconsciously the writer got several yards in advance, but Lieut. A. B. Barnett, Dick Salsbury, Robt. Bonner, now of Sedalia, Mo., and Sergt.

COLONEL HUGH A. GARLAND COMMANDED THE 1ST/4TH MISSOURI
AFTER THE DEATH OF A. C. RILEY IN MAY 1864 UNTIL HE WAS
KILLED IN ACTION AT FRANKLIN, TENNESSEE, IN NOVEMBER.

FRANKLIN, TENNESSEE

Denny Callahan caught up with him, and, without intending to do so, we led the line over the last few steps up to the ditch, where we all went down together. I made a stroke at a bluecoat, felt my leg give way and fell on top of the works. He was too quick for me, my sword flying from my hand. In another second our men were on top of the parapet. The enemy's fire ceased abruptly and I crawled forward and picked up my sword; then, finding that I could walk a little, started back to hunt for a surgeon, but my wound was too severe and I fell. Two slightly wounded men of the 5th Missouri assisted me off the field and placed me in an ambulance of General Quarles.[24]

The enemy gave way and we made another successful assault. It may sound boastful, but it is true, that never, during the entire war, did our Missouri command fail to carry a line we were ordered to take, and never did the enemy succeed in breaking our line. This can be said of very few commands in all the history of war, but the official reports of both sides agree in confirming the statement. It is my first boast and shall be my last.

But our triumph was very short. With empty guns, without officers, out of breath, our thin line rested a few seconds, when it was assailed by the enemy's second line. The scene inside the fatal fortifications of Corinth was repeated. A solid wall of blue infantry advanced at the double-quick and poured in a volley. It was too much. Our brave fellows came out of the works as quickly as they had entered them and sought refuge behind the rifle pits a short distance back.

As we moved forward to charge, two guns of Guibor's St. Louis battery, under command of Lieuts. A. W. Harris and Sam Kennard, advanced with us and opened fire at close range.[25] As I limped back, I saw the cannoneers pushing their guns by hand to the front, right up to the rifle-pits, where the infantry rallied upon them, and all opened fire for a short time, when night put a stop to the slaughter. During this last firing nearly all of our wounded lying in front were killed by the enemy's fire. Poor fellows! Their cries for help and for water could occasionally be heard, but no one could reach them, and they were gradually silenced by the fire from that awful parapet.

After midnight the enemy withdrew, leaving his dead and severely wounded in our possession. Following the custom of the federal authorities in similar battles, this might be claimed as a Confederate victory. Well, I can safely say, just two such victories will wipe out any army the power of man can organize. Surely, "the path of glory leads but to the grave."[26]

Our appalling loss was not generally realized until next morning, when a ghastly sight was revealed to those still living. Among the dead of our regiment was Col. Hugh A. Garland, brave and daring in battle, in camp gentle as a child and always in good humor; Capt. Cadmus Bray, Lieuts. A. B. Barnett, [George Riley] Cannon, Sergt. William Hopkins. Of the wounded I remember Lieut. Harry Thompson and Sergt. Jones.

The heroic bravery and thorough discipline of our brigade on the field of Franklin almost lost them their organization as Missourians. Those remaining did not make a good sized regiment, while the regiments looked like companies. Our regiment had but three officers left for duty, Capt. James Wickersham (now of Lebanon, Mo.) and Lieuts. James Kennerly and Patrick Collins.[27] This loss was proportionate throughout the brigade.

Our army was a wreck. Our comrades were lying in the embrace of death. So many young hearts were stilled forever, which a few hours ago beat high in the prospect of soon being at home in Missouri. The sad news was quickly carried to our people and many, many families of our friends bowed their heads in sorrow for the poor boys laid low on the ill-fated field of Franklin.

Gen. F. M. Cockrell was badly wounded in two places; despite this he led his brigade to the works.[28] Col. Elijah Gates was severely wounded in both arms, losing one by amputation. Maj. James M. Loughborough of St. Louis rode at the front, and dashed his horse upon the works, brave as a lion, waving his hat and cheering us on. Battle is a strange place. Those who appear to be in the most danger escape without injury. Such was Loughborough's case. I think he was the only one of Gen. Cockrell's staff who escaped unhurt.[29]

It is a well-known fact that one man behind a well-intrenched line is equal to five men in front. Thus we were confronted at Franklin. The "War Records" state that Schofield had 25,400 and Hood had 21,874 men without artillery, except two guns brought with him, Guibor's battery.

FRANKLIN, TENNESSEE

The sad duty of burying the dead was commenced and continued through the day until the work was finished. The wounded were sent into Franklin and made as comfortable as possible. Among the killed was General Cleburne, the model soldier. We felt his loss as deeply as the men of his own division. The men would say to one another, "Why, Cleburne is killed!" and appeared to doubt it, as if such a calamity could not befall the army.

Then the death of Capt. Patrick Canniff, commanding the Fifth Missouri, caused us great grief. He was also a model soldier. After passing through so many battles, he was killed when needed most. It appears he was killed after he was wounded, near the works. He was too badly hurt to crawl away to a place of safety, and received his death wound later on.[30] Among the killed were Lieut. William A. Crow, Patrick Marnell, and Thomas Hogan, all from St. Louis.[31]

The day after burying the dead the command took up the line of march towards Nashville, passing to the right of the town of Franklin. After arriving at Nashville the brigade, under command of Col. Peter C. Flournoy, now of Linneus, Mo., was sent to the mouth of Duck River on the outpost duty, passing through Franklin on its way. It did not remain long at this point, as another overwhelming disaster befell what remained of our army at Nashville. It was routed by the enemy and driven off in awful confusion. Couriers brought the news to the brigade and it was hurried off, joining the retreating forces of Hood near Columbia.

On that dreadful retreat, in the midst of winter, the weather turning suddenly and intensely cold, we were followed by a victorious foe who showed no signs of fatigue or desire to let us rest. Our rear guard was engaged all the time and met him with the same unflinching courage they showed in attacking him at Franklin. The men were distressed by hunger and exhaustion. Bloody foot tracks in the frozen show and upon the icy roads were to be seen in many places. Yet, like Napoleon's Old Guard on the retreat from Moscow, they presented a front for fight at all times. The weather was not as severe as a Russian winter, it is true, but the hardships our poor fellows had to endure were similar, because they were so poorly clad and fed. The patriotism of the Confederate soldier can never be doubted by any one familiar with the horrors of that retreat. All his troubles would end if he were to fall out of the ranks and allow himself to be taken. The Federals would clothe him, feed him, administer the oath of loyalty (or royalty, as we used to call it), and send him to his home. In fact many a man marched wearily along within sight of his home. No; he would rather die by exposure than desert his flag. Those who were taken fell overcome by fatigue and hunger. After many days of hardship and nights of suffering, the command reached Bainbridge and recrossed the Tennessee river. At this point the enemy abandoned the pursuit, and Hood and his suffering men proceeded on their way unmolested.

The Missouri troops took a prominent part in the rear guard under Gens. Forrest and Walthall. Col. Bob McCulloch and his Second Missouri Cavalry was always on the alert, while Bledsoe and his noble battery thundered defiance at the enemy almost continuously during the retreat.[32]

All the attempts of the enemy to break the line of the rear guard were in vain. The most remarkable face in connection with the veterans composing this heroic body of men was that when the retreat ended they had as trophies more Federal prisoners than their entire number, and about twelve more pieces of artillery than when they began to fall back from Nashville.

ENDNOTES

1. Brian Steel Wills, *A Battle from the Start: The Life of Nathan Bedford Forrest* (New York: HarperCollins Publishers, 1992), 111–119.

2. French, *Two Wars*, 287.

3. Thomas Robson Hay, *Hood's Tennessee Campaign* (New York: Walter Neale, 1929; reprint: Dayton, OH: Press of Morningside Bookshop, 1976), 46, 57.

4. John B. Hood, *Advance and Retreat: Personal Experiences in the United States and Confederate States Armies* (1880; reprint, Secaucus, NJ: Blue and Grey Press, 1985), 266–267.

5. Cassville, Georgia, was burned on November 5, 1864. Rome followed on November 10, and Marietta on November 13. Sporadic fires had broken out throughout the city over the previous few days, but on November 15, after three days of determined preparation supervised by Sherman's chief engineer, Atlanta went up in flames. Bonds, *War Like the Thunderbolt*, 342–357.

6. Anderson, *Memoirs*, 395. French, *Two Wars*, 290.

7. Hood's army concentrated at Tuscumbia on the southern bank of the Tennessee River on October 31. Hay, *Hood's Tennessee Campaign*, 57.

8. The pontoon bridge was completed on November 2. Lee's corps crossed that day and moved to Florence, Alabama. Heavy rain the next day delayed other troops from crossing. Stewart's corps, including the 1st/4th Missouri Infantry, crossed the Tennessee River on November 19. Hood's army, now reinforced by Forrest's cavalry, resumed its march toward Tennessee early on November 21. Hay, *Hood's Tennessee Campaign*, 62–64.

9. Robert McCulloch was born in Albemarle County, Virginia, in 1820 and later moved to Missouri. Before the war, he was "a plain, blunt farmer... of hard common sense." McCulloch joined the Missouri State Guard in 1861. He became colonel of the 2nd Missouri Cavalry in 1862 but was often detailed to lead a cavalry brigade. "Dark skinned, sun-browned, and black-haired," Colonel McCulloch was known as "Black Bob" to distinguish him from "White Bob": his light complexioned and fair-haired cousin and lieutenant colonel of the 2nd Missouri Cavalry, Robert A. McCulloch. "The 2nd Missouri Cavalry," *The Land We Love* 3 (1867): 276, 279.

10. King's Missouri Battery was originally known as Clark's battery and commanded by Captain Samuel Churchill Clark, grandson of explorer William Clark. Clark was killed at Elkhorn Tavern (Pea Ridge) in 1862, and First Lieutenant Houston King was promoted to command the battery. In November 1864 King was promoted away from the battery, and First Lieutenant James L. Farris was promoted to captain on November 18 to lead the unit. The battery received new guns and harness at Crawfordsville, Mississippi, shortly before meeting Hood's army. Jo. A. Wilson, "The Services of 'Clark's Battery' Through Sixty Engagements," *Missouri Republican*, November 28, 1885.

11. John Russell Dougherty was eighteen and a student in St. Charles, Missouri, before he enlisted and joined the Missouri artillery. An examination of the historic roll of King's battery shows that most of the cannoneers were from western Missouri, not St. Charles. "Historic Roll of Capt. King's Battery, originally known as the Clark Battery or 2nd Missouri," Joint Collection, University of Missouri, Western Historical Manuscript Collection–Columbia and State Historical Society of Missouri Manuscripts.

12. Boyce avoids discussion of Hood's attempt to head off Union major general John Schofield's retreating force at Spring Hill, Tennessee, on November 29–30. At the time Boyce was writing, tempers still flared among Confederate veterans over this "lost opportunity." A modern historian has called Hood's personal version of events "a most erroneous story." Boyce's corps commander, A. P. Stewart, concluded: "The truth is, the failure at Spring Hill was General Hood's own fault." Hay, *Hood's Tennessee Campaign*, 94, 98.

13. Stewart's corps approached Franklin moving roughly from southeast to northwest in the angle formed by the Lewisburg Turnpike and the Harpeth River on the corps' right and the Columbia Pike to its left. Jacob D. Cox, *The Battle of Franklin, Tennessee* (New York: Charles Scribner's Sons, 1897; reprint Dayton, OH: Press of Morningside Bookshop, 1983), endpaper map.

14. French's division formed the left of Stewart's corps, with Sears' brigade in the first line and Cockrell's brigade in the second. Cheatham's and Stewart's corps moved on converging courses. As they drew nearer to Franklin, Cheatham's right (Cleburne's division) overlapped French's troops (Stewart's left). Cox, *The Battle of Franklin*, 148–151.

15. Early on the morning of October 21, 1805, British vice admiral Lord Horatio Nelson retired to the cabin of HMS *Victory* to compose what has become the famous Trafalgar prayer: "England expects that every man will do his duty." The message was signaled to the fleet, which then proceeded to destroy eighteen ships of the French and Spanish navies without the loss of a single British ship. Nelson was killed in the action. David G. Chandler, *Dictionary of the Napoleonic Wars* (New York: MacMillan Publishing Co., 1979), 311–312, 450. Entries for "Nelson" and "Trafalgar."

16. In Irish folklore, crows (rooks) may bring good luck or bad, but "the curse of the crows" is a powerful curse, wishing that no good may come to the person so accursed. "Some Irish Superstitions about Birds," *The Month: A Catholic Magazine and Review* LXXVI (September–December 1892), 37. Rev. Charles Swainson, *The Folk Lore and Provincial Names of British Birds*, vol. 17 (London: Folk-Lore Society, 1886), 87.

17. The corps of Stewart (not Lee) and Cheatham made the initial attack. Lee's corps was still arriving from Spring Hill. The four brigades of Major General Edward Johnson's division of Lee's corps moved an hour after dark to assist Cheatham's corps, entering the combat on Cheatham's left. Hay, *Hood's Tennessee Campaign*, 119. Cox, *The Battle of Franklin*, 151.

18. At Allatoona, the Missouri regiments had been initially aligned left to right as follows: $2^{nd}/6^{th}$ Infantry, $1^{st}/4^{th}$ Infantry, $3^{rd}/5^{th}$ Infantry, and $1^{st}/3^{rd}$ Cavalry (Dismounted). Scaife, *Hood's Campaign for Tennessee*, 13–14.

19. Captain John M. Hickey, Company B, $2^{nd}/6^{th}$ Missouri Infantry, also remembered the band: "Our lines of battle were readily formed, and under the soul-stirring strains of music from our brigade band—'Bonnie Blue Flag' and 'Dixie'—we were ordered to the assault." James E. Payne, too, recalled the role of the band: "Cockrell, leading the well-formed line, advanced to the music of 'The Bould Sojer Boy' played by the brigade band. Reaching a point within two hundred yards of the enemy, the line halted and dressed, the band was sent to the rear and the order to charge at the double was given." William Kavanaugh of Company G, $2^{nd}/6^{th}$ Missouri Infantry, remembered too that "a splendid brass band" advanced in line and "cheered us on with the strains of Dixie and the Bold Soldier Boy," but recalled that "they never played another air after this day; they were entirely put out of business." Bevier, *History of the First and Second Missouri Confederate Brigades*, 251. James E. Payne, "Cockrell's Missouri Brigade, C.S.A.," *Confederate Veteran* 37 (1929): 419–420. William H. Kavanaugh Papers, Joint Collection, University of Missouri, Western Historical Manuscript Collection–Columbia and State Historical Society of Missouri Manuscripts.

20. John S. Harris, a native of Kentucky, enlisted with Company E, 1st Missouri, when the regiment was in Kentucky in September 1861 and rose to the rank of corporal. Wounded during the Vicksburg campaign, he was twenty years old when he died of wounds received at Franklin on November 30, 1864. *CSR—Confederate, Missouri.*

Robert M. Bentley was nineteen years old and a resident of Mount Vernon in Jefferson County, Illinois, when he enlisted in Company G, $1^{st}/4^{th}$ Missouri Infantry, at Tuscaloosa, Alabama, in May 1864. Not long after enlisting, he was in hospital for nearly a month, returning to the regiment in July. He died at Franklin on November 30. *CSR—Confederate, Missouri.*

21. Callahan was captured during the Franklin battle and sent north to prison camp, first to Camp Douglas in Chicago and then to Point Lookout, Maryland. *CSR—Confederate, Missouri.*

22. A veteran of the $2^{nd}/6^{th}$ Missouri Infantry remembered that the converging Confederate attack resulted in the Missouri regiments occupying "nearly the center of the lines of the attacking party." "We went over the first line of works without a halt," he recorded, but "before we reached the second line more than 50 per cent of our men had fallen." William H. Kavanaugh Papers, Joint Collection, University of Missouri, Western Historical Manuscript Collection–Columbia and State Historical Society of Missouri Manuscripts.

23. Boyce added the sentence "Our colonel, Garland…" to his account of Franklin when it was published in *Confederate Veteran* 24 (1916): 103. His

account elicited a response from veteran James K. Merrifield, a member of Company C, 88th Illinois Infantry: "Colonel Garland…went down about fifty feet in front of the works….The flag of the regiment went down about the same time. Colonel Garland was not killed when he fell, but was wounded in the knee, and had he been taken off the field at once he doubtless would have recovered; but in the many charges made after he fell he received his death wounds." Merrifield helped Garland with his canteen and returned to the fight.

In his response, Merrifield addressed an account concerning Garland's death by Union General Jacob Cox (*The Battle of Franklin, Tennessee*, 1897) and by Boyce, saying "Both are wrong." In the margin of his copy of *Confederate Veteran*, now in the possession of the MHM Archives, Boyce clearly wrote: "I know my statement is correct." He signed his name following the remark to leave no doubt concerning its veracity.

Garland was the son of Hugh A. Garland Sr. who, with his partner Lyman Decatur Norris, successfully argued *Scott v. Emerson* in June 1852 before the Supreme Court of Missouri, whose decision confirmed Dred Scott's status as a slave. The decision in Missouri led to the United States Supreme Court case of *Scott v. Sandford*. J. K. Merrifield, "Col. Hugh Garland—Captured Flags," *Confederate Veteran* 24 (1916): 551–552. Marshall D. Hier, "Garland & Norris, Slaveowner Emerson's 'Dream Team'—Part I," *St. Louis Bar Journal* (Fall 1999): 45–47.

On March 28, 1896, Merrifield was awarded the Medal of Honor for capturing two flags during the battle at Franklin and returning them to Federal lines. United States Army, Medal of Honor at http://www.history.army.mil/html/moh.

24. Brigadier General William Andrew Quarles led a brigade in Walthall's division and was severely wounded in the advance against Franklin. Cox, *The Battle of Franklin, Tennessee*, 151.

25. Samuel M. Kennard was born at Lexington, Kentucky, in 1842 and moved to St. Louis as a youth. He joined the Missouri Volunteer Militia in February, 1861, and when war came, he enlisted in the 1st Missouri Infantry. Six months later, he transferred to Guibor's battery. Moore, *Confederate Military History: Missouri*, 333–334. Harris has not been identified.

26. Boyce quotes a line from English poet Thomas Gray's "Elegy Written in a Country Church-Yard," first published in 1751.

27. James H. Wickersham had been a lieutenant in the 4th Missouri Infantry at its organization in 1861 and served continuously with the consolidated 1st/4th Missouri Infantry.

Patrick William Collins was one of the original members of Boyce's company, enlisting at Memphis in July 1861 and serving as a sergeant in Company D. A native of Limerick, Ireland, he was a grocer in St. Louis before the war. He was twenty-five years old when he enlisted. In November 1863, he was promoted to second lieutenant for "gallantry at Baker's Creek and the siege of Vicksburg." His service records are unusual in that they note that he served in all of the battles of the 1ˢᵗ Missouri "through all of which he passed without receiving a wound." *CSR—Confederate, Missouri*.

28. Cockrell was shot twice in the right arm. His more serious wounds were through the left leg, just missing the bone, and in the right ankle, where a bullet broke a bone. He received his wounds while on the front line in the middle of the fight. Francis M. Cockrell III, *The Senator from Missouri: The Life and Times of Francis Marion Cockrell* (New York: Exposition Press, 1962), 23–24.

Gates remained mounted after being wounded, and his horse had the sense to move away from the fight. An observer remembered: "His rider was powerless to guide him, both arms shot through and hanging limp by his side." Bevier, *History of the First and Second Missouri Confederate Brigades,* 253.

29. Before the war, James Loughborough was publisher of the *New Era*, a newspaper serving Carondelet, a suburb south of St. Louis. In Carondelet, Loughborough and his wife, Mary, were neighbors of John Bowen, the first colonel of the 1ˢᵗ Missouri Infantry. Loughborough transferred to Confederate service after service in the Missouri State Guard in April 1862, serving as a captain on Price's staff. In July 1864, Loughborough became the assistant adjutant general for Cockrell's Missouri brigade. Files, Carondelet Historical Society, St. Louis. *CSR—Confederate, Missouri.*

30. Veteran George Warren remembered: "Captain Caniff was knocked from his horse by a shot in the right shoulder, and it must have been while lying on the ground, that he was struck in the top of the head, the ball coming out under the chin." Warren quoted in Bevier, *History of the First and Second Missouri Confederate Brigades,* 255.

31. Thomas Hogan had been "my schoolmate during our boyhood years," Boyce reminisced in 1914. Like Boyce, Hogan had been a member of the Missouri Volunteer Militia in St. Louis. He was a sergeant in Company A, 3ʳᵈ/5ᵗʰ Missouri Infantry when he was killed at Franklin.

In May 1864, Hogan wrote to his sister Ellen to make a request: "I hope you, as well as my friends, will remember me in their prayers, as it is to their prayers I owe, through the mercy of God, my almost miraculous escapes from the dangers that surround me...." Hogan's father, William, was so moved to remember his son that he had the text of his letters printed and framed to hang in his home as a constant reminder of his loss. On William Hogan's death, the letters were given to Boyce, then a neighbor. Boyce placed the memento for safekeeping with the Missouri Historical Society. Thomas Hogan Papers, Civil War Collection, MHM Archives.

32. Another who knew the six foot, three inch Hiram Bledsoe described him as "one of the most distinguished battery captains of Price's Missourians." Dabney Herndon Maury, *Recollections of a Virginian in the Mexican, Indian, and Civil Wars*, 3ʳᵈ ed. (New York: Charles Scribner's Sons, 1894), 168.

CHAPTER 15
THE LAST BATTLE

———◆◆◆◆◆———

JANUARY–APRIL 1865

DECADES LATER, WHEN A FRIEND WOULD INQUIRE ABOUT HIS HEALTH, CAPTAIN BOYCE WOULD RESPOND: "I AM ALL RIGHT EXCEPT FOR MY 'FRANKLIN KNEE.'" [1] AT THE TIME, HOWEVER, HIS FRANKLIN WOUND COULD EASILY HAVE PROVED FATAL. BOYCE WAS LEFT BEHIND WITH THE WOUNDED WHEN HOOD'S ARMY MOVED NORTH FROM FRANKLIN TO NASHVILLE. FROM "MR. REECE'S HOUSE 6 MILES SOUTH OF FRANKLIN," BOYCE WROTE TO A FRIEND ON DECEMBER 4, 1864, JUST A FEW DAYS AFTER THE BATTLE. BOYCE HAD BEEN SHOT IN THE RIGHT THIGH, BUT THE FEDERAL BULLET FIRST HIT HIS KNIFE BEFORE GLANCING INTO HIS LEG, MISSING THE BONE. "HAD IT NOT BEEN FOR GOD ALMIGHTY AND MY KNIFE, MY THIGH BONE WOULD HAVE BEEN CRUSHED & I A 'GONNER,'" BOYCE WROTE. THE PAIN OF THE SURGERY TO REMOVE THE BALL HAD CAUSED HIM TO FAINT. THE NERVES WERE CUT, AND HIS SUFFERING WAS INTENSE.

BOYCE CLOSED HIS LETTER BY RECOUNTING THE NAMES OF THE KILLED, DEATHS HE HAD EITHER WITNESSED OR LEARNED OF FROM OTHER WOUNDED MEN. "GOD HAVE MERCY ON US," HE CONCLUDED. "NEARLY THE WHOLE BRIGADE WAS KILLED." [2] BOYCE'S BRIGADE MADE THE ASSAULT AT FRANKLIN WITH 696 OFFICERS AND MEN, AND ONLY 277 REMAINED WHEN IT WAS OVER. NINETEEN OFFICERS AND 79 MEN WERE KILLED, AND 31 OFFICERS AND 198 MEN HAD BEEN WOUNDED. THIRTEEN OFFICERS AND 79 MEN WERE MISSING AFTER THE BATTLE. MORE THAN 60 PERCENT OF THE BRIGADE'S SOLDIERS WERE COUNTED AS CASUALTIES. [3]

THE LAST BATTLE

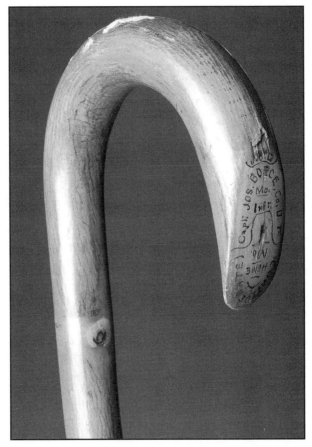

POSTWAR CANE PRESENTED TO CAPTAIN BOYCE, PERHAPS TO
AID HIS "FRANKLIN KNEE," 1905.

HOOD'S WEAKENED ARMY ARRIVED AT NASHVILLE ON DECEMBER 7. UNABLE
TO FORCE THE CITY'S EXTENSIVE ENTRENCHMENTS, HOOD SETTLED IN TO A
DEFENSIVE POSITION SOUTH OF THE CITY. AS A HEAVY FOG LIFTED ON THE
MORNING OF DECEMBER 15, TROOPS FROM FEDERAL MAJOR GENERAL GEORGE
THOMAS'S ARMY STRUCK HOOD'S RIGHT, BUT THE PRIMARY ATTACK CAME ON
HOOD'S LEFT SHORTLY BEFORE MIDDAY. BY NIGHTFALL, HOOD'S ARMY WAS
DRIVEN TO A PRECARIOUS POSITION. THE CONFEDERATES PRESENTED AN EFFEC-
TIVE DEFENSE FOR MOST OF THE DAY ON DECEMBER 16, BUT ANOTHER UNION

MOVE AGAINST THEIR LEFT NEAR SUNDOWN BROKE THE ARMY AND TURNED IT INTO A DISORGANIZED RABBLE. ONLY LEE'S CORPS RETAINED SOME COHESION, AND IT COVERED THE RETREAT SOUTH.[4] THE MISSOURI BRIGADE, REDUCED TO THE SIZE OF A SMALL REGIMENT, HAD EARLIER BEEN ORDERED TO THE EXTREME LEFT FLANK OF THE ARMY AND WAS NOT ENGAGED IN THE BATTLE.[5]

WHEN HOOD'S ARMY RETREATED AFTER THE DEFEAT AT NASHVILLE, BOYCE WAS MOVED TO A HOSPITAL AT UNIONTOWN, ALABAMA. TO THE DISMAY OF THE BOYCE FAMILY, NEWS REACHED THEM IN ST. LOUIS THAT CAPTAIN BOYCE WAS NUMBERED AMONG THE DEAD. ACCORDING TO ANTHONY BOYCE, JOE'S BROTHER, AN OFFICER OF THE REGIMENT HAD BEEN CAPTURED AFTER THE BATTLE AT FRANKLIN AND SENT TO THE PRISON AT ALTON, ILLINOIS. WHILE A PRISONER OF WAR, THE OFFICER WAS VISITED BY HIS OWN BROTHER WHO IN TURN RELATED "THE SAD INTELLIGENCE" OF JOE'S DEATH TO THE BOYCE FAMILY. SEVERAL MONTHS PASSED BEFORE CAPTAIN BOYCE LEARNED OF THE SITUATION.[6]

THE REMNANTS OF HOOD'S ARMY WOULD SOON BE DISPERSED, AND THE MISSOURIANS WOULD BE SENT TO MOBILE. SLOWLY, THE WOUNDED FROM FRANKLIN RETURNED TO THE BRIGADE. GENERAL COCKRELL, THOUGH FAR FROM FULLY RECOVERED FROM HIS WOUNDS, RETURNED TO COMMAND THE DIVISION. COLONEL GATES, FORMERLY COMMANDER OF THE 1ST/3RD MISSOURI CAVALRY (DISMOUNTED), WAS NOW MISSING HIS LEFT ARM, BUT HE TOOK COMMAND OF THE BRIGADE. THE EIGHT PROUD REGIMENTS OF MISSOURIANS COULD NOW MUSTER ONLY FOUR HUNDRED SOLDIERS.

IN THE SUMMER OF 1864, MOBILE WAS IMPORTANT AS ONE OF THE TWO MAJOR CONFEDERATE PORTS OPEN FOR BLOCKADE RUNNERS. A COMBINED EFFORT BY THE UNION NAVY AND ARMY CLOSED THE LOWER END OF MOBILE BAY IN AUGUST. IN MARCH 1865, UNION GENERAL E. R. S. CANBY AND A FLEET OF TRANSPORTS LEFT NEW ORLEANS FOR DAUPHIN ISLAND, THE COLLECTION POINT FOR HIS ATTACK ON MOBILE. CANBY DETERMINED TO USE HIS OVERWHELMING STRENGTH TO ATTACK THE EASTERN LAND DEFENSES OF MOBILE FIRST.

THE LAST BATTLE

MAJOR GENERAL DABNEY H. MAURY COMMANDED THE CONFEDERATE DEFENSES OF MOBILE. OF THE FIVE FOOT, THREE INCH TALL MAURY, ONE VETERAN OBSERVED THAT HE WAS "EVERY INCH A SOLDIER, BUT THERE WERE NOT MANY INCHES OF HIM."[7] BRIGADIER GENERAL ST. JOHN RICHARDSON LIDDELL COMMANDED THE LAND DEFENSES ON THE EASTERN SIDE OF MOBILE BAY. MAURY GAVE LIDDELL, AN EXPERIENCED INFANTRY COMMANDER, COMMAND OF THE DEFENSES ON THE EASTERN SIDE OF MOBILE BAY IN MID-SEPTEMBER, 1864. HE QUICKLY BECAME AWARE OF THE DIFFICULTIES OF HIS POSITION.[8] THE EASTERN DEFENSES WERE A COLLECTION OF UNCONNECTED STRONG POINTS MUCH TOO LARGE FOR THE EFFECTIVE USE OF THE AVAILABLE FORCES. THE TWO MOST IMPORTANT POINTS IN HIS LINE OF DEFENSES WERE SPANISH FORT AND FORT BLAKELY. THE FORT BLAKELY GARRISON INCLUDED THREE SMALL INFANTRY BRIGADES AND THE ARTILLERISTS FOR ITS MORE THAN FORTY GUNS. LIDDELL ESTIMATED THE FORCE TO NUMBER APPROXIMATELY 2,500 MEN. THE SMALL BRIGADE OF MISSOURIANS HELD THE CENTER OF THE FORT BLAKELY DEFENSES, "THE STRONGEST AND BEST FORTIFIED PART OF THE LINE," WITH BRIGADIER GENERAL BRYAN M. THOMAS'S ALABAMA RESERVES TO THEIR RIGHT AND BRIGADIER GENERAL CLAUDIUS SEARS' MISSISSIPPI BRIGADE (NOW COMMANDED BY COLONEL WILLIAM S. BARRY) TO THEIR LEFT. FOUR GUNBOATS PATROLLED THE WATERS OF MOBILE BAY, GIVING SUPPORT TO THE CONFEDERATE LAND DEFENSES.[9]

———◆◆◆◆———

As the writer was not in this campaign, owing to the wounds he received at Franklin, Tenn., and having not fully recovered until after the war had closed, he believes it best to state this fact here, and to say in addition that this paper is written at the urgent request of his comrades so that this series of papers may complete the term of service of the First Missouri Infantry during the entire war. To make this paper complete he will have to quote from Gen. Maury's report of the battle in this vicinity (Mobile), and to use information given by the members of the regiment and brigade who served during this campaign, which was the last of the war.

After crossing the Tennessee river at Bainbridge, the command proceeded on its way to Verona, Miss., where it arrived early in January, after long and tedious marches through stormy and rainy weather, suffering all the time from cold and hardships.[10] It is remarkable the devotion the Missouri Confederate manifested to the Southern confederacy. No danger was too great for him; hardships had no terrors. He was always ready for fight and up to the last moment had an undying belief that his side would ultimately win. Never a complaint about the length of the march or the scarcity of food and clothes, but he drew the line at tobacco. He knew the government had plenty of the weed, and when this portion of his ration was not forthcoming there was trouble in camp "sure enough." No excuse from the commissary would allay his indignation. It was often said by the men while drawing their scanty rations: "You may run short of grub, Mr. Commissary, and we will overlook it, but if you want to see h–ll just run out of tobacco."

The command remained at Verona a month, where it was recruited in health and numbers. Quite an addition was made to the brigade by the wounded from Allatoona and Franklin returning for duty, and the ranks began to grow by these additions until the command mustered nearly 1,000 muskets. Battle-scarred veterans were those Missourians.

Gen. Maury, commanding the department with headquarters at Mobile, wrote the brigade the following letter:

> As for you, you have deserved well of your country. You have been such soldiers as the world has never seen. Three years have passed since first we met in the Boston mountains of Arkansas and marched through the driving snow to attack the enemy's army. From that hour to this you have been voluntary exiles from the land of your birth and the homes of all you love. You were then a mighty host; you are now a remnant of battle-scarred veterans. But your hearts are brave and true; your eyes are bright, and your noble purposes are unshaken. [11]

General Maury was a great favorite with the Missouri troops. He commanded them in one of their early battles, and they were in his department in their last engagement at Blakely.[12]

THE LAST BATTLE

Early in February, 1865, the command was ordered to Mobile. In the meantime, at his own request, Gen. Hood was relieved of the command of the Army of Tennessee, and when the order came for our command to go to Mobile this army was scattered, part of it going to North Carolina to join Gen. Joseph E. Johnston and some to reinforce Maury at Mobile.[13]

Gen. Cockrell took command of the brigade on its way to Mobile. He had only partly recovered from his wounds. Col. Gates came to the brigade about the same time, looking anything but well. He left an arm at Franklin. It was hard to see the men coming in, not yet well from their wounds. When asked why they did not stay away longer they replied: "We were kindly treated by all the people we were with, but we know Mobile is going to be attacked and everyone who is able to load and fire a musket must join his command. There are so few of us left now that every man must come to the front. If we go down we will all go together." This was the spirit that animated Missouri's sons.

Mobile was reached about the second week in February, and the brigade was placed in camp on the shell road, about three miles from town, where it remained until the middle of the following month. Prior to this Gen. Cockrell was placed in command of the division (French's), and Col. Gates took command of the brigade.[14]

About this time the enemy was making demonstrations towards Fort Blakely, when the brigade was sent across Mobile Bay and added its strength to the garrison already there. It was placed on the Pensacola road and did picket duty for several weeks. All wore a saddened, softened look. Friend spoke to friend in a subdued tone of quiet affection, and at the social gatherings around the camp-fires conversation drifted to the past. The loss of so many comrades at Franklin had tinged the thoughts of every man with sorrow, for there is no such genuine affection known to man as that existing between those who have faced death and shared hardships during years of war. This little band of a few hundred men were the survivors of a large division, which division was the select of Missouri's soldiers and patriots, for none others remain in distant states, fighting four long years after their own state is irretrievably lost. Sentiment alone can produce such devotion. All the gold ever coined can not produce it.

Battles and brave deeds were no longer discussed. Such had for a long time been too common to excite attention. The nearest approach to this that can now be called to mind was one night at Gen. Cockrell's tent, where a number of officers had assembled to greet a visiting friend and former comrade. Some one raised the question: "Is there a man in the brigade who has not been wounded?" Each one of the four (formerly eight) regiments was represented, and a careful sifting of evidence resulted in the unanimous opinion that there was not one present for duty in the brigade, from the general to drummer boy, who had not been wounded once. A few had been struck six times. This is a remarkable statement to make, and I should hesitate to make it if many of that group were not living to corroborate it.

As said above, conversation drifted to the past, but battles were not mentioned. The non-military reader will ask, what else could old veterans, after four years of such life, talk about? It is interesting now to recall this peculiarity, that, as the military past and the military future were alike too sombre for social intercourse, the general effort was to recall some pleasant event, where the hospitable homes of our Gulf state friends had been thrown open to us for entertainment when well, or shelter when disabled. And the tender tone of brotherly affection with which each addressed the other easily glided into one of reverence and gratitude to the noble women of the South, who had, far more than they knew, smoothed our path and cheered us to dare everything for ultimate success.

A very large number of these men had wives and children at home in Missouri, or it is more proper to say, in Missouri, but not at home, for many were dependent upon others for shelter. But the husband and father thought of this in silence, never intruding his troubled anxieties upon others, well knowing that each had his own burthen to carry.

It seems strange now to recall the calm, matter of course, way in which the enemy was faced.

When at Blakely, opposite Mobile, the last ditch for our brigade, when the enemy deployed at 800 yards, our men discovered they were new troops from the careful manner in which their skirmishers lay upon the ground with knapsacks placed in front for shelter, while our skirmishers were lounging around, not returning the light, scattering fire. In consequence our skirmishers, five paces apart in the usual rifle pit, had orders to hold their line against a single line of battle, but to fall back before two lines.

Capt. O. F. Guthrie of Gates' regiment was to command this line the next morning. All agreed that the assault was to be made then, and also concurred with his expressed opinion that it was probably his last day, for skirmishers with such orders seldom live to run in. As death was almost certain before the war ended, it made little difference to Guthrie whether he was killed tomorrow or a few months later. The assault was delayed one day and Guthrie still lives.[15]

The situation in this section of country at this time was really deplorable. The army for the defence of the territory embracing Mobile was in a wretched state. The largest part of it had been in Hood's Tennessee campaign, and had met with hardships and defeat, while the commands were so reduced in numbers that it looked like refined cruelty to ask men to fight again. But the necessities of the Confederacy were so great that the expression of Gen. Grant that we were "robbing the cradle and the grave" was too true. Old men, whose hairs had silvered many years ago, whose sons and grandsons had battled for the South under Lee and Stonewall Jackson in Virginia, many of whom were lying in bloody graves far away from Alabama, carried their muskets alongside the cadets—boys ranging in age from 14 to 16 summers. Poor boys, they knew only the bright side of war, waving flags, martial music, smiles from the ladies whose hearts were sore at the many sorrows imprinted by former losses of husbands, sons, brothers and sweethearts.[16] The veterans from the Atlanta and Tennessee campaigns looked kindly on these men and boys who were to help drive back the enemy. It's true it showed the resisting power of the southern people, and what a people can do when pressed, but still possessed of brave hearts. Nevertheless the scene was a sad one, and to this day call up sorrowful memories of a brave and noble people who fought to the last ditch, and true of the Missourians who said when leaving home, we shall fight until we reach the Gulf of Mexico. How many true things are said in jest. They had reached the Gulf.

From Gen. Maury's report the writer takes the following:

"Immediately after the battle of Nashville preparations were commenced by the federals for the reduction of Mobile. Two corps, which had been sent to reinforce Thomas at Nashville, were promptly returned to Canby in New Orleans, and the collection of material and transportation for a regular siege of Mobile commenced. Gen. 'Dick' Taylor agreed with me in the opinion that 10,000 men in Mobile would compel a siege by regular approaches, would occupy the federal troops in the southwest for a long time, and would be as much as the confederacy could spare for such objects. He thought he could send me such a force, and believed that the cavalry under Forrest would be able to defeat Wilson and succor me, and prevent the successful siege of the place if I could hold out for seven days.

"The orders given me by Gen. Beauregard and Gen. Taylor were to save my garrison, after having defended my position as long as was consistent with the ultimate safety of my troops, and to burn all the cotton in the city except that which had been guaranteed protection against such burning by the confederate authorities. Canby organized his forces in Mobile bay and at Pensacola. Two army corps assembled at Pensacola under Gen. Steele. The whole expeditionary force against Mobile consisted of 50,000 infantry, 7,000 cavalry, a very large train of field and siege artillery, a fleet of more than twenty men-of-war and about fifty transports, mostly steamers. The preparation having commenced in December the attack began on the 25th of March.

"My total effective force was 7,700 excellent infantry and artillery, 1,500 cavalry and about three hundred field and siege guns. A naval force of four small gunboats co-operated with my troops.

"The column under Canby marched from Fish river against the position of Spanish Fort. On March the 25th information received through the advanced cavalry induced me to believe that the column from Fish river was not more than 12,000 strong, and expecting it would march by the river road with its left covered by the fleet, I organized a force of 4,500 infantry and ten guns and resolved to give battle to Canby at the crossing of D'Olive creek about two miles distant from the works of Spanish Fort. The troops ordered for this service were the Missouri brigade of Cockrell, Gibson's Louisiana brigade, Ector's Texas and North Carolina brigade and Thomas' brigade of Alabama boy-reserves, and the Third Missouri battery and Culpepper's battery.[17]

THE LAST BATTLE

"I felt confident, and the light of experience justifies the confidence, that had Canby marched upon us with only 12,000 men, we should have beaten him in the field; but he moved by a road which turned our position far to the left, and his force was near 40,000 men. I therefore moved the troops into Spanish Fort and Blakely, and awaited attack in them. I assigned Gen. St. John Liddell to the immediate command of Blakely and Gen. Randall Gibson to the immediate command of Spanish Fort.

"On the 26th of March Canby invested the latter position with a force of one corps, two divisions of infantry, and a large siege train. Another division of infantry invested Blakely at the same time, and the siege of Spanish Fort was prosecuted with the greatest energy."[18]

About this time, the writer received a letter from Capt. A. C. Danner, which he managed to save and unearth after looking through old papers for data, and as an indication of the feeling prevailing in the brigade I insert it. For some time prior to this Danner was serving as paymaster on Gen. Cockrell's staff, and by the way, he was another one of those brave boys who literally grew up to manhood in the army. There were two serious obstacles to his holding a commission as quartermaster. First he was under age, a fact carefully concealed from the war department at Richmond; and second, he would always desert his money wagons when the fun commenced and go into battle with the brigade, in violation of peremptory orders from the war department.[19]

April 3, 1865   Quartermaster's Office
                                   Missouri Brigade
                                   Mobile

Dear Joe:

Your very welcome letter of the 31st ult. has just been received, and I take pleasure in answering.

I am truly glad to hear of the improvement in your wounds and to know that you can get along without your crutches. Be patient, and I hope you will soon be O.K. again.

Truly, this is a great country for rumors. You have heard that our brigade was so cut up, when it had not lost a man at that time, and we hear just as strange rumors about matters in your country. The train yesterday brought the following news:

First—Forrest met the raid (Wilson's) and completely used it up.

Second—Forrest met the raid and got terribly whipped.

Third—Forrest had been driven through Selma and the Yanks had the place.

Fourth—Forrest had gone towards Tuscaloosa to meet the raid; hadn't found it yet, etc.

Of course I believe it all.[20]

Our brigade has been in but little fighting here as yet. They were on outpost two days ago, quietly lying down or strolling around, guns empty, there being a cavalry regiment (Forty-third or Four Hundred and Thirtieth Alabama) in their front. Yank cavalry came along, ammunition being scarce our cavalry regiment surrendered without firing a gun, and our boys were awakened from their slumbers by what some at first supposed to be a stampede of wild buffalos, but when they got good awake found a great many gentlemen dressed in blue galloping their fine horses over and around and among them as if they were so many logs. Guns being empty, could only kill three before they got out of reach. We lost two officers wounded, no men hurt. If we had had any intimation of it there would have been many a saddle emptied. As long as our government permits conscripts to be recruited we must look for such work. They have since dismounted most of the cavalry and put them in the ditches.[21]

The fighting at Spanish Fort is pretty constant, sounds something like "New Hope" or "Lattimer House." They will take the fort in a couple of weeks, I think, unless we get outside help.

Your friends are all doing well. Col. Gates is here and will take command of the brigade in a day or two. Write frequently.

Yours very truly, A. C. Danner[22]

After several days' skirmishing with the enemy, which was only preliminary to the attack and without much loss to the command, the federal lines were drawn closer and closer until the 9th of April when the position held by the Confederates was attacked in force in front of the Missouri command and was held in check and driven back repeatedly, notwithstanding the troops on the right and left of the Missourians had given way.[23] The men felt able to repulse any force which could be massed in their front. At this moment the men of the First Missouri regiment were amazed to see a line of the enemy at their rear with guns levelled and crying out, Surrender! They hesitated only a moment, when Lieut. Harry Thompson of Co. "E" cried out to Maj. Chas. L. Edmondson, commanding the regiment, "Is it fight or surrender? Talk—quick, major."[24] Poor Edmondson, brave-hearted always, took a look at the enemy (who, by the way, were really magnanimous), dropped his sword point to the ground, saying "surrender."[25] The fight was over, and with it I may say the war, for Lee, as was afterwards learned, surrendered this day at Appomattox.

Gen. Maury in his report adds:

> Blakely was attacked by regular siege on the first of April. Steele's corps came down from the direction of Pollard, and with the division that had been lying before Blakely since the 26th, broke ground very cautiously against the place.[26] The position of Blakely was better defence than that at Spanish Fort. The works consisted of nine lunettes connected by good rifle-pits and covered in front by a double line of abattis and of an advanced line of rifle-pits. The crest was about 3,000 yards long. The flanks rested on Apalachee river and on the marsh. No part of the line was exposed to enfilade fire. The garrison was the noble brigade of Missourians, Elijah Gates commanding, the survivors

of more than twenty battles, and the finest troops I have ever seen; the Alabama boy-reserve brigade, under Gen. Thomas, part of Holtzclaw's brigade, Barry's Mississippi brigade, the First Mississippi light artillery, armed as infantry, several light batteries, with about thirty pieces of field and siege artillery, beside Cohorn and siege mortars.[27] The whole effective force was about 2,700 men under Gen. St. John Liddell. The gallant Gen. Cockrell of Missouri was next in command.

During Sunday, the day after the evacuation of Spanish Fort, the enemy was continually moving troops from below toward Blakely, and on Sunday evening, about 5 o'clock, he assaulted the centre of the line with a heavy column of eleven brigades (about 22,000 men in three lines of battle), and carried the position, capturing all of the material and troops except about 150, who escaped over the marshes and river by swimming.

Capt. O. F. Guthrie of Col. Elijah Gates' Regiment—First and Third Missouri Cavalry, dismounted—favors me with the following incidents of Blakely and Ship Island.

On the morning of the assault on Blakely the Spanish Fort garrison marched in on our right, down to our landing and took transports for Mobile. Then we knew we were "gone up" unless the enemy deferred the attack on our position until the transports (steamboats) could return for us. I was commanding the three left companies, and Capt. Joe Neal of Marion county, Missouri, commanding the regiment, came over and we sat down on a log and talked the matter over. We knew our brigade could hold its lines, but we also knew that the old men and boys to our right, who had never been under fire, would get excited when the assault came, and shoot the tops of the trees off, and the Yanks would bulge right in on them. Joe suggested that if captured we escape by running through their lines and taking to the swamp near by, and I agreed. He wore a handsome new uniform coat which he threw away when the time came to start, and I suppose the Yanks took him for a brigadier, for one of them shot him dead in front of the regiment. Joe had about half of his jaw shot out at New Hope, Ga., and carried the bones in a box in his pocket, calling it his "menagerie."[28]

Cockrell's brigade had the biggest half of the lines to hold. The First and Fourth regiments, commanded by Maj. Chas. L. Edmondson, on the extreme left; next was the Third and Fifth, Col. McCown, then the Second and Sixth, Col. Flournoy, and next came our regiment (Gates') Capt. Joe Neal commanding. Our regiment had the best works we ever fought behind, with nice head-logs, and a battery on each flank. Our men were in single rank but they were tolerably close together, and in such a position it was just fun to beat back the Yanks when they charged. We had stretched a telegraph wire close in front, and they thought it was a torpedo wire, and trying to run back, tumbled over it again. I saw an officer, leading his men, trip over this wire, and trying to run back, tumble over it again.

Our right was held (or rather occupied, for they did not hold it) by the Alabama reserves, made up of old men and boys called out from home for the occasion. As they had never seen an enemy before, we knew this was our weak point, but yet when I saw a white flag up there, I thought some of the federals had got it too hot and were surrendering to us. But I knew better in a minute, as they came pouring in around us.

The day before the assault I had charge of a bridge away out in front, with two companies. My orders were to hold on until dark if possible, but if driven in to burn the bridge. During the day federal cavalry got in our rear and had a fight with our main skirmish line and we were given up as lost, but Col. Gates, then commanding the brigade, said: "I know he is obeying orders and won't come in until dark." He then asked for a volunteer to go out and order me in. Lieut. Fred. M. A[n]derson, now with Orr & Lindsl[e]y of this city, came to us and found us facing both ways, ready to fight either side.[29]

Capt. Davis Lanter was on the skirmish line and got a piece of skin knocked off the top of his head.[30] He and Joe Slem[m]ons led the federal charge on our works, running in ahead of them.[31] During the excitement of surrendering a federal officer stepped up to Col. Steve Cooper of Howard County, Missouri, and demanded his sword, which was then offered him, point first. "Reverse it!" was the order, and Col. Cooper threw the sword away as far as he could, saying "Go and get it, I hand nothing to a federal soldier."[32]

In the fight one of my men was shot in the head and the brains were spattered over the breast of my coat. After the surrender, while washing off this mess, an old schoolmate of mine in federal blue, Marcus Cox, of Bloomington, Ill., came up and shook hands with me, and we had a long talk about old school days.[33] Davy Walker, now of Ely, Walker & Co. of St. Louis, had told Cox if he met me down south to treat me well.[34]

A lot of federal officers surrounded Col. Gates and asked him to point out where torpedoes were planted. He replied, "I don't know where they are, and by the lord Harry if I did I would not tell you." They threatened to take him along, and he said, "All right, I have the satisfaction of knowing you will be blown up with me."[35]

ENDNOTES

1. "Memoirs of Deceased Members of the Society: Joseph Boyce," *Missouri Historical Society Collections* 6, no. 1 (1928): 132. Boyce was wounded in the left leg at Shiloh, in the neck at Allatoona, and in the right thigh at Franklin.

2. Joseph Boyce to Edward Warren, Richmond, Virginia, December 6, 1864. Boyce Family Papers, MHM Archives.

3. French, *Two Wars*, 296.

4. Connelly, *Autumn of Glory*, 507–512.

5. Bevier, *History of the First and Second Missouri Confederate Brigades*, 256.

6. Anthony Boyce to Mrs. Dr. McKeage, February 3, 1865, Boyce Family Papers, MHM Archives.

7. Hughes, *Philip Daingerfield Stephenson*, 358.

8. Nathaniel C. Hughes, ed., *Liddell's Record: St. John Richardson Liddell, Brigadier General, C.S.A.* (Dayton, OH: Morningside House, 1985), 189.

9. Hughes, *Liddell's Record*, 193–194. James W. Farley, *Forgotten Valor: The First Missouri Cavalry Regiment, C.S.A.* (Shawnee Mission, KS: Two Trails Publishing, 1996), 189. Sean Michael O'Brien, *Mobile, 1865: The Last Stand of the Confederacy* (Westport, CT: Praeger Publishers, 2001), 70, 72.

10. The Missourians recrossed the Tennessee River on the evening of December 27, 1864. The army retreated slowly south, arriving at Verona, Mississippi, on January 27, 1865. Bradley, *The Confederate Mail Carrier*, 223. Bradley was a member of Company K, 3rd/5th Missouri Infantry.

11. Boyce's access to Maury's letter is not known, but the text had been published in 1879 in Bevier, *History of the First and Second Missouri Confederate Brigades*, 261.

12. Maury was first associated with Price's Missourians when he served as a staff officer for Van Dorn in northwestern Arkansas in early 1862.

13. It was the second week of January 1865 before Confederate authorities realized that Hood had only about fifteen thousand infantry remaining in the ranks. Hood soon asked to be relieved, and he was replaced by Lieutenant General Richard Taylor, son of President Zachary Taylor. Taylor retained Stewart's corps and the cavalry near Tupelo, Mississippi, sending the other two corps east to join in the attempt to resist Sherman. Connelly, *Autumn of Glory*, 513–514. Warner, *Generals in Gray*, 299–300.

14. An infection or similar ailment developed in French's eyes in early December, and after a week of suffering in cold, snowy weather, French was granted a leave of absence on December 13, 1865. Command of his small division was given to Claudius Sears, but Sears lost his right leg in the battle at Nashville and was taken prisoner. Command of Sears' brigade at Fort Blakely went to Colonel William S. Barry. When Cockrell recovered from his wounds from the battle at Franklin, he was given command of the small division. French, *Two Wars*, 302. O'Brien, *Mobile, 1865*, 69–70.

15. Orlando F. Guthrie was born in Scotland County, Missouri, and living in St. Louis when he enlisted in the Missouri State Guard in 1861. After a year of service with the State Guard, he enlisted in Confederate service in September 1862. He quickly became a lieutenant in Company B, 3rd Missouri Cavalry Battalion. In 1863, he was promoted to first lieutenant and now served with Company H, 1st/3rd Missouri Cavalry (Dismounted). In 1878, he was making his living as a merchant in San Francisco, California. Farley, *Forgotten Valor*, 397. Bevier, *History of the First and Second Missouri Confederate Brigades*, Appendix, 3. *CSR—Confederate, Missouri.*

16. The Alabama Reserve Brigade included the 62nd and 63rd Alabama Infantry, also known as the 1st and 2nd Alabama Reserve Regiments. Twenty cadets from the University of Alabama were initially assigned as drillmasters to the two regiments, and many of them were later elected officers. Most of the enlisted men of the 62nd Alabama were underage volunteers but most of the soldiers in the 63rd Alabama were youthful conscripts. Both regiments were recognized as "boy soldiers." O'Brien, *Mobile, 1865*, 80–82.

17. On reaching their positions on the north bank of D'Olive's Creek south of Spanish Fort on March 26, Cockrell's brigade deployed to the left, and the Louisiana brigade moved to the right. The remainder of the force held the Confederate center. The Federal XVI Corps was their antagonist. O'Brien, *Mobile, 1865*, 43–44.

Randall Lee Gibson, a graduate of the law school at Yale University in 1853, served on the staff of Louisiana governor Thomas Overton Moore before leading the 13th Louisiana Infantry at Shiloh and in subsequent battles. He was promoted to brigadier general for his service in the Atlanta campaign. At Spanish Fort, his garrison included the 1,800 soldiers of Ector's Texas brigade, the Alabama Reserves under Thomas, and their supporting artillery. Warner, *Generals in Gray*, 104.

Bryan Morel Thomas graduated from the U.S. Military Academy in 1858 and was commissioned in the 8th Infantry. He resigned to join the Confederacy in April 1861 and served in staff positions until promoted to brigadier general in August 1864. He led the brigade of Alabama Reserves in the defense of Mobile. Warner, *Generals in Gray*, 304–305.

18. Major General Edward Richard Sprigg Canby began the Federal offensive against Mobile on March 17, 1865. Major General Gordon Granger led two divisions of the XIII Corps from Fort Morgan. Major General Andrew Jackson Smith led the veteran XVI Corps. Together, they began the siege of Spanish Fort on March 27.

Major General Frederick Steele and a force of 13,000 began their march from Pensacola, Florida, on March 20, arriving in front of Fort Blakely on April 1. His force included one division of XIII Corps, the 1st Division of United States Colored Troops, and a cavalry brigade. Richard B. Irwin, "Land Operations Against Mobile," in *Battles and Leaders of the Civil War*, ed. Johnson and Buel, vol. 4, 411.

19. Albert C. Danner was appointed captain and quartermaster on July 2, 1862. Before the war, he lived in Chariton County, Missouri. His records state that he was twenty-two when he entered the Missouri State Guard in May 1861. He entered Confederate service in January 1862. In 1878, Danner was living in Mobile making his living as a merchant. *CSR—Confederate, General and Staff Officers.* Bevier, *History of the First and Second Missouri Confederate Brigades,* Appendix, 3.

20. Five Federal divisions totaling 22,000 men—16,000 of them mounted—were assembled in northwest Alabama under Brigadier General James H. Wilson. Some 13,000 of the troopers were armed with Spencer repeating carbines. By March 22, 1865, they had crossed the Tennessee River and were moving south toward Selma, Alabama, and a final clash with Nathan Bedford Forrest. Robert Selph Henry, *"First with the Most" Forrest* (Indianapolis: Bobbs-Merrill Company, 1944; reprint, Westport, CT: Greenwood Press, 1974), 421–422, 427.

21. The 43rd (or 430th) Alabama Cavalry is mythical, but the circumstances are not. On the afternoon of April 1, 1865, the 2nd Maine Cavalry and the 2nd Illinois Cavalry overran the 46th Mississippi Infantry on outpost duty. The Union horsesoldiers pursued to the outer lines of Fort Blakely, where they were abruptly checked by the fire of the Missourians and their supporting artillery. O'Brien, *Mobile, 1865,* 67–68.

22. The letter from Danner to Boyce is in the Boyce Family Papers, MHM Archives.

23. The Missouri regiments held the center of the line, between Thomas's Alabama brigade on their right and Adair's Mississippi brigade on their left. From left to right, the Missouri regiments were in line as follows: 1st/4th Infantry, 3rd/5th Infantry, 2nd/6th Infantry, 1st/3rd Cavalry (Dismounted). Farley, *Forgotten Valor,* 189.

24. Henry (Harry) D. Thompson was twenty-four years old and a resident of St. Louis when war broke out. He enrolled for service with the 1st Missouri Infantry in August of 1861 and mustered in as a corporal in Company E. He was promoted to sergeant major of the consolidated 1st/4th Missouri on November 25, 1863, and he was promoted lieutenant for "valor and skill" at the Baker's Creek (Champion Hill) battle more than a year before. He had been wounded in the assault at Franklin. *CSR—Confederate, Missouri.*

25. Charles L. Edmonson enlisted in the 1st Missouri at Memphis in June 1861. A resident of St. Louis, he was twenty-four years old and identified his occupation as "merchant." Serving as captain since June 1861, Edmonson was severely wounded by a musket ball through the right thigh during the Atlanta campaign, but he recovered and took command of the 1st/4th Missouri on February 19, 1865. *CSR—Confederate, Missouri.*

26. Steele's column left Pensacola, Florida, on March 20 and moved toward Pollard, Alabama, as if to attack Montgomery. The last of Steele's command

reached Pollard on March 26. Canby's campaign against Mobile did not produce the city's swift collapse; Steele's column was directed west to help. O'Brien, *Mobile, 1865*, 61, 64.

27. James Thaddeus Holtzclaw was an attorney in Montgomery, Alabama, when he entered Confederate service as a lieutenant of a local infantry company. During his service in the Atlanta campaign in 1864, he was promoted to brigadier general. After taking part in the battles at Franklin and Nashville, he was sent to Mobile to assist in the city's defense. Warner, *Generals in Gray*, 141–142.

28. Joseph H. Neal, a native of Marion County, Missouri, left his farm in 1861 to enlist in the Missouri State Guard. He became captain of Company A, 1st/3rd Missouri Cavalry in June 1863. Casualties in the combined regiments had been so heavy that he was now the commanding officer. Lieutenant Charles B. Cleveland, Company C, 1st/3rd Cavalry, reported that Neal and four others of his regiment were killed in the firing that persisted after the unit had surrendered at Fort Blakely. Farley, *Forgotten Valor,* 189–190, 193.

29. Before the war, Frederick M. Anderson was a merchant in St. Louis. A member of the Missouri Volunteer Militia captured at Camp Jackson in May 1861, he served in the Missouri State Guard before enlisting in Company D, 6th Missouri Infantry, in the Confederate service at Ripley, Mississippi, in October 1862. Wounded, he was left behind when the Confederates were forced from Port Gibson, Mississippi, in May 1863. He returned to the regiment and in 1864 was promoted to lieutenant "for valor and skill" effective January 6. After the surrender, as a paroled prisoner he signed his Amnesty Oath before the provost marshal in St. Louis on June 2, 1865, indicating his intention to pursue "clerking or some mercantile business." *CSR—Confederate, Missouri.*

30. Davis Lanter was forty years old and a resident of Platte City, Missouri, when he became a lieutenant in the 1st Missouri Cavalry in December 1861 after service in the Missouri State Guard. He was now captain of Company C in the consolidated 1st/3rd Missouri Cavalry. Lanter was afflicted with partial paralysis in his right hand, allowing him only to draw a rough "X" as his mark when he appeared before the provost marshal in St. Louis on May 20, 1865. Farley, *Forgotten Valor,* 249. *CSR—Confederate, Missouri.*

31. Joseph Martain Slemmons was a farmer living at Iowa Point in Doniphan County, Missouri, when he enlisted at age twenty-two on December 25, 1861, in the 1st Missouri Cavalry. Slemmons was a native of Barron County, Kentucky. In February 1863, he was identified as a deserter but appears to have suffered no punishment on his return to service in July. In 1878, he resided in Pleasureville, Missouri. *CSR—Confederate, Missouri.* Bevier, *History of the First and Second Missouri Confederate Brigades,* Appendix, 23.

32. Transferring from service in the Missouri State Guard to the 6th Missouri Infantry in March 1862, Stephen Cooper was quickly promoted to captain.

In the battle at Corinth, Cooper received a severe wound to his left arm, resulting in its amputation above the elbow. Promoted to major in November 1862, he served in the Atlanta campaign, during which he was wounded again in July 1863. In November, he was promoted to lieutenant colonel of the 2nd/6th Missouri Infantry, ranking from June 23, 1863. He survived the war to return to farming in Howard County, Missouri, his pre-war home. *CSR—Confederate, Missouri*. Bevier, *History of the First and Second Missouri Confederate Brigades*, Appendix, 2.

33. William Marcus Cox was born in Bloomington Township, Illinois, in 1836 and lived there until enlisting in the 99th Illinois Infantry in 1862. Wounded slightly by shell fragments at Fort Blakely, Cox survived his wounds to return to Bloomington, marry, and return to farming. *Portrait and Biographical Album of McLean County, Illinois* (Chicago: Chapman Brothers, 1887), 291 transcribed at http://genealogytrails.com/ill/mclean/coxWilliamMarcus.html.

34. David "Davy" Davis Walker, also a native of Bloomington, Illinois, came to St. Louis at age seventeen in 1857 after a short attendance at Beloit College in Wisconsin. He entered the dry goods business, and by war's end he had become a partner in one of the city's largest enterprises. In 1880, he formed a new company, Ely & Walker Dry Goods, and remained its president until 1892. Hyde and Conard, *Encyclopedia of the History of St. Louis*, 2395.

A son of David and Martha Beakey Walker, George Herbert, was the great-grandfather of President George Herbert Walker Bush and the great-great-grandfather of President George W. Bush. "News: President Bush's Roots Extend to Beloit," *Beloit College Magazine* (Spring 2001), at http://www.beloit.edu/belmag,

35. Gabriel James Rains, an 1827 graduate of West Point, experimented extensively with explosives during his career in the U.S. Army. When he joined the Confederacy in 1861, he was appointed a brigadier general. He became a pioneer in the development of the land mine, or "torpedo," first employing them in the roads in Virginia in 1862. Typically, a pressure-sensitive fuse detonated its powder when something—or someone—put at least seven pounds of pressure on it. Late in the war, he assisted with the mine and torpedo defenses at Richmond, Charleston, and Mobile. Warner, *Generals in Gray*, 240 – 250. Time-Life Books, *Echoes of Glory*, 302–303.

CHAPTER 16
PRISONERS OF WAR
APRIL–MAY 1865

THE MISSOURIANS HAD BEEN SURRENDERED BEFORE, AFTER THE SIEGE OF VICKSBURG. THE CONDITIONS OF THEIR PAROLE CAMP AT DEMOPOLIS, ALABAMA, HAD BEEN MUCH DIFFERENT FROM THOSE THEY NOW EXPERIENCED AT SHIP ISLAND OFF BILOXI, MISSISSIPPI. AT DEMOPOLIS, THE MISSOURIANS REMAINED UNDER THE SUPERVISION OF THEIR OWN COMMANDERS WHILE THEY AWAITED EXCHANGE BEFORE FIGHTING AGAIN. NOW THE WAR WAS OVER, AND THE MISSOURIANS RUDELY REALIZED THAT THEIR KEEPERS WERE THE WHITE OFFICERS AND BLACK SOLDIERS OF THE UNITED STATES COLORED TROOPS.

AT WAR'S END, THE U.S. COLORED TROOPS PROVIDED MORE THAN 10 PERCENT OF THE STRENGTH OF THE UNION ARMY. INITIALLY DEPLOYED IN REAR-AREA GARRISON DUTY OR ON CONSTRUCTION OR LOGISTICS TASKS, BLACK TROOPS BEGAN ASSUMING AN EVER GREATER SHARE OF THE BURDENS OF ACTIVE CAMPAIGNING AS THE WAR WORE ON. IN THE ASSAULT ON FORT BLAKELY, BRIGADIER GENERAL JOHN HAWKINS'S DIVISION WAS UNIQUE. THE NINE REGIMENTS OF ITS THREE BRIGADES WERE EXCLUSIVELY REGIMENTS OF THE U.S. COLORED TROOPS. RARELY HAD SO MANY BLACK SOLDIERS BEEN DEPLOYED TOGETHER IN COMBAT. OF THE DIVISIONS IN THE ATTACKING FORCE, HAWKINS'S DIVISION SUSTAINED THE HIGHEST NUMBER OF CASUALTIES.[1] ONE WHITE OFFICER WAS SO IMPRESSED (OR PERHAPS SURPRISED) BY THE BEHAVIOR OF HIS SOLDIERS UNDER FIRE AT FORT BLAKELY THAT HE DESCRIBED THEIR PERFORMANCE WHEN HE WROTE TO HIS PARENTS A FEW DAYS AFTER THE BATTLE:

PRISONERS OF WAR

AS SOON AS OUR NIGGERS CAUGHT SIGHT OF THE RETREATING
FIGURES OF THE REBS THE VERY DEVIL COULD NOT HOLD THEM
THEIR EYES GLITTERED LIKE SERPENTS AND WITH YELLS & HOWLS
LIKE HUNGRY WOLVES THEY RUSHED FOR THE REBEL WORKS—THE
MOVEMENT WAS SIMULTANEOUS—REGT. AFTER REGT. AND LINE
AFTER LINE TOOK UP THE CRY AND STARTED UNTIL THE WHOLE
FIELD WAS BLACK WITH DARKEYS.[2]

ANOTHER OFFICER CONCLUDED, "THE FORMER SLAVES OF THE SOUTH CANNOT
BE EXCELLED AS SOLDIERS."[3]

FEDERAL FORCES HAD GARRISONED SHIP ISLAND SINCE THE FALL OF 1861
AFTER IT WAS ABANDONED BY THE CONFEDERATES. ITS PRINCIPAL VALUE WAS AS
A BASE TO INTERDICT COASTAL TRAFFIC BETWEEN MOBILE AND NEW ORLEANS.[4]
NOW, SOLDIERS OF THE FORMER 2ND LOUISIANA NATIVE GUARD WAITED
THERE TO STAND GUARD OVER THE ARRIVING PRISONERS. THE REGIMENT WAS
ORGANIZED IN LATE 1862, AND ELEMENTS WERE FIRST SENT TO GARRISON SHIP
ISLAND IN JANUARY 1863. IN JUNE OF THAT YEAR, THE REGIMENT'S DESIGNATION
WAS CHANGED TO 2ND REGIMENT, CORPS D'AFRIQUE, AND IN APRIL 1864, THE
NAME WAS CHANGED AGAIN TO NUMBER THE REGIMENT AS THE 74TH U.S.
COLORED TROOPS.[5] COLONEL ERNEST W. (VON) HOLMSTEDT, FORMERLY AN
OFFICER IN THE 41ST NEW YORK INFANTRY, COMMANDED THE REGIMENT AND
THE PRISON CAMPS ON SHIP ISLAND.[6]

AT THE END OF MARCH 1865, SHIP ISLAND HELD 410 PRISONERS, INCLUDING
79 CIVILIANS. THE MISSOURIANS SURRENDERED AT FORT BLAKELY ON APRIL
9 AND ARRIVED AT SHIP ISLAND AS PRISONERS OF WAR ON APRIL 16. BY THE
END OF THE MONTH, THE PRISONER POPULATION WOULD GROW TO MORE THAN
4,000.[7]

WHEN THE MISSOURIANS ENTERED CAPTIVITY, THE EIGHT REGIMENTS
MUSTERED NOT MORE THAN A FEW HUNDRED MEN. CAPTAIN BOYCE'S ONCE-
PROUD REGIMENT WAS NOT AS LARGE AS ONE OF ITS TEN COMPANIES WOULD
HAVE BEEN FOUR YEARS EARLIER. THEY DID NOT KNOW IT AT THE TIME, BUT

THEIR STAY AT SHIP ISLAND WOULD BE BRIEF. THE PRISONERS WOULD SOON BE TRANSFERRED TO NEW ORLEANS TO BEGIN THEIR JOURNEY HOME.

BOYCE, STILL CONVALESCING, WAS NOT AMONG THE MISSOURIANS WHO SURRENDERED AT FORT BLAKELY. IN PREPARING HIS HISTORY OF THE 1ST MISSOURI INFANTRY, BOYCE TURNED TO THOSE WHO HAD PERSONAL EXPERIENCE OF LIFE ON SHIP ISLAND. AS PRISONERS OF WAR, THE OFFICERS WERE SEPARATED FROM THE ENLISTED MEN. CONSEQUENTLY, BOYCE INCLUDED ACCOUNTS FROM TWO OTHER MISSOURIANS, CAPTAIN ORLANDO GUTHRIE OF THE 1ST/3RD MISSOURI CAVALRY (CONSOLIDATED) AND SERGEANT JOHN CORKERY OF THE 1ST/4TH MISSOURI INFANTRY, TO TELL THE STORY OF THEIR BRIEF IMPRISONMENT ON SHIP ISLAND, "NOTHING BUT A BLEAK SAND–BAR, WITHOUT ANY SHADE OR SHELTER UPON IT OF ANY KIND."[8]

Capt. O. F. Guthrie has given me these further incidents of Blakely and Ship Island.

> On our way to Ship Island we would have captured the ship and run off, but we had no navigator among us and knew we would lose the course going to Cuba. On the island officers and men were put in separate camps, about a half mile apart. My mess had seven in it, but Col. Gates having only one arm we did not allow him to do any work. We cast lots for cook and dishwasher, and I was the first cook. We had a frying-pan, three tin plates and two or three tin cups. The dishwasher had an easy time, for he just rubbed the dishes in the sand and water, then left them to dry in the sun.

> Ship Island is a narrow sand-bar, surrounded by salt water, and you would wonder where to get fresh water. We just dug a hole and sunk a cracker barrel, and fresh water seeped in. In two days it got brackish, then we shifted our well five or six feet and got fresh water again.

PRISONERS OF WAR

Next week Capt. Lanter and Lieut. Harry Thompson were cook and dishwasher. While cooking dinner a detail of negro soldiers passed with some of our officers under guard, cursing them at every step. Thompson said, "Just listen to them niggers cursing." "Who said nigger?" bawled the black sentry on post, bringing his gun down on us. Thompson quickly replied it wasn't him, and then of course it must be Lanter, who threw up his hands, and in a pleading, pitiful way yelled, "It wasn't me, oh, it wasn't me!" Col. Gates lay there on his blanket laughing himself hoarse. A negro corporal came up and pompously asked, "What's the matter?" "Some d——d rebel said nigger." The corporal eyed us sternly, then said: "If another says nigger, shoot him. That's my order," and strutted away.[9]

Our camps were so close together that when bathing, officers and men would get mixed. Lieut. J. B. Slo[ne] could never hold on to his money long enough to buy a uniform, so he wore a private's jacket or a piece of one.[10] One day Slone, returning from his daily swim, was halted by a negro sentry, who thought he belonged in the other camp. "Is you an officer?" "Yes, sir!" "Why, you dirty scoundrel, you ought to be ashamed of yourself. I'm a notion to kill you for being so dirty!" The joke was so good that Slone told it on himself.

The federal commander of the island required the men to carry wood on their backs through sand over shoe deep, three to six miles away, for their own cooking and for the officers too. We petitioned for the privilege of bringing our own wood, which was granted. I volunteered on the first detail and we were marched about three miles, the negro guards cursing us all the way. I picked out a big stick so as to have plenty for my mess. An Alabama major, well dressed and dignified, picked up a little stick as big as my wrist when a negro yelled, "Here, you long, gray-coated, slick rascal, come here. I'll get you a load." "Speaking to me, sir?" "You knows who I'm speaking to, —— you," and he loaded the major up to our great amusement. The abuse of those black rascals was so foul that it became laughable. "Black Frank" put in his whole time, from morning until night, cursing us. Their officers were mostly foreigners who came over to learn the art of war or for the pay, and seemed generally to be pretty good fellows and heartily disgusted with the negroes.[11]

Now about the starving of prisoners. I am told that the men in the other camp suffered a great deal, and it is reasonable to suppose they were not treated as well as the officers. But I believe that in general the starving of prisoners at Ship Island or Andersonville, or in any military prison on either side, was due, in a great measure, to mismanagement by the prisoners. We drew three days' rations at a time, divided this supply into three piles and made it last. While we could have eaten the three days' rations easily in one day, yet there was enough to keep men up in fair condition living as we did, with no work to do. Some of our Alabama neighbors ate all their rations the first day, starved the second and on the third all who had received precisely the same amount as they, divided with them.

I am indebted to Jno. J. Corkery, first sergeant, Co. D., First Missouri Infantry, for the following—his experience on Ship Island, and at Blakely.[12]

The Federals in their assault of Blakely broke through on our flank, but we were so busy beating back the lines in our front that they surrounded us before we knew it, and we surrendered. We held a redoubt, and the federals raised the cry that it was mined with torpedoes. To test this we were ordered inside, and luckily, too, for just as we got under cover the Fifth Missouri, under Col. McCown, changed front and fired into our captors, knocking over a good many of them. As we laid down behind the parapet the bullets went over us.[13]

PRISONERS OF WAR

Soon after the fighting ended we were formed in column and marched south, halting near Gen. Canby's headquarters. One of our guards was Joe Emmet[t] of St. Louis, now famous as 'Our Fritz,' who recognized me, marched with me a couple of miles while we exchanged news about old friends in each army. Joe knew every St. Louis boy in our regiment.[14]

At Canby's headquarters our officers were separated from the men. A fancy dressed officer rode up, and seeing Col. Gates sitting on a log, said, "Hello, what in the h—l are you doing here with one arm? I should think you had got enough before this!" Col. Gates, too mad to talk much, gave him an equally rough reply, which stopped the conversation.

Rations were then issued, and we slept there on the ground through the night. The next morning our regiment was placed under command of our sergeant-major, Jno. K. Newman, and about noon we were marched to Hollywood, I think the wharf is called, on the eastern shore of Mobile bay, and embarked on the old Missouri river steamboat, *White Cloud*, for Ship Island.[15] It was Easter Sunday and some one recalling the old superstition that the sun danced on the water this morning, remarked that he did not dance for us this time.[16]

We were placed in camp on Ship Island, near the fort, on the bare sand, without tents, cover or cooking utensils. The officers were placed a half mile or so from us up the island, which is simply a sandbar seven or eight miles long and about a half mile wide. We were guarded by the First Louisiana regulars (colored), commanded by Col. Holm[stedt].[17]

As we had no cooking utensils we were served with cooked rations. The ration for one day was a piece of bacon one inch thick and one and a half to two inches square, with one pint of mush to four men, but we seldom got our full measure. I was appointed commissary, and when issuing the mush would commence with a pint, then reduce as I got lower down, and often could give the last only about a teacupful, with none left for myself. We carried the chunks of bacon to camp on barrel heads or strung like beads on hoops. The mush was carried in all sorts of old tin-cans as we could pick them up, and was usually well filled by showers of sand blown in by the wind.

I drew our rations from a dandy nigger in velvet slippers. At the first issue I saw he was swindling in weight, and objected. He called in another nigger with his gun and put me out in a hurry. I soon learned the great danger I was in at this moment, for a day or two after one of my detail, Doc Stearns, a jolly good fellow, called "Doc" because he always had a remedy for the sick, was standing at the commissary with arms resting on his hips, when "Black Frank" yelled, "git down dat arm," and plunged a bayonet into him.[18]

The starvation rations immediately told on the men. Men were sent every day to the other end of the island, six miles away, to cut wood for cooking and bring it to camp on their backs, tramping through the deep, hot sand, surrounded by abusive negro guards. From the first, the men would drop from exhaustion and would usually be prodded with a bayonet by a negro soldier, because they did not get up when ordered. Each day, as the men grew weaker, more would drop from weakness and more would get the bayonet.

At the sundown bell all had to go inside our camp lines. One evening a Texas sergeant stepped out from under his little shelter of boards and shook the sand out of his blanket, and a negro sentry, taking deliberate aim, shot him dead.[19] We finally got desperate, and a committee—Jno. K. Newman, Ed Stiles and myself—was appointed to petition Col. Holmstedt for protection as prisoners of war.[20] We drafted a respectful petition and it was signed by two thousand men. We drew up a second petition to Col. Holmstedt for permission to write to friends in St. Louis for money to purchase provisions to save us from starving to death, and I was selected to present both.

Putting on the most respectful smile possible, I walked up to headquarters and was promptly captured by two negro sentries. A Massachusetts captain came out and told me I could not see the colonel commanding, but when I explained that my errand was to get permission to send home for money, he and the two black guards took me right in. Col. Holmstedt was a German. In broken English he asked me my business. I explained our starving condition, and presenting the second petition first, was requesting that we be allowed to write home for money with which to buy food at the sutler's, when he broke in: "You choost tell dem boys to write open letters , and if dey is all right I let 'em go oult. Dem letters moost be sent to me. I open dem an' take de money oult, an' den I open an agount mid each man, an' gif him dickets to de sutler, an' id'll be all right yet."

Then I drew out my other paper, and said: "Aside from our money wants, we have another and more important one. We, as prisoners of war, ask of you as a soldier and a man, the protection due to prisoners. I hope the petition is respectfully worded, and that you will notice it."

"What ish dat?"

"A petition from the prisoners for your protection, which I hope will receive your favorable consideration," and I handed it to him. He threw it carelessly on the table and said: "You choost be sure an' tell dem boys to tell their frients in St. Louis to send dat money to me, an' you get your tickets an' get all you want from the sutler's." I again attempted to call his attention to the petition, when he called his negro orderly, and motioning at me, said, "Show him quick oult," and "quick oult" I went.

John Newman owned *The Last Days of Pompeii* but loaned it to Dr. Vaughn, with the officers at the other end of the island.[21] It was the only novel in camp. I asked a Massachusetts captain to get it for me. He did, and kept it.

On the 20th of April a ship arrived at the fort with flags at half-mast. A great commotion followed among the negro soldiers and white officers, and we commenced wondering what it was all about. We did not know of Lee's surrender, and some thought there had been a big battle and Gen. Grant was killed. At 9 o'clock that night the guards were doubled, and a few minutes after they opened fire on us. "Pop, pop" they commenced, then a general rattling fire. A New York surgeon galloped up and stopped the firing. Our camp was full of wild rumors, but in the morning we learned that only two men were wounded. As we were all lying down the guards could not see us at night and shot over us. We also heard that Lincoln was assassinated, but got no particulars.[22]

Lights were ordered out at taps. One night a campfire was blazed up by the wind and the sentries fired at it, wounding three men. Col. Gates went to Col. Holmstedt and told him if we were to be killed for nothing we would very soon give him a chance to kill us for something. This stopped the shooting.

About the 23rd of April we were ordered aboard the gulf steamer *St. Mary*, transported to New Orleans, and anchored in midstream. Then we hauled alongside the old *Henry Chouteau*. On the levee we saw a beautiful young lady in a red jacket, with a number of servants, bringing us provisions and fruit. Some of the boys asked for tobacco, and she went uptown and got a big lot of it. We went on board the *Chouteau* and were soon off for Vicksburg, where we arrived in a few days and marched to Jackson, Miss., where we remained in camp until early in May when we were surrendered again by Gen. Dick Taylor. Paroles were issued and we started for our homes.[23]

ENDNOTES

1. Dudley Taylor Cornish, *The Sable Arm: Black Troops in the Union Army, 1861–1865* (Lawrence: University Press of Kansas, 1956), 285.

2. Joseph T. Glatthaar, *Forged in Battle: The Civil War Alliance of Black Soldiers and White Officers* (New York: The Free Press, 1990), 167–168.

3. Cornish, *The Sable Arm*, 262.

4. John D. Winters, *The Civil War in Louisiana* (Baton Rouge: Louisiana State University, 1963), 49–50.

5. Dyer, *A Compendium of the War of the Rebellion*, 1214, 1718, 1734–1735.

6. U.S. Department of the Interior, National Park Service, Civil War Soldiers and Sailors System, accessed at www.itd.nps.gov.

7. Abstract from the monthly returns of the principal U.S. military prisons, *OR* ser. II, vol. 8, 1001–1002.

8. Anderson, *Memoirs*, 400.

9. The threats from the guards were more serious than the new prisoners may have recognized. On December 15, 1864, a soldier of the 74th U.S. Colored Troops shot and killed a prisoner for repeatedly annoying the cooks by cooking his own food on their stove and not responding to repeated orders to stop. Colonel Ernest W. Holmstedt, the regiment's commander, exonerated the guard, noting that the incident "has had a good effect on the surviving, undisciplined crew." Report of Ernest W. Holmstedt, Colonel, Commanding Post, Ship Island, Miss., December 19, 1864, *OR* ser. II, vol. 7, 1246.

10. John B. Slone, a Kentucky native then living in Platte County, Missouri, was serving in the Missouri State Guard when his unit, Hughes' Battalion, transferred to the Confederate service to become Company G, 6th Missouri Infantry. He was wounded at Corinth in October 1862 and in May 1863 became the first lieutenant of Company C in the consolidated 2nd/6th Missouri Infantry. He served with the regiment through the Vicksburg and Atlanta campaigns, although his service record for August 1864 notes that he was absent on "secret service" by the authority of General Hood. In June 1865, in response to a requirement of his amnesty oath, he indicated his intention to follow the avocation "of farming if I can't do any better." Slone's service record frequently spells his name "Sloan" and files his records under that spelling. His signature on his Vicksburg parole, however, clearly reads "Slone." *CSR—Confederate, Missouri.*

11. After an inspection, post commander Holmstedt reported that prisoners on the island did, indeed, have to walk about 3.5 miles to pick up their firewood but noted that "on pleasant days it is rather beneficial for them." Report of Colonel Ernest W. Holmstedt, Commanding Post, Ship Island, Miss., December 22, 1864, *OR* ser. II, vol. 7, 1259.

12. Writing in 1913, Boyce noted: "Jno. J. Corkery was for many years with the Anheuser-Busch Brewing Co. At present he is in Washington, D. C. looking after their affairs in the Internal Revenue Department." Corkery

was then in poor health, living with his sister, the widow of Captain Martin Burke, who died in 1869. Joseph Boyce to Isaac Fowler, May 10, 1913, Boyce Family Papers, MHM Archives.

13. The Federal attackers at Fort Blakely broke through the Mississippi brigade immediately to the left of the Missourians. In response, from its position at the left center of the brigade, the $3^{rd}/5^{th}$ Missouri turned about and wheeled right to assist the $1^{st}/4^{th}$ Missouri in holding the brigade's crumbling left flank. Farley, *Forgotten Valor*, 189.

14. Joseph K. Emmett, later known as the entertainer "Old Fritz," had marched as a drummer with the Missouri Guards of the St. Louis militia before the war. As an entertainer, he became noted for writing his own songs for his comedies in which he portrayed Fritz von Vonderblinkinstoffen, a German immigrant. Boyce, "Military Organizations," typescript, MHM Archives, 78. Russell Sanjek, *American Popular Music and Its Business, the First Four Hundred Years, Volume II—From 1790 to 1909* (New York: Oxford University Press, 1988), 307.

15. John K. Newman was an eighteen-year-old student in St. Louis when he enlisted in Company E, 1st Missouri Infantry, in August 1861 and became the unit's third sergeant. On June 3 of the following year, Newman was promoted to second sergeant. His promotion to sergeant major came on March 10, 1864. *CSR—Confederate, Missouri.*

16. In 1865, Easter Sunday fell on April 16.

17. The 1st Louisiana Native Guard participated in the assault at Fort Blakely, but it was likely the 2nd Louisiana Native Guard watching over the Missourians at Ship Island. Though participating in sorties along the Gulf coast from time to time, the regiment was part of the Ship Island garrison until the men were mustered out in October 1865. Dyer, *A Compendium of the War of the Rebellion,* 1214, 1718, 1734–1735.

Colonel Ernest W. (von) Holmstedt, formerly a field officer in the 41st New York Infantry, commanded the 74th USCT on Ship Island. Civil War Soldiers and Sailors System, www.itd.nps.gov.

18. "Doc" Stearns may be B. F Stearnes, D. F. Starnes, or B. F. Sternes, all variations appearing in the records of Wade's, now Walsh's, Missouri Light Artillery. *CSR—Confederate, Missouri.*

19. Shelter for the prisoners was minimal. Colonel Holmstedt appended a note to his monthly report for February 1865 to indicate that "the tents now occupied by the prisoners are so rotten that a norther tears them down by the dozen." He requested authorization of funds to build barracks, but by mid-April, when the Missourians arrived, he was still trying to obtain permission to proceed with the work. Report of Ernest W. Holmstedt, Colonel, 74th U.S. Colored Troops, Commanding Ship Island, Miss., March 1, 1865, and endorsements of March 28 and April 18, *OR* ser. II, vol. 8, 323.

20. Edward J. Stiles enlisted in Company F, 1st Missouri, in September 1861 while the regiment was stationed at Camp Beauregard. Born in St. Joseph, Missouri, Stiles was eighteen and a student living in Leavenworth, Kansas, prior to his enlistment. He was severely wounded at Shiloh on April 7, 1862, and was appointed first corporal while recuperating from his wound. As color corporal, he was commended for bravery at Baker's Creek (Champion Hill) where on May 16, 1863, he was again wounded. Promoted to sergeant on May 1, 1864, Stiles was again severely wounded in the assault on Allatoona, Georgia. *CSR—Confederate, Missouri.*

21. *The Last Days of Pompeii*, a novel by Sir Edward Bulwer-Lytton, was published by G. Routledge and Sons in London and New York in 1834 and reprinted several times. http://hollisweb.harvard.edu.

Dr. Vaughn is likely John W. Vaughn, surgeon for the 2nd Missouri Infantry. After the war, Vaughn practiced medicine in Waverly, Missouri. Bevier, *History of the First and Second Missouri Confederate Brigades*, Appendix, 7.

22. Robert E. Lee surrendered the Army of Northern Virginia to Ulysses S. Grant at Appomattox Court House, Virginia, on April 9, 1865. Maury evacuated Mobile on April 11 and retreated with this remaining force toward Meridian, Mississippi. Canby entered the city the next day. On the evening of April 14, 1865, President Abraham Lincoln was shot by an assassin. He died the next day. Joseph E. Johnston agreed to surrender the Army of Tennessee to William T. Sherman near Durham Station, North Carolina, on April 18 but terms were not finalized until April 26. Long, *The Civil War Day by Day*, 670, 673, 675, 678, 682.

23. On May 4, Lieutenant General Richard Taylor surrendered the Confederate forces in the Department of Alabama, Mississippi, and East Louisiana to Canby, the last major Confederate command east of the Mississippi River to surrender. Long, *The Civil War Day by Day*, 685.

CHAPTER 17
WAR ECHOES

1887

To conclude his history of the 1ST Missouri Infantry, Joseph Boyce wrote a coda plaintively entitled "War Echoes." Boyce may well have agreed with British author and critic G. K. Chesterton who in 1911 made the following ironic observation:

> For the great Gaels of Ireland
> Are the men that God made mad,
> For all their wars are merry,
> And all their songs are sad.[1]

In his history of the 1ST Missouri Infantry, Boyce frequently demonstrates that amid the strain of combat he and his fellow Missourians were successful in using good humor to maintain their morale. Boyce also recognizes that the causes for which the men of the 1ST Missouri fought were costly ones. John Bowen, the regiment's organizing force and its first colonel, died of sickness contracted during the Vicksburg siege. Lucius L. Rich, leading the regiment after Bowen advanced to lead the brigade, died from a wound received at Shiloh in April 1862, the regiment's first fight. When the 1ST and 4TH Regiments were consolidated, Archibald MacFarlane of the 4TH Missouri was to become commander, but he was too incapacitated from wounds received at Corinth months before to accept the honor. His successor, Amos Camden Riley, was killed at New Hope Church in

241

WAR ECHOES

THE ATLANTA CAMPAIGN WHILE CONVERSING WITH BOYCE. BRADFORD KEITH WENT DOWN AT EZRA CHURCH LATER THAT SUMMER, AND HUGH GARLAND DIED IN THE ASSAULT AT FRANKLIN. THE CASUALTIES AMONG THE COMPANY OFFICERS AND THE MEN IN THE RANKS WERE NO LESS TERRIBLE. ACCORDING TO BOYCE, HIS COMPANY—THE ST. LOUIS GREYS—"EARLY IN THE WAR WAS 110 STRONG, LOST BY KILLED IN ACTION, DISEASE, ETC., OVER 90 MEN, LESS THAN 20 OF ITS MEMBERS RETURNING TO ST. LOUIS." EVEN THOSE SURVIVORS "WERE SEVERAL TIMES SEVERELY WOUNDED."[2]

WITHIN HIS STORY, BOYCE RARELY TOUCHES ON THE WAR'S CAUSES OR THE MOTIVATIONS OF THE MEN WHO SERVED IN THE 1ST MISSOURI. IN HIS LATER YEARS, CAPTAIN JOSEPH BOYCE WOULD BE ASKED WHAT MOTIVATED HIM—THEN BARELY OUT OF HIS TEENS—TO ENTER CONFEDERATE SERVICE. HIS REPLY: "WE HAD NO SLAVES; SLAVERY DID NOT MEAN A THING TO ME, AND I KNEW NOTHING ABOUT THE PROBLEM OF STATE SOVEREIGNTY, BUT I WAS SO OUTRAGED AT THE ATTACK OF CAPTAIN LYON ON OUR STATE MILITIA IN ITS REGULAR ANNUAL ENCAMPMENT AT ST. LOUIS THAT I MADE UP MY MIND THEN AND THERE TO TAKE UP ARMS AGAINST THE FEDERAL GOVERNMENT AT MY FIRST OPPORTUNITY."[3]

IRONICALLY, WHEN BOYCE PENNED HIS CLOSING CHAPTER—"WAR ECHOES"—IN 1887, IT MAY HAVE BEEN DIFFICULT FOR THE UNINITIATED OBSERVER IN MISSOURI TO DETERMINE WHO WON THE WAR. THE STATE ADMINISTRATION WAS SAFE IN CONSERVATIVE HANDS, MOST OF THEM DEMOCRATS AND MANY OF THOSE EX-CONFEDERATES. FRANCIS MARION COCKRELL, THE LEADER OF THE MISSOURI BRIGADE FROM VICKSBURG TO THE END OF THE WAR, WAS SENT TO THE UNITED STATES SENATE FROM MISSOURI IN 1874. HE WOULD SERVE THERE FOR THIRTY YEARS.[4] ATTORNEY GEORGE GRAHAM VEST, WHO HAD BEEN ELECTED TO THE MISSOURI HOUSE OF REPRESENTATIVES IN 1860 AND BECAME AN OUTSPOKEN SUPPORTER FOR SECESSION, REPRESENTED MISSOURI IN THE CONFEDERACY'S HOUSE OF REPRESENTATIVES AND, IN 1865, THE CONFEDERATE SENATE. FOURTEEN YEARS LATER, IN 1879, MISSOURI SENT

VEST TO THE UNITED STATES SENATE, A POST HE WOULD HOLD UNTIL 1903.[5] THOMAS CAUTE REYNOLDS WAS ELECTED MISSOURI'S LIEUTENANT GOVERNOR IN 1860 AND WAS A DRIVING FORCE IN THE MOVE TOWARD SECESSION. ON GOVERNOR CLAIBORNE JACKSON'S DEATH IN LATE 1862, REYNOLDS BECAME MISSOURI'S SECOND CONFEDERATE GOVERNOR. IN 1868, HE RETURNED TO ST. LOUIS TO ESTABLISH A VERY SUCCESSFUL LAW PRACTICE, WINNING A SEAT IN THE STATE LEGISLATURE IN 1874.[6] FORMER CONFEDERATE MAJOR GENERAL JOHN SAPPINGTON MARMADUKE WAS ELECTED GOVERNOR IN 1884, JUST AS BOYCE BEGAN PRESENTATION OF HIS HISTORY OF THE 1ST MISSOURI INFANTRY.[7]

CAPTAIN JOSEPH BOYCE AND MANY OTHERS OF THE SURVIVING CONFEDERATE VETERANS HAD WEATHERED THE DIFFICULT PERIOD OF RECONSTRUCTION AND RECONCILIATION. THEY WERE WELL ON THEIR WAY TO ASSURING THAT THEIR CONTRIBUTIONS TO MISSOURI'S HISTORY WERE REMEMBERED WITH PRIDE.

The parting of old friends and comrades was affecting, indeed. Some remained in the South, others returned to Missouri.

It was our hope, fondly cherished during the darkest day of the war, that we would in time march as victors through the streets of St. Louis and stack our arms on Camp Jackson's ground, but fate decreed otherwise, we accepted the situation, took the oath of allegiance to support the government of the United States, and have faithfully observed this obligation, and I have yet to see an old comrade who has regretted the results of the war.

And now my task is done. I have related as best I could the heroic actions of my fellow soldiers. I am proud of my connection with the First Missouri Infantry, and claim for it that it was the best organized and disciplined volunteer regiment the war produced. Missourians, whether they were for the North or South, can take pride in the prowess of the First Missouri. We represented our state, and despite our failure, we were Missourians, and stood to our guns from the first to the last.

Of the 1,400 men enlisted during the war in this regiment, less than 160 surrendered, and not 150 survived. Nearly all met death by the bullet. Not many died from disease. I can only name one officer who died from disease, Lieut. Thomas T. Tunstall of the writer's company. He died at

WAR ECHOES

Meridian, Miss., in [December] 1863. He was a young St. Louis lawyer, who entered the regiment with us at Memphis. He was the writer's friend and companion, and I cannot close these papers without referring to him as one of the bravest boys I ever saw—and the most even-tempered—a cheery word for all, and after twenty years I miss him yet. God rest him![8]

As the figures above will show, a very large majority of the poor fellows were left behind in their Southern graves. Their lot was a sad one. They were exiled from their homes during the war, and gave up their lives for their convictions. As the poet O'Hara says in his "Bivouac of the Dead,"

> The muffled drum's sad roll has beat
> The soldier's last tattoo;
> No more on life's parade shall meet
> the brave and daring few.
> On Fame's eternal camping-ground
> Their silent tents are spread,
> And glory guards with solemn round
> The bivouac of the dead.
>
> Their shivered swords are red with rust,
> Their plumed heads are bowed,
> Their haughty banners trailed in dust
> Is now their martial shroud.
> And plenteous funeral tears have washed
> The red stains from each brow,
> And their proud forms in battle gashed
> Are free from anguish now.
>
> The neighing steed, the flashing blade,
> The trumpet's stirring blast,
> The charge, the dreadful cannonade,
> The din and shout are past;
> Nor war's wild note, nor glory's peal,
> Shall thrill with fierce delight
> Those breasts that never more shall feel
> The rapture of the fight.[9]

I desire to make a special acknowledgement to Captain William P. Barlow of our society for the help he gave me in these papers. I will say that I faltered from time to time, but he kept me up and urged their completion.

Since these scenes were enacted sufficient time has elapsed to enable many of us to view them in an impersonal light; that is in relating one's personal experiences it does not usually appear to the old soldier that it was himself who participated, but rather some younger, more reckless, and often foolish acquaintance. Viewed in this light as an affair in which we were not individually concerned, but where some faint, dimly recognizable shadow of self starved, fought, got wounded or sick, went to the hospital, thence hurried back to be in time for the next battle, often praying for a wound just severe enough to give one a furlough, and when it was received then reversing the prayer and longing to be back with the boys in camp; looked at through the mellowing influences of time, is it not now a pertinent inquiry, Why?

Professional politicians, imitating our common British foe of a hundred years ago, easily dismiss the subject with the epithet, "traitor," but with the great thinking, reasoning class of the American people this off-hand solution does not appear quite sufficient; there seems to be a missing link in the reasoning.

Young men may leave their homes, old men their wives and children for adventure, or out of that pure cussedness with which we are charged, but will such motives hold millions of people to a death-struggle of four long years? Is not some higher incentive than a criminal desire to be a villain required to enable men to undergo such a period of semi-starvation, unsheltered, half-clothed, unpaid, when a few miles' midnight tramp through the lines and the signing of the always-ready blank oath would have given them free transportation home, and permission to toil for their suffering loved ones there? And when to this is added what at last seemed the only natural and inevitable ending, an unmarked grave in a strange land, what peculiar force, moral or immoral, enabled the soldier to cheerfully face death, bury his comrades and go into battle again and again?

Companies originally 100, reduced to eight or ten men by three and a half years of this life, who made three charges through the horrible slaughters of Corinth and Franklin, leaving the last survivors wounded in the ditch of the Union parapets, must have long since lost, if they ever possessed, any mere fiendish desire to be "traitors" or "rebels."

We can easily see that only the highest of all motives—patriotism—could have brought the Union Army of the Potomac through the unprecedented carnage of the Wilderness, Spotsylvania and Cold Harbor, after their years of defeat, uncheered by a single victory, only lightened by their gallant repulse of Lee at Gettysburg and the drawn battle of Antietam. But I have never conversed with a real veteran Union soldier who felt that his side entirely monopolized that ennobling sentiment, the love of country.

If the Confederate soldier was nerved to do his work only by mere perversity in conscious wrong, then the Supreme Being who created him must have taken a vacation, or resided only on the north side of Mason and Dixon's line during the thirty or forty years preceding 1861; and a proper reverence for that All-Wise Creator seems to forbid the assumption that He could have inspired the noble women of the South with that heartlessness

THE BOYCE FAMILY PLOT IN CALVARY CEMETERY, ST. LOUIS, MISSOURI.
PHOTO BY WILLIAM C. WINTER.

1887

which, in default of prayerful sense of duty, could have enabled them to send husbands and sons to the front.

These are some of the reasons why the Confederate soldier, as he passes in review those dear friends who gave life to duty, is not yet ready to acknowledge that they were simply brigands, who knew they were wrong. And we can still decline to apologize, while acknowledging that it is probably better for the country, better for ourselves, that our cause failed.

The great mass of our Northern brethren, with the noble magnanimity of a high civilization, are beginning to see that the heroism and endurance of each side is alike illustrative of American national character.

With this humble attempt to represent the actions and feelings of the Confederate soldier in war, and his opinions in peace, I conclude the reminiscences of the First Missouri Confederate Infantry.

—Joseph Boyce

WAR ECHOES

ENDNOTES

1. G. K. Chesterton, *The Ballad of the White Horse* (New York: John Lane, 1911).

2. Joseph Boyce, "Military Organizations," 14.

3. "Memoirs of Deceased Members of the Society: Joseph Boyce," *Missouri Historical Society Collections* 6 (1928): 131.

4. Ruth Warner Towne, "Cockrell, Francis Marion," in *Dictionary of Missouri Biography*, ed. Christensen, 197–198. In 1887, as the Boyce family prepared for a European tour, Senator Cockrell arranged for the State Department to provide Boyce with a letter of introduction "to the Diplomatic and Consular Officers of the United States," requesting their "official courtesies." St. Louis mayor David Francis also wrote "to whom it may concern" to recommend Boyce as a citizen "whose responsibility cannot be questioned." Department of State, Washington, D.C., May 7, 1887, and Mayor's Office, St. Louis, Missouri, May 7, 1877, Boyce Family Papers, MHM Archives.

5. Lynn Wolf Gentzler, "Vest, George Graham," in *Dictionary of Missouri Biography*, ed. Christensen, 772–773.

6. Lawrence O. Christensen, "Reynolds, Thomas Caute," in *Dictionary of Missouri Biography*, ed. Christensen, 647–648.

7. Lynn Morrow, "Marmaduke, John Sappington," in *Dictionary of Missouri Biography*, ed. Christensen, 519–521.

8. On January 18, 1864, Boyce wrote to Smith Hawes, a friend from St. Louis and former member of the regiment now serving in Texas, bringing him up to date on the changes since his departure. Among those changes, Boyce reported "Our friend Tom Tunstall died at Meridian Miss. Dec. 12, 1863 of typhoid pneumonia. Poor Tom, his death cast a gloom over all of us. May he rest in peace." Captain Joseph Boyce to Captain Smith N. Hawes, January 18, 1864, typescript, Boyce Family Papers, MHM Archives.

9. Theodore O'Hara, a native of Danville, Kentucky, penned "The Bivouac of the Dead" in 1847 to honor the American dead at the battle of Buena Vista in the war with Mexico. In 1856, he moved to Mobile, Alabama, and became editor of the *Mobile Register*, a position he held until entering Confederate service at the head of the Mobile Light Dragoons in 1861. He subsequently served in the 12th Alabama Infantry as a lieutenant colonel. O'Hara died from malaria in 1873 in Alabama but was buried in Frankfort, Kentucky. www.nps.gov/archive/gett/gettncem.bivouac.htm.

APPENDIX

ROSTERS OF THE ST. LOUIS GREYS

THE ST. LOUIS GREYS, COMPANY A, 1ST REGIMENT,
MISSOURI VOLUNTEER MILITIA
Officers and Non-Commissioned Officers
Southwest Expedition, Winter 1860–1861[1]

Captain: M. Burke

1st Lieutenant: Stephen O. Coleman

1st Sergeant: Wm. Barlow

2nd Sergeant: Samuel Gilfillan

3rd Sergeant: Wm. J. Pentland

1st Corporal: M. Morris

2nd Corporal: Henry Guibor

3rd Corporal: F. Glichhart

4th Corporal: Joseph Boyce

THE ST. LOUIS GREYS, COMPANY A, 1ST REGIMENT,
MISSOURI VOLUNTEER MILITIA
Spring 1861

Captain: M. Burke

1st Lieutenant: S. O. Coleman

2nd Lieutenant: H. B. Belt

3rd Lieutenant: R. U. Lenori

1st Sergeant: W. B. Craft

2nd Sergeant: Samuel M. Gilfillin

3rd Sergeant: Francis Glickart

4th Sergeant: not identified

5th Sergeant: Robert McKenna

1st Corporal: not identified

2nd Corporal: M. Morris

3rd Corporal: not identified

4th Corporal: Joseph Boyce

CAPTAIN JOSEPH BOYCE

Privates

Bartling, H. E.

Breed, Stanley M.

Brown, Wm.

Carmelich, George

Coleman, M. J.

Colston, E.

Connell, J. W.

Conrey, Geo. M.

Corkery, J. J.

Coss, A.

Craig, M.

Craig, R.

Dausman, Geo.

Dean, Geo. C.

Duchring, H. P.

English, E. O.

Ferguson, C. D.

Fisher, James Matthews

Gallagher, A.

Gardner, M.

Gaylord, A.

Gorin, Frank

Haley, Wm.

Johnston, James M.

Keith, Thos.

Kelly

Kennedy, A.

Koniuszeski, E. M.

Lehan, Coman

Lenori, Henry J.

Lockett, John

Malloy, James

Martin

Maston, S.

May, W.

Merrill, John

Mullery, John

O'Connell, Daniel

Overbeck, Chs.

Pentland, W. J.

Pife, Geo.

Price, John A.

Robinson, W. J.

Shephard, Elihu

Slaughter, J. C.

Smith, A.

Sullivan, Jas.

Vienna, Stephen

Virden, J.

Wooley, Oliver

Young, John

Martin Burke was elected captain of the company on July 27, 1860. As the city's senior company, the St. Louis Greys counted more than one veteran member. Elihu Shepard, for example, was a veteran of the War of 1812 and "upwards of three score and ten years of age." Stephen O. Coleman had served with the unit for more than twenty-five years.[2]

APPENDIX

The St. Louis Greys, Company D, 1st Missouri Infantry, C.S.A.
Muster Roll made at Lumpkin's Mill, Mississippi, October 1862[3]

Officers, Sergeants, and Corporals

Captain: Martin Burke

1st Lieutenant: Lewis H. Kennerly

2nd Lieutenant: Wm. C. P. Carrington

Brevet 2nd Lieutenant: Jos. Boyce

Brevet 2nd Lieutenant: Thos. Tunstall

Brevet 2nd Lieutenant: Patrick W. Collins

1st Sergeant: Jno. J. Shea

2nd Sergeant: Jno. J. Corkery

3rd Sergeant: Wm. Carnes

4th Sergeant: Thos. Dwyer

5th Sergeant: James M. Johnston

1st Corporal: Jerry J. Horan

2nd Corporal: Wm. Hodnett

3rd Corporal: Francis X. Jones

4th Corporal: Frank Trapp

Color Corporal: Malcolm M. MacDonald

4th Corporal: Chas. McDonnell

4th Corporal: Wm. Dowdall

1st Corporal: Jno. F. Crowley

Color Corporal: Jos. T. Donovan

Privates

Beakey, Lewis B.

Bloomfield, James

Boucher, Patrick

Buckley, William

Burch, William W.

Burke, John

Butler, William

Cannell, James

Carver, James H.

Chilton, William

Conner, Anthony

Crawla, Patrick

Cunningham, James

Dailey, Thomas

Dalton, Enoch

Davis, James

Davis, Thomas

Dillon, Thomas

Doolan, Patrick

Elder, J. Scott

Feagan, Edward B.

Fitzwilliam, Peter L.

Galloway, Thomas

Gardner, Michael A.

Green, George

Green, Joseph H.

Hall, Reuben B.

Harris, Francis Marion

Harrison, James T.

Hollihan, John

Keener, Jesse

Kennett, Ferdinand B.

Lambshire, Otto K.

Logan, Dudley

Matthews, Jos. R.

McCloud, James

Mercer, Eugene

Moriarty, Patrick

Morris, James X.

Mulligan, John

Murray, Edward

O'Connell, Daniel

O'Donnell, Patrick

O'Neal, Michael

Sandford, John W.

Sill, Eudora G.

St. Clair, George

Stanton, Thomas

Stone, James W.

Summers, William

Taylor, Edward

True, Alfred H.

Weaver, Jos.

Wheat, Jonas, Jr.

Wheat, Jonas, Sr.

Wheat, Solomon

White, Henry K.

Young, John

ENDNOTES

1. Hopewell, *Camp Jackson*, 26.

2. Hopewell, *Camp Jackson*, 16.

3. The roster is found in Boyce Family Papers, MHM Archives, to which Joseph Boyce adds the following note: "This roll was with Capt. James W. Allen, Mo. Trust Bldg., Nov. 22/07, and was to be sent to Washington, D.C., tomorrow 23rd inst."

RESOURCES

ARTICLES BY JOSEPH BOYCE IN *Missouri Republican,* ST. LOUIS, MISSOURI

November 10, 1883: "Personal Reminiscences: The First Regiment of Missouri Infantry, C.S.A."

January 7, 1884: "Personal Reminiscences."

May 3, 1884: "Second Day's Fight at Shiloh, April 7, 1862."

September 6, 1884: "Battle of Corinth, October 3 and 4, 1862."

December 5, 1884: "The Battles of Baker's Creek, Big Black and the Siege of Vicksburg."

May 11, 1885: "Paroled Camp at Demopolis, Ala.—Operations in Mississippi: Prize Drill at Mobile—In Front of Sherman Through Georgia, Etc."

September 5, 1885: "Capt. Joseph Boyce Relates Incidents of Hood's Georgia Campaign; The Fall of Atlanta and the Bloody Assault at Allatoona."

January 30, 1886: "The Affair at Tilton, Ga., and the Battle at Franklin, Tenn."

February 12, 1887: "Capt. Joe Boyce Continues the History of the First Missouri Regiment—Incidents of Its Capture at Fort Blakely Near Mobile."

March 12, 1887: "Capt. Jos. Boyce Closes His Record of the First Missouri— Rough Experience While Confined as Prisoners at Ship Island."

March 26, 1887: "He was the Soldier's Friend" (Chaplain Arthur J. Durbin).

CAPTAIN JOSEPH BOYCE

ARTICLES BY JOSEPH BOYCE IN *Confederate Veteran*

"Cockrell's Brigade Band at Franklin," XIX, no. 6 (June 1911): 271.

"Missourians in Battle of Franklin," XIV, no. 3 (March 1916): 101–103, 138.

"What Flag Was This?" XXVII, no. 6 (June 1919): 235.

"The Evacuation of Nashville," XXVIII, no. 2 (February 1920): 60–62.

"In the Missouri Infantry," XXXIII, no. 4 (April 1925): 158.

OTHER WRITINGS BY JOSEPH BOYCE

"Rev. John Bannon, Chaplain, Price's Missouri Confederate Division." A paper read at a meeting of Camp St. Louis No. 731, United Confederate Veterans, March 9, 1914. Boyce Family Papers, MHM Archives.

"Now About Myself and Why I Was Not in Vicksburg during the Siege...." Undated manuscript, ca. September 1863. Boyce Family Papers, MHM Archives.

"When St. Louisans Fought Their Bloodiest Battle for the Confederacy." *The St. Louis Republic,* November 28, 1914.

"Military Organizations." In *Encyclopedia of the History of St. Louis: A Compendium of History and Biography for Ready Reference*, edited by William Hyde and Howard Louis Conard. New York: The Southern History Company, 1899, 1489–1518.

"Military Organizations Describing the Uniforms and the Action That These Organizations Took in the Civil War." Typescript, 1897. MHM Archives.

BIBLIOGRAPHY

MANUSCRIPTS AND COLLECTIONS

Carondelet Historical Society, St. Louis
    File, John S. Bowen
    File, James M. Loughborough

Joint Collection, University of Missouri, Western Historical
Manuscript Collection–Columbia and State Historical Society of
Missouri Manuscripts
    Goah W. Stewart Papers (R699)
    "Historic Roll of Capt. King's Battery, originally known as the Clark
        Battery or 2nd Missouri"
    William H. Kavanaugh Papers (SUNP1189)
    The United Daughters of the Confederacy, Missouri Division, comp.,
        Record of Missouri Confederate Veterans

Kennesaw Mountain National Battlefield Park
    "Guibor's Missouri Battery in Georgia." *The Kennesaw Gazette*, May 15,
        1889.
    Letter, Walter A. Rohr to My Dear Cousin Susan, March 22, 1864.

CAPTAIN JOSEPH BOYCE

Missouri History Museum Archives, St. Louis
  William R. Babcock Scrapbook
  Boyce Family Papers
      "Funeral Services for Joseph Boyce to Be Held Tomorrow." *St. Louis Globe Democrat*, July 30, 1928.
  Boyce Scrapbooks
      "Capt. Joe Boyce." *St. Louis Merchant*, March 31, 1901.
      Captain W. T. DeWitt, "The Last Shots at Vicksburg." *Missouri Republican* (St. Louis), undated clip ca. 1885.
  Civil War Collection
      John T. Appler Diary
      Camp Jackson Papers
      "Volunteer Reviews History of the First Missouri Regiment." *St. Louis Republican*, July 26, 1908.
      Fisher, Theodore D. "A Confederate Veteran's Diary as Written During the Siege of Vicksburg 1863." Typescript.
      Guibor's Battery, Battle Roll
      Thomas Hogan Papers
  Kearny–Kennerly Scrapbook
  Necrologies of Missouri Historical Society Members

U.S. Army Military History Institute
  Harrisburg Civil War Round Table Collection
      William A. Ruyle Diary

NEWSPAPERS

Daily Appeal (Memphis)
Missouri Democrat (St. Louis)
Missouri Republican (St. Louis)
St. Louis Post-Dispatch

BIBLIOGRAPHY

STATE AND FEDERAL GOVERNMENT RESOURCES

Civil War Centennial Commission of Tennessee. *Tennesseans in the Civil War.* Nashville: n.p., 1964.

Compiled Service Records of Confederate General and Staff Officers and Nonregimental Enlisted Men. Publication No. M331. National Archives and Records Administration.

Compiled Service Records of Confederate Soldiers Who Served in the Organizations from the State of Missouri. Publication No. M320. National Archives and Records Administration.

Hewitt, Jane B., ed. *Supplement to the Official Records of the Union and Confederate Armies.* Wilmington, NC: Broadfoot Publishing Company, 1996.

Ohio Battlefield Commission. *Ohio at Shiloh.* Cincinnati: C. J. Krehbiel & Co., 1903.

United States War Department. *The War of the Rebellion: A Compilation of the Official Records of the Union and Confederate Armies.* Washington, D.C.: Government Printing Office, 1881–1901.

United States War Department, Record and Pension Office. *Organization and Status of Missouri Troops (Union and Confederate) in Service During the Civil War.* Washington, D.C.: Government Printing Office, 1902.

PRIMARY SOURCES: BOOKS

Anderson, Ephraim McDowell. *Memoirs: Historical and Personal; Including the Campaigns of the First Missouri Confederate Brigade.* St. Louis: Times Printing Company, 1868.

Bevier, Robert S. *History of the First and Second Missouri Confederate Brigades, 1861–1865.* St. Louis: Bryan, Brand & Company, 1878; reprint, n.p.: Walworth Publishing Company, 1985.

Bogle, Joseph, and William L. Calhoun. *Historical Sketches of Barton's (later Stovall's) Georgia Brigade: Army of Tennessee, C.S.A.* Atlanta, n.p., 1900; reprint, William Stanley Hoole, ed., Dayton, OH: Morningside House, 1984.

Bradley, James. *The Confederate Mail Carrier; Or, From Missouri to Arkansas through Mississippi, Alabama, Georgia and Tennessee.* Mexico, Missouri: n.p., 1894; reprint, Bowie, MD: Heritage Books, 1990.

Cox, Jacob D. *The Battle of Franklin, Tennessee.* New York: Charles Scribner's Sons, 1897; reprint, Dayton, OH: Press of Morningside Bookshop, 1983.

Duke, Basil Wilson. *The Civil War Reminiscences of General Basil W. Duke, C.S.A.* Garden City, NY: Doubleday, Page, 1911; reprint, Cooper Square Press, 2001.

Franklin, Ann York, transcriber. *The Civil War Journal of Lt. George R. Elliot, 2nd & 6th Missouri Infantry, Company F, 1862–1864.* Louisville, KY: privately printed, 1997.

French, Samuel Gibbs. *Two Wars: An Autobiography of General Samuel G. French.* Nashville: Confederate Veteran, 1901; reprint, Huntington, WV: Blue Acorn Press, 1999.

Hammond, Otis G., ed. *The Utah Expedition, 1857–1858: Letters of Capt. Jesse A. Gove, 10th Inf., U.S.A. of Concord, N.H.* Concord: New Hampshire Historical Society, 1928.

Hood, John B. *Advance and Retreat: Personal Experiences in the United States and Confederate States Armies.* 1880; reprint, Secaucus, NJ: Blue and Grey Press, 1985.

Hughes, Nathaniel Cheairs, Jr., ed. *The Civil War Memoir of Philip Daingerfield Stephenson, D. D.* Baton Rouge: Louisiana State University Press, 1998.

———, ed. *Liddell's Record: St. John Richardson Liddell, Brigadier General, C.S.A.* Dayton, OH: Morningside House, 1985.

Johnson, Robert Underwood, and Clarence Clough Buel, ed. *Battles and Leaders of the Civil War.* 4 vols. 1887; reprint, NY: Thomas Yoseloff, 1956.

Lehr, Suzanne Staker, ed. *Fishing on Deep River: Civil War Memoir of Pvt. Samuel Baldwin Dunlap, C.S.A.* St. Joseph, MO: Platte Purchase Publishers, 2006.

Loughborough, Mary Ann Webster. *My Cave Life in Vicksburg, with Letters of Trial and Travel.* D. Appleton and Company, 1864; reprint, Wilmington, NC: Broadfoot Publishing Company, 1989.

Maury, Dabney Herndon. *Recollections of a Virginian in the Mexican, Indian, and Civil Wars.* 3rd ed. New York: Charles Scribner's Sons, 1894.

BIBLIOGRAPHY

Sherman, William T. *The Memoirs of William T. Sherman*. 2nd ed., 1885; reprint, New York: The Library of America, 1990.

Urquhart, Kenneth Trist, ed. *Vicksburg, Southern City Under Siege: William Lovelace Foster's Letter Describing the Defense and Surrender of the Confederate Fortress on the Mississippi*. New Orleans: Historic New Orleans Collection, 1980.

PRIMARY SOURCES: ARTICLES

Bock, H. Riley, ed. "Confederate Col. A. C. Riley, His Reports and Letters, Part I." *Missouri Historical Review* 85 (1991): 158–181.

———, ed. "Confederate Col. A. C. Riley, His Reports and Letters, Part II," *Missouri Historical Review* 85 (1991): 264–287.

———, ed. "One Year at War: Letters of Capt. Geo. W. Dawson, C.S.A." *Missouri Historical Review* 73 (1979): 165–197.

Castel, Albert, ed. "The Diary of General Henry Little, C.S.A." *Civil War Times Illustrated* (1972): 4–11, 41–47.

"Diary of Lieut. Col. Hubbell, of 3d Regiment Missouri Infantry, C.S.A.," *The Land We Love* 6 (1868): 97–105.

Grant, Ulysses S. "The Vicksburg Campaign." In *Battles and Leaders of the Civil War*, edited by Robert Underwood Johnson and Clarence Clough Buel, vol. 3, 493–539. 1887; reprint, New York: Thomas Yoseloff, 1956.

Irwin, Richard B. "Land Operations Against Mobile." In *Battles and Leaders of the Civil War*, edited by Robert Underwood Johnson and Clarence Clough Buel, vol. 4, 410–411. 1887; reprint, New York: Thomas Yoseloff, 1956.

Lockett, Samuel H. "The Defense of Vicksburg." In *Battles and Leaders of the Civil War*, edited by Robert Underwood Johnson and Clarence Clough Buel, vol. 3, 482–492. 1887; reprint, New York: Thomas Yoseloff, 1956.

Merrifield, J. K. "Col. Hugh Garland—Captured Flags." *Confederate Veteran* 24 (1916): 551–552.

Moss, James E., ed., "A Missouri Confederate in the Civil War: The Journal of Henry Martyn Cheavens, 1862–1863," *Missouri Historical Review* 57 (October 1962): 16–52.

Payne, James E. "Cockrell's Missouri Brigade, C.S.A.," *Confederate Veteran* 37 (1929): 419–420.

Snead, Thomas L. "With Price East of the Mississippi." In *Battles and Leaders of the Civil War,* edited by Robert Underwood Johnson and Clarence Clough Buel, vol. 2, 717–734. 1887; reprint, New York: Thomas Yoseloff, 1956.

"The Opposing Forces at Shiloh." In *Battles and Leaders of the Civil War,* edited by Robert Underwood Johnson and Clarence Clough Buel, vol. 1, 537–539. 1887; reprint, New York: Thomas Yoseloff, 1956.

Wilson, Jo. A. "The Services of 'Clark's Battery' Through Sixty Engagements." *Missouri Republican* (St. Louis), November 28, 1885.

SECONDARY SOURCES: BOOKS

Arnold, James R. *Grant Wins the War: Decision at Vicksburg.* New York: John Wiley & Sons, 1997.

Bearss, Edwin C. *The Campaign for Vicksburg, Volume I: Vicksburg Is the Key.* Dayton, OH: Morningside House, 1985.

———. *The Campaign for Vicksburg, Volume II: Grant Strikes a Fatal Blow.* Dayton, OH: Morningside House, 1986.

———. *The Campaign for Vicksburg, Volume III: Unvexed to the Sea.* Dayton, OH: Morningside House, 1986.

Boatner, Mark M., III. *The Civil War Dictionary.* New York: David McKay Company, 1959.

Bonds, Russell S. *War Like the Thunderbolt: The Battle and Burning of Atlanta.* Yardley, PA: Westholme Publishing, 2009.

Burton, William L. *Melting Pot Soldiers: The Union's Ethnic Regiments.* Ames: Iowa State University Press, 1988.

Castel, Albert. *General Sterling Price and the Civil War in the West.* Baton Rouge: Louisiana State University Press, 1968.

———. *Kansas: A Frontier State at War.* Lawrence: Kansas Heritage Press, 1958.

Chandler, David G. *Dictionary of the Napoleonic Wars.* New York: MacMillan Publishing Co., 1979.

BIBLIOGRAPHY

Christensen, Lawrence O., et al., eds. *Dictionary of Missouri Biography*. Columbia: University of Missouri Press, 1999.

Cockrell, Francis M., III. *The Senator from Missouri: The Life and Times of Francis Marion Cockrell*. New York: Exposition Press, 1962.

Cockrell, Monroe F., ed. *The Lost Account of the Battle of Corinth and Court-Martial of Gen. Van Dorn*. Jackson, TN: McCowat-Mercer Press, 1955; reprint, Wilmington, NC: Broadfoot Publishing Company, 1987.

Coggins, Jack. *Arms and Equipment of the Civil War*. Garden City, NY: Doubleday, 1962; reprint, Wilmington, NC: Broadfoot Publishing Company, 1990.

Conard, Howard L. *Encyclopedia of the History of Missouri*. New York: The Southern History Company, 1901.

Connelly, Thomas Lawrence. *Autumn of Glory: The Army of Tennessee, 1862–1865*. Baton Rouge: Louisiana State University Press, 1971.

Constitution and By-Laws of the Veteran Volunteer Fireman's Historical Society of the City of St. Louis, Mo. St. Louis: n.p., 1893.

Cornish, Dudley Taylor. *The Sable Arm: Black Troops in the Union Army, 1861–1865*. Lawrence: University Press of Kansas, 1956.

Corwin, Edward T., D.D. *A Manual of the Reformed Church in America (formerly Ref. Prot. Dutch Church), 1628–1902*. New York: Board of Publication of the Reformed Church in America, 1902.

Cozzens, Peter. *The Darkest Days of the War: The Battles of Iuka and Corinth*. Chapel Hill: University of North Carolina Press, 1997.

Crute, Joseph H., Jr. *Units of the Confederate States Army*. Midlothian, VA: Derwent Books, 1987.

Cullum, George W. *Biographical Register of the Officers and Graduates of the U.S. Military Academy at West Point, N.Y., From Its Establishment, March 16, 1802, to the Army Re-Organization of 1866–67*. New York: D. Van Nostrand, 1868.

Culmer, Frederick A. *A New History of Missouri*. Mexico, MO: McIntyre Publishing Company, 1938.

Davis, William C. *Breckinridge: Statesman, Soldier, Symbol*. Baton Rouge: Louisiana State University Press, 1974.

———. *The Orphan Brigade: The Kentucky Confederates Who Couldn't Go Home*. Garden City, NY: Doubleday & Company, 1980.

Downer, Edward T. "Johnson's Island." In *Civil War Prisons*, edited by William B. Hesseltine, 98–113. Kent, OH: The Kent State University Press, 1962.

Dyer, Frederick H. *A Compendium of the War of the Rebellion*. Des Moines, IA: Dyer Publishing Company, 1908; reprint, Dayton, OH: Morningside Bookshop, 1978.

Eakin, Joanne Chiles, and Donald R. Hale, comps. *Branded as Rebels: A List of Bushwhackers, Guerillas, Partisan Rangers, Confederates and Southern Sympathizers from Missouri During the War Years.* Independence, MO: Wee Print, 1993.

Elliott, Sam Davis. *Soldier of Tennessee: General Alexander P. Stewart and the Civil War in the West.* Baton Rouge: Louisiana State University Press, 1999.

Faherty, William Barnaby, S.J. *Exile in Erin: A Confederate Chaplain's Story.* St. Louis: Missouri Historical Society Press, 2002.

———. *The Fourth Career of John B. Bannon.* Portland, OR: C&D Publishing, 1994.

Farley, James W. *Forgotten Valor: The First Missouri Cavalry Regiment, C.S.A.* Shawnee Mission, KS: Two Trails Publishing, 1996.

Faust, Patricia, ed. *Historical Times Illustrated Encyclopedia of the Civil War.* New York: Harper & Row, 1986.

Fullenkamp, Leonard, Stephen Bowman, and Jay Luvaas. *Guide to the Vicksburg Campaign.* Lawrence: University of Kansas Press, 1998.

Glatthaar, Joseph T. *Forged in Battle: The Civil War Alliance of Black Soldiers and White Officers.* New York: The Free Press, 1990.

Gottschalk, Phil. *In Deadly Earnest: The History of the First Missouri Confederate Brigade, C.S.A.* Columbia: Missouri River Press, 1991.

Grabau, Warren E. *Ninety-Eight Days: A Geographer's View of the Vicksburg Campaign.* Knoxville: The University of Tennessee Press, 2000.

Griffith, Paddy. *Battle in the Civil War: Generalship and Tactics in America 1861–1865.* Mansfield, England: Fieldbooks, 1986.

———. *Battle Tactics of the Civil War.* New Haven: Yale University Press, 1989.

Hartje, Robert G. *Van Dorn: The Life and Times of a Confederate General.* Nashville: Vanderbilt University Press, 1967.

BIBLIOGRAPHY

Hattaway, Herman. *General Stephen D. Lee*. Jackson: University Press of Mississippi, 1976.

Hay, Thomas Robson. *Hood's Tennessee Campaign*. New York: Walter Neale, 1929; reprint: Press of Morningside Bookshop, 1976.

Henry, Robert Selph. *"First with the Most" Forrest*. Westport, CT: Greenwood Press, 1944; reprint, Indianapolis: Bobbs-Merrill, 1974.

History of Vernon County, Missouri. St. Louis: Brown & Co., 1887; reprint, Clinton, MO: The Printery, 1974.

Hopewell, M., M.D. *Camp Jackson: History of the Missouri Volunteer Militia of St. Louis*. St. Louis: George Knapp & Company, 1861.

Horn, Stanley F. *The Army of Tennessee*. Norman: University of Oklahoma Press, 1952.

Howell, H. Grady, Jr. *Going to Meet the Yankees: A History of the "Bloody Sixth" Mississippi Infantry, C.S.A.* Jackson, MS: Chickasaw Bayou Press, 1981, softcover 2002.

Hughes, Nathaniel Cheairs, Jr. *The Battle of Belmont: Grant Strikes South*. Chapel Hill: University of North Carolina Press, 1991.

———. *The Pride of the Confederate Artillery: The Washington Artillery in the Army of Tennessee*. Baton Rouge: Louisiana State University Press, 1997.

Hyde, William, and Howard Louis Conard. *Encyclopedia of the History of St. Louis: A Compendium of History and Biography for Ready Reference*. New York: The Southern History Company, 1899.

Johnston, William Preston. *The Life of General Albert Sidney Johnston*. 1879; reprint, New York: DaCapo Press, 1997.

Jones, Archer. *Confederate Strategy from Shiloh to Vicksburg*. Baton Rouge: Louisiana State University Press, 1961; 2nd. ed., 1991.

Keating, J. M. *History of the City of Memphis, Tennessee*. Syracuse, NY: D. Mason & Co., 1888.

Kennedy, Robert V. *Kennedy's Saint Louis City Directory for the Year 1857, Containing a General Directory of Citizens*. St. Louis: R.V. Kennedy, 1857.

———. *Kennedy's Saint Louis City Directory for the Year 1859, Containing a General Directory of Citizens*. St. Louis: R.V. Kennedy, 1859.

Kitchens, Ben Earl. *Rosecrans Meets Price: The Battle of Iuka, Mississippi*. Florence, AL: Thornwood Publishers, 1985.

Long, E. B., and Barbara Long. *The Civil War Day by Day: An Almanac.* Garden City, NY: Doubleday & Company, 1971.

Losson, Christopher. *Tennessee's Forgotten Warriors: Frank Cheatham and His Confederate Division.* Knoxville: University of Tennessee Press, 1989.

McMurry, Richard M. *John Bell Hood and the War for Southern Independence.* Lexington: University Press of Kentucky, 1982.

McPherson, James M. *The Atlas of the Civil War.* New York: Macmillan, 1994.

McWhiney, Grady. *Braxton Bragg and Confederate Defeat, Volume I.* Tuscaloosa: University of Alabama Press, 1969.

McWhiney, Grady, and Perry D. Jamieson. *Attack and Die: Civil War Military Tactics and the Southern Heritage.* Tuscaloosa: University of Alabama Press, 1982.

Merrill, James M. *Battle Flags South: The Story of the Civil War Navies on Western Waters.* Rutherford, NJ: Fairleigh Dickinson University Press, 1970.

Miles, Jim. *Fields of Glory: A History and Tour Guide of the Atlanta Campaign.* Nashville, TN: Rutledge Hill Press, 1995.

Monaghan, Jay. *Civil War on the Western Border, 1854–1865.* Lincoln: University of Nebraska Press, 1955.

Moore, John C. *Confederate Military History Extended Edition, Volume XII: Missouri.* N.p.: Confederate Publishing Company, 1899; reprint, Wilmington, NC: Broadfoot Publishing Company, 1988.

O'Brien, Sean Michael. *Mobile, 1865: The Last Stand of the Confederacy.* Westport, CT: Praeger, 2001.

Parks, Joseph H. *General Leonidas Polk, C.S.A.: The Fighting Bishop.* Baton Rouge: Louisiana State University Press, 1962.

Parrish, William E. "Fletcher, Thomas Clement." In *Dictionary of Missouri Biography*, edited by Lawrence O. Christensen et al. Columbia: University of Missouri Press, 1999.

Quaife, M. M., ed., *Absalom Grimes: Confederate Mail Runner.* New Haven, CT: Yale University Press, 1926.

Rombauer, Robert J. *The Union Cause in St. Louis in 1861.* St. Louis: Nixon-Jones Publishing Co., 1909.

BIBLIOGRAPHY

Sanjek, Russell. *American Popular Music and Its Business, the First Four Hundred Years, Volume II*. New York: Oxford University Press, 1988.

Scaife, William R. *Hood's Campaign for Tennessee*. Atlanta: Author, 1986.

———. *War in Georgia: A Study of Military Command and Strategy*. Atlanta: Author, 1994.

Seematter, Mary E. "McDonald, John." In *Dictionary of Missouri Biography*, edited by Lawrence O. Christensen, et al. Columbia: University of Missouri Press, 1999.

Sergent, Mary Elizabeth. *They Lie Forgotten: The United States Military Academy 1856–1861*. Middletown, NY: The Prior King Press, 1986.

Sons of Confederate Veterans, Tilghman–Beauregard Camp No. 1460. *A History of Camp Beauregard, Graves County, Kentucky*. Mayfield, KY: privately printed, 1988.

Swainson, Rev. Charles. *The Folk Lore and Provincial Names of British Birds*. The Folk-Lore Society for Collecting and Printing Relics of Popular Antiquities, vol. 17. London: Folk-Lore Society, 1885.

Symonds, Craig L. *Joseph E. Johnston: A Civil War Biography*. New York: W. W. Norton & Company, 1992.

Thomas, Dean S. *Cannons: An Introduction to Civil War Artillery*. Arendtsville, PA: Thomas Publications, 1985.

Time-Life Books. *Echoes of Glory: Arms and Equipment of the Confederacy*. Alexandria, VA: Author, 1998.

Troiani, Don. *Don Troiani's Regiments and Uniforms of the Civil War*. Mechanicsburg, PA: Stackpole Books, 2002.

Warner, Ezra J. *Generals in Blue: Lives of the Union Commanders*. Baton Rouge: Louisiana State University Press, 1964.

———. *Generals in Gray: Lives of the Confederate Commanders*. Baton Rouge: Louisiana State University Press, 1959.

Wiley, Bell Irvin. *The Life of Billy Yank: The Common Soldier of the Union*. Baton Rouge: Louisiana State University Press, 1952, 1978.

———. *The Life of Johnny Reb: The Common Soldier of the Confederacy*. Baton Rouge: Louisiana State University Press, 1943, 1978.

Willis, James. *Arkansas Confederates in the Western Theater*. Dayton, OH: Morningside House, 1998.

Wills, Brian Steel. *A Battle from the Start: The Life of Nathan Bedford Forrest.* New York: HarperCollins, 1992.

Winter, William C. *The Civil War in St. Louis: A Guided Tour.* St. Louis: Missouri Historical Society Press, 1994.

Winters, John D. *The Civil War in Louisiana.* Baton Rouge: Louisiana State University, 1963.

Woodworth, Steven E. *Nothing but Victory: The Army of the Tennessee, 1861–1865.* New York: Alfred A. Knopf, 2005.

Wynne, Ben. *A Hard Trip: A History of the 15th Mississippi Infantry, C.S.A.* Macon, GA: Mercer University Press, 2003.

Young, Peter, *Napoleon's Marshals.* New York: Hippocrene Books, 1973.

SECONDARY SOURCES: ARTICLES

"Death of Dr. Sylvester L. Nidelet." *St. Louis Medical Review* 54 (1906): 517.

Drumm, Stella M. "The Kennerlys of Virginia." *Missouri Historical Society Collections* 6 (1928): 98–123.

Hier, Marshall D. "Garland & Norris, Slaveowner Emerson's 'Dream Team'—Part I." *St. Louis Bar Journal* (Fall 1999): 45, 48–49.

———."Garland & Norris, Slaveowner Emerson's 'Dream Team'—Part II." *St. Louis Bar Journal* (Winter 2000): 32–35.

Hyde, William. "Gay and Festive Times in Old Carondelet." *Bulletin of the Missouri Historical Society* 6 (1950): 330.

"Irish Immigrants Fought Back in Nativist Riots of 1854." *St. Louis Post-Dispatch*, August 8, 2010.

"Many Mourned Death of Iconic Senator." *St. Louis Post-Dispatch*, April 18, 2010.

"Memoirs of Deceased Members of the Society: Joseph Boyce." *Missouri Historical Society Collections* 6 (1928): 131–133.

"Some Irish Superstitions about Birds." *The Month: A Catholic Magazine and Review* 76 (1892): 37.

"The 2nd Missouri Cavalry." *The Land We Love* 3 (1867): 272–282.

Winter, William C. "The Zouaves Take St. Louis." *Gateway Heritage* 19

BIBLIOGRAPHY

ONLINE REFERENCES AND RESOURCES

Christian Brothers College High School, St. Louis
  http://www.cbchs.org
Missouri State Archives, Missouri Birth and Death Records Database
  http://www.sos.mo.gov/archives/resources/birthdeath/
"News: President Bush's Roots Extend to Beloit," *Beloit College Magazine*
  (Spring 2001).
  http://www.beloit.edu/belmag
Portrait and Biographical Album of McLean County, Illinois. Chicago: Chapman
  Brothers, 1887.
  http://genealogytrails.com/ill/mclean/coxWilliamMarcus.html
State of Wisconsin, Adjutant General's Office. *Roster of Wisconsin Volunteers,*
  War of the Rebellion, 1861–1865. 1886.
  http://www.wisconsinhistory.org/roster
The Tennessee Encyclopedia of History and Culture
  http://tennesseeencyclopedia.net
United States Army, Medal of Honor
  http://www.history.army.mil/html/moh
United States Department of the Interior, National Park Service, Civil War
  Soldiers and Sailors System
  http://www.itd.nps.gov
United States Department of the Interior, National Park Service, Gettysburg
  National Military Park
  http://www.nps.gov/archive/gett/gettncem/bivouac.htm

INDEX

Alabama Reserves, 210

Allatoona, Georgia, battle at, 178–180; map, 179

Appler, John T., 100, 112–113

Arkansas units, C.S.A.; 9th Infantry, 60–65; 10th Infantry, 44, 60–65

Army of Mississippi; creation, 59

Army of the Department of Mississippi and East Louisiana, 97

Atlanta, battles for, 164, 174

Averill, John C., 37

Bannon, Father John B., *102*, 113, 123

Barlow, William P., 27, 89, 92, 245

Bass, Joseph H., 35

Beauregard, P. G. T., 59 63

Black Plume Rifle Cadets, 16

Blair, Francis Preston, Jr., 22, 121, 128

Bowen, John S., 31, *33*, 35, 44, 48, 53, 55, 59, 72–89, 95–98, 101, 103, 108, 110, 120, 125; commands division, 99; raises regiment, 10, 32; death, 126, 131

Boyce, Anthony, 209

Boyce, Joseph, *23*; at Camp Jackson, 22; funeral, 15; joins 1st Missouri Infantry, C.S.A., 22; on board of Missouri Historical Society, 26; paroled, 125, 131; promoted to first lieutenant, 76; reasons for fighting, 241–247; sick, 135; wounded at Franklin, 198, 207; wounded at Shiloh, 69; writes history of 1st Missouri Infantry, 10–11, 24

Boyce, Mary Elizabeth Casey, 24

Boyce Brothers, 24

Boyce Realty Company, 24

Bragg, Braxton, 59, 75, 83–84

Breckinridge, John C., 53, 56, 59, 77, 81

Britts, John Henry, 123, 129

Buckley, William, 35

Buckner, Simon Bolivar, 51

Buell, Don Carlos, 59, 66. 73

Burke, Martin, 20, 36, 98, 99, 105–107, *107*, 110, 126, 142

Bush, Robert, 121

Butler, Benjamin, 79, 81

Butler, Wallace, 135

Byrne, Gregory, 36

Camp Beauregard, Kentucky, 44–47; illnesses, 44–45

Camp Jackson, St. Louis, 21–22, 64; massacre, 10

Campbell, Charles C., 35, 69

Canniff, Patrick, 105, 115, 200

Cannon, William, 35

Carrington, W. C. P., 36, 41, 69, 126

Carter, E. S., 47

Casey, John, 24

Casey, Juliette, 24

Champion Hill, battle at, 105–109

Cheatham, Benjamin F., 176

Cockrell, Francis M., 101, 106, 112, 116, 124, 140, *142*, 145, 180, 199, 209, 212, 242

INDEX

Conklin, William (Billy), 53, 56
Corinth, battle at, 83–89
Corkery, John J., 63, 71, 112, 231, 237
Corkery, William, 101, 112, 128
Corwin, Charles, 35
CSS *Arkansas*, 77

Danner, Albert C., 216, 224
Daughters, James M., 37
Daughtry, James, 69
Davis, Jefferson, 141, 143, 177
Dawson, George Washington, 36, 44
Deane, Joseph, 36, 69
Demopolis, Alabama, camp of parole, 133, 137
Donovan, John T., 157, 161, 184, 196
Douglass, John C., 36
Duffy, Robert J., 36, 69, 92
Duke, Basil, 55
Durbin, Father Arthur J., 46
Dwyer, Thomas, 73

Edmondson, Charles L., 37, 218, 224
Elder, John Scott, 63, 72

Farrell, Michael, 88, 92
1st Missouri Infantry; at Champion Hill, 105–109; at Fort Blakely, 210, 212; at Kennesaw Mountain, 153; at Ship Island, 227; casualties, 69, 119, 126, 132, 164, 172, 207, 242; companies, 35–37; defense of Vicksburg, 76; formation, 10; in Allatoona, 178–180; in Bowling Green, 53; in Corinth, 59, 83–89; in Georgia, 151–185; in Mayfield, 44; in Mobile, 212; in Nashville, 52; in New Madrid, 34; in Shiloh, 61–70; in Tennessee, 189–201; in Vicksburg, 95–127; merge with 4th Missouri Infantry, 96; paroled, 125, 131, 227; praised by Jefferson Davis, 141, 143–144; prisoners of war, 227–236
Fletcher, Thomas C., *99*, 111
Flournoy, Peter C., 140, *181*, 186, 200
Floyd, John B., 52, 55, 57

Foote, Andrew H., 51
Forrest, Nathan Bedford, 52, 140, 192, 193, 217
Fort Blakely, 210, 212, 227, 238
Fort Donelson, 52–54
Fort Henry, 51
Fowler, Isaac, 37
Franklin, battle at, 194; map, *194*
French, Samuel G., 140, 178, 222
Frost, Daniel M., 18

Galbaugh, Augusta "Gus," 36
Gardner, Michael, 37
Garland, Hugh A., 36, 98, 110, 142, 196–197, *197*, 199, 204
Gates, Elijah, 141, 199, 209
Gordon, George C., 36
Gordon, John A., 36
Grant, Ulysses S., 43, 60–70, 114, 119, 134
Green, Martin E., 95, 110, 120
Guibor, Henry, 62, 71, 91, 101–102, 108, 128, 141
Guthrie, Orlando F., 219, 223, 229

Haines, William F., 35
Hardee, William J., 41, 51, 59, 66–68, 171, 176
Hargett, Joseph T., 36, 69, 71
Hawes, Cary N., 35
Hawes, Smith N., 36, 69
Haynes, Lloyd A., 36
Healy, Tim, 35
Hirsch, David, 36
Hogan, Thomas, 200, 206
Hogan, Tilford, 37
Hood, John Bell, 163–166, 203
Hubbell, Finley L., 97, 106, 115
Hutchinson, Randolph R., 36

Jackson, Mississippi, Boyce at, 77, 99
Jackson, Claiborne F., 20, 31
Johnston, Albert Sidney, 39, 43, 54, 59, 63, 125, 134, 141, 152, 153, 159, 177; death, 65

Johnston, Joseph E., 98, 114, 124, 133, 148, 163

Johnston's Army of Relief, 134–137

Kavanaugh, William H., 111
Kearney, John, 102
Kearny, William, 68, 73
Keith, Bradford, 37, 168, 174
Kelly, Joseph, 20, 105
Kennerly, James A., 35, 46, 48, 199
Kennerly, Lewis H., 35–36, 69, 146, 149
Kennerly, Samuel A., 37, 126, 171, 175
Kennesaw Mountain, battle at, 157–158
Kerr, James, 35, 69
Knight, George C., 37

Ladd, John A., 167, 173
Lalor, James, 35
Landis, John C., 105, 108, 115
Leavy, John A., 123, 130
Lewis, Jerry, 53
Liddell, St. John Richardson, 210
Loring, William W., 105, 108, 114, 140, 152
Louden, Robert, 86, 91
Louisiana units, C.S.A.; 3rd Infantry, 68, 74; 24th Infantry (Crescent Regiment), 67, 73; Watson's battery, 76, 83, 87–88, 92; Washington Artillery, 67–68
Lovell, Mansfield, 83, 90
Lyon, Nathaniel, 22, 90

MacFarlane, Archibald, 98, 110, 241
Marmaduke, John Sappington, 111, 243
Marr, Patrick, 35
Maury, Dabney H., 145, 149, 210–211
McArthur, William J., 36
McConlogue, William, 53, 56
McCown, James C., 105, 115, 140
McCoy, Arthur, 35
McCulloch, Ben, 90
McDonald, John, 49
McDowell, James K., 156, 160
McFarland, James H., 36, 126

McIntosh, John, 35
Miller, Mordecai, 37
Minute Men, 34
Mississippi units; 6th Infantry, 76, 83, 91; 15th Infantry, 83, 91, 92; 22nd Infantry, 83, 91; Caruthers's battalion, 83, 91; Hudson's battery, 60, 62, 71
Missouri Historical Society, 26–27
Missouri Republican, 11; Boyce's writings, 10
Missouri State Guard, 10; creation, 31
Missouri units (except 1st and 1st/4th Infantry); 2nd Infantry, 91, 97, 114, 115, 140, 186; 2nd/6th Infantry, 140, 163, 204, 224, 237; 3rd Infantry, 91, 97, 115, 129, 140; 3rd/5th Infantry, 140, 186, 204, 224, 238; 5th Infantry, 48, 91, 115, 140, 198; 6th Infantry, 91, 130, 140, 237
Missouri Volunteer Militia, 16, 40
Montgomery, James Edward, 78, 80
Mulholland, Jabez, 37
Muse, John M., 36

Nicholson, John Page, 11
Nidelet, Sylvester L., 124, 129

O'Neil, John, 68, 73

Pemberton, John, 95–97, 101, 110, 120, 125
Phillips, Thomas J., 36
Pillow, Gideon J., 41, 43, 52, 55, 57
Polk, Leonidas, 40, 43, 59, 140, 151–152
Port Gibson, battle at, 100–103; map, *104*
Prentiss, Benjamin M., 64, 72
Price, Sterling, 10, 31, 75, 84–90, 98, 111
Pritchard, James, 36

Quinlan, James M., 35, 69

Ragland, John, 181, 187
Reynolds, Joseph, 35
Rice, Olin F., 36, 146, 149
Rich, Lucius L., 35, 42, 46, 48, 64, 69; death, 75

INDEX

Riley, Amos C., 36, 45, 74, 76, 80, 87, 98, 142; assumes command of 1st Missouri Infantry, 75
Rosecrans, William S., 84

Sansom, Emma, 189
Schaffer, Chris, 37
Shaw, Frank, 35
Shelby, Joseph O., 98, 111
Sherman, William T., 134, 151, 159
Shiloh, battle at, 61–70; map, 62
Ship Island, prisoners of war, 227–236
Shoup, Francis A., 121, 128
Smith, Guy P., 36
Southern Historical and Benevolent Society of St. Louis, 10
Southern Mothers' Association, 70, 74
Sprague, J. Kemp, 35, 69
St. Louis Greys, 16, 19, 36; roster, 249
"St. Louis Greys Quick Step, The," 16
Stevenson, Carter L., 105, 108, 114, 116
Stewart, Alexander P., 152, 177
Stewart, Goah W., 37, 180, 186

Tate, Mr. and Mrs. Sam, 69
Thompson, Harry, 230
Toledano, Edmund A., 88, 93

Ungerer, Rev. Mr., 35
U.S. Colored Troops, 227–236; 2nd Regiment, Corps d'Afrique, 228; 44th Infantry, 188; 74th Infantry, 228, 237, 238

Van Dorn, Earl, 75–78, 83–89, 95, 110
Veteran Volunteer Fireman's Historical Society, 25
Veterans of the Blue and Gray, 25
Vicksburg, battles and siege, 119–127
Villepigue, John B., 85, 91

Wade, William, 91, 102, 113
Walker, David, 36, 55
Walsh, Dudley A., 35
Walsh, Henry H., 35
Walsh, Richard C., 105, 115, 128
Watson, Augustus C., 92
Woods, Ed. P., 102

Yergin, George W., 36

ABOUT THE AUTHOR

WILLIAM C. WINTER is the author of *The Civil War in St. Louis: A Guided Tour* (1994), one of the Missouri History Museum's most popular books. His work on Civil War topics has also appeared in *Gateway Heritage*, *Missouri Historical Review*, and other periodicals. He has led tours of Civil War St. Louis for a variety of organizations.

Bill holds a bachelor of science from the University of Illinois and an MBA from Michigan State University. Among his family's ancestors are a Prussian immigrant who served in the 12th Missouri Infantry, U.S.A., and an Irish immigrant who served in the 9th Illinois Infantry, killed in action at Fort Donelson, Tennessee.